D0518940

BURNS NOW

TO G. ROSS ROY

bon vivant, raconteur extraordinaire, and most generous of scholars, this book is dedicated, in warm appreciation of his contribution to Burns scholarship and Scottish literary studies

BURNS NOW

Edited by
Kenneth Simpson

CANONGATE ACADEMIC

First published in 1994 by Canongate Academic
an imprint of Canongate Press Ltd
14 Frederick Street, Edinburgh EH2 2HB, Scotland

ISBN 1 898410 13 5

British Library Cataloguing-in-Publication Data
A catalogue record for this book is available on request from the British Library

The publisher gratefully acknowledges subsidy from the Scottish Arts Council
towards the publication of this volume.

Typeset by Hewertext Composition Services
Printed and bound by Bookcraft Ltd, Midsomer Norton.

Contents

Acknowledgements

The following have kindly granted permission for the publication of material from their collections: The Mitchell Library; The Burns Federation; The Bodleian Library; The Thomas Cooper Library, University of South Carolina; Professor G. Ross Roy; Lady Stair's House Museum.

For all their help in organising the Burns Conferences I am most grateful to Cath Wales and Allison MacDonald of the Centre for Scottish Studies at the University of Strathclyde. Dr. A. M. Fleming and the staff of the Centre for Continuing Education have been highly supportive. Thanks are due also to Dr. Andrew Noble who proposed the first conference. The publicising of the Conferences by *The Herald* is greatly appreciated.

My greatest debt of gratitude is to Val and John Tuckwell of Canongate Academic. By combining dedication, patience, good-humour, and unflappability in equal – and immense – measures, they ensured that this book appeared.

Notes on Contributors

R.D.S. Jack is professor of Scottish and Mediaeval Literature at the University of Edinburgh. He edited Volume I of *The History of Scottish Literature* (1988) and his books include *Scottish Prose 1550–1700* (1972); *The Italian Influence on Scottish Literature* (1972); *Scottish Verse 1560–1660* (1978); *Alexander Montgomerie* (1985); and *Patterns of Divine Comedy* (1989). He is the author of a major re-evaluation of Barrie, *The Road to the Never Land: A Reassessment of J.M. Barrie's Dramatic Art* (1991).

Donald A. Low is Professor in the Department of English Studies at the University of Stirling and Director of the Centre for Scottish Literature and Culture. In 1990 he was the first recipient of the W. Ormiston Roy fellowship at the University of South Carolina. His many publications on Burns include *Robert Burns: The Critical Heritage* (1974); *Critical Essays on Robert Burns* (1975); and *Robert Burns* (1986). His most recent work, *The Songs of Robert Burns* (1993), is a landmark in Burns studies.

Carol McGuirk taught English at Rutgers University and she is now Professor at Florida Atlantic University. In 1989 she was British Academy Visiting Professor at the University of Strathclyde, and in 1993 Ormiston Roy Fellow at the University of South Carolina. Author of *Robert Burns and the Sentimental Era* (1985), she is editor of the forthcoming Penguin edition of the Poems of Burns. She is also compiling a comprehensive bibliography of Burns criticism.

Jo Miller performs and teaches Scottish music. Currently on the staff of the Royal Scottish Academy of Music and Drama, Glasgow, she has among her research interests music and identity, and music in the life of rural communities.

Edwin Morgan is Emeritus Professor of English Literature at the University of Glasgow, and from 1987 to 1990 he was Visiting Professor at the University of Strathclyde. Author of over thirty volumes of poems, he published his *Collected Poems* in 1990. He is also a librettist, a translator, and an essayist; his criticism includes *East European Poets* (1976); *Hugh MacDiarmid* (1976); and *Crossing the Border: Essays in Scottish Literature* (1990). Communicado Theatre Company's production of his Glaswegian translation of Rostand's *Cyrano de Bergerac* was one of the theatrical triumphs of 1992. Edwin Morgan received the OBE in 1982.

Andrew Noble is Senior Lecturer and head of the English section of the Department of English Studies at the University of Strathclyde. With R.D.S. Jack he edited *The Art of Robert Burns* (1982). Editor of *Edwin Muir: Uncollected Scottish Criticism* (1982) and *Robert Louis Stevenson* (1983), he is working on a study of Burns and English Romanticism.

Donny O'Rourke, a graduate of the University of Glasgow, is Head of Arts at Scottish Television. His first poetry collection, *Second Cities*, was published in 1991 to critical acclaim. He has since edited *Dream States: An Anthology of Young Scottish Poets*.

G. Ross Roy, a graduate of the Sorbonne and the Universities of Montreal and Strasbourg, is Distinguished Professor Emeritus at the University of South Carolina, where he was Chair of Comparative Literature. He is founding editor of *Studies in Scottish Literature*, and among his particular interests are the chapbooks, Macpherson's *Ossian*, and the work of Hugh MacDiarmid. His revised edition of *The Letters of Robert Burns*, ed. J. De Lancey Ferguson, appeared in 1985. The Roy Collection of Scottish texts has made the Thomas Cooper Library at the University of South Carolina, Columbia, the foremost centre of Scottish literary study in North America.

Kenneth Simpson is Senior Lecturer in the Department of English Studies at the University of Strathclyde and Director of the Centre for Scottish Cultural Studies. In 1992 he was Ormiston Roy Fellow at the University of South Carolina. Editor of *Henry Fielding: Justice Observed* (1985), he is the author of *The Protean Scot: The Crisis of Identity in Eighteenth-Century Scottish Literature* (1988) and *The Poetry of Robert Burns* (1994). With G. Ross Roy he is editing a comprehensive collection of the letters written to Burns.

Iain Crichton Smith was born in Lewis and is a graduate of the University of Aberdeen. Novelist, playwright, translator, and short-story writer, he is a distinguished poet in both Gaelic and English. Among his awards are the Queen's Jubilee Medal and the OBE. His *Collected Poems* (1992) won the Saltire Literary Award. His recent publications include the essays, *Towards the Human* (1986); the novel, *An Honourable Death* (1992); and *Thoughts of Murdo* (1993). Since 1990 Iain Crichton Smith has been Visiting Professor at the University of Strathclyde.

John Strawhorn taught History at Ayr Academy and he is renowned as the foremost authority on the history of Ayrshire. Among his many publications are *Ayrshire, The Story of a County* (1975); *History of Ayr* (1989); and *Ayrshire at the Time of Burns* (1959), which he edited. With Nellie P. Hankins he is editing *Correspondence of James Boswell with his Estate Overseers* in the Yale Research Editions.

Christopher A. Whatley, a graduate of the University of Strathclyde, was Lecturer in Scottish History at the University of St Andrews until 1992, when he took up a similar post at the University of Dundee. Interested principally in the eighteenth and early nineteenth centuries, he includes among his most recent publications *The Manufacture of Scottish History* (1992), which he co-edited, and a co-authored history of Dundee. Currently he is writing a short book on the Union of 1707.

Introduction

Burns Now reflects what Burns means to us today, almost two centuries after his death, and also represents the current state of Burns scholarship. These essays are offered as a celebration of the richness and the range of Burns's achievement. Their aims replicate those of their source — the Burns conferences held annually since 1990 under the auspices of the Centre for Scottish Cultural Studies at the University of Strathclyde in Glasgow.[1]

There is so much to celebrate in Burns. His letters, here used incidentally but worthy of a full-length study in themselves, testify to his mastery of a wide range of voices and styles. For proof of Burns's bilingualism one need only compare 'Tam o' Shanter' with the prose account to Francis Grose of the material which inspired the poem.[2] In his modulation of the rhythms and syntax of English Burns is revealed in his letters as a prose writer of distinction. In a letter of 14 July 1790 Burns informed Dr John Moore, author of the novel, *Zeluco*, 'I have gravely planned a Comparative view of You, Fielding, Richardson, & Smollet (*sic*), in your different qualities & merits as Novel-Writers' (*Letters*, II, 37). We can only speculate as to what he might have accomplished himself in the way of fiction, had circumstances been more favourable to him.

An important part of Burns's activity was his contribution to Scottish song, and scholarship in this area is much facilitated by the recent publication of *The Songs of Robert Burns* by Donald A. Low. If Burns's first visit to Edinburgh, in the winter of 1786, acquainted him with the vogue of antiquarianism, his tours of the Borders and the West Highlands in the following summer both alerted him to the need to preserve the native oral tradition and provided him with much of its material. By the autumn of 1787 he was collaborating with James Johnson on the second volume of the *Scots Musical Museum* and he later became involved increasingly in the compilation of George Thomson's *Select Collection*. Burns wrote many songs, but he reset or adapted many more. In two respects his achievement was distinguished — his adeptness in writing words for existing music (the opposite of the normal practice, and altogether more challenging), and his ability to range widely in terms of subject and mood.

Burns's finest love lyrics are unrivalled in direct emotional appeal. Though there were chapbook models for each stanza of 'A Red, Red Rose', Burns made the material his own, enriching the most trite of similes by the intensifying effect of the repetition of 'red'. Likewise, 'Ae Fond Kiss', for Scott 'the essence of a thousand love tales',[3] exemplifies the perfect union of words and music. The political songs, too, resonate with authentic feeling. Typical of Burns's powers of empathy, 'Such a Parcel of Rogues in a Nation' offers the response of an aged patriot to the Union of Parliaments in 1707. Burns conveys the speaker's scorn and outrage in that most telling of metaphors: the 'rogues', the thirty-one Scottish Commissioners, are a 'parcel' — all packed up together for protection and safety. In 'Auld Lang Syne' Burns communicates with moving simplicity the remembrance of shared childhood experience:

> We twa hae run about the braes,
>   And pou'd the gowans fine;
> But we've wander'd mony a weary fitt,
>   Sin auld lang syne.
>
> We twa hae paidl'd in the burn,
>   Frae morning sun till dine;
> But seas between us braid hae roar'd
>   Sin auld lang syne.

In each of these stanzas the earlier experience is vividly evoked, re-lived almost, only to be succeeded by the adult perspective; thus Burns presents simultaneously what it is to be young and to have been young. Carol McGuirk's research into illustrations of Burns has produced a fascinating insight into this song: George Harvey's illustration identifies 'Auld Lang Syne' as 'one of Burns's elegies for displaced Highlanders . . . All Harvey's illustrations for this song assume that Burns is dramatizing the chance reunion of two exiled Jacobites, or at any rate two reluctant emigrants'.

Two of the essays deal exclusively with Burns and song. In offering a singer's view, Jo Miller meets a long-felt need. Focusing on 'how singers feel and perform songs, and how they are received', she highlights the differences between text and performance, recognising, for instance, that certain of Burns's songs are especially challenging for singers because the airs derive from instrumental (mainly fiddle) settings. Jo Miller illuminates Burns's relationship to the song-culture by means of the concept of 'participant observation' and what she terms his 'creative engagement with the oral and literary environments of his time'. Donald A. Low deals with the various representations of the relationships between love and money in Burns's songs. Characteristically of Burns, 'the balance of sympathy is on the side of romantic love, rather than of mere prudential reasoning'.

Professor Low points to an essential quality of Burns when he writes, 'In song, as in the rest of his creative work, he does nothing by halves'. Burns himself had acknowledged, 'Poets are not very famous for their prudence' (*Letters*, I, 461). His intense creative energy resulted in an immense output for a relatively short life; the creative period was little more than a decade, and all the while farm or excise duties had to be fulfilled. The vitality and charisma which Maria Riddell identified (she alluded to Burns's 'sorcery . . . of fascinating conversation' and his '*vivida vis animi*'[4] ('lively force of mind')) found expression in the vigour and the technical range of his verse.

Multi-faceted as a personality, Burns was a poet of many voices. In both literature and life he was a chameleon; hence apparent contradictions abound. While exuding rarefied sensibility in his passionate correspondence as 'Sylvander' to Mrs Agnes McLehose's 'Clarinda', he was simultaneously fathering a child to Jenny Clow, an Edinburgh servant-girl. To society ladies he read extracts from Henry Mackenzie's *The Man of Feeling* ('a book I prize next to the Bible' (*Letters*, I, 17)); yet one of his qualities which its author felt worthy of remark was his 'sarcastic humour'.[5] The poet who could empathise with a mouse and address with compassion a flower whose stem he had severed was also the poet who threatened to unleash on the opponents of Dr William McGill 'the faulcons of Ridicule . . . [and] the bloodhounds of Satire' (*Letters*, I, 175); who relished the use of 'fair, candid ridicule' (*Letters*, II, 345); and who in 'To the Rev. John McMath' envied Pope in these terms:

> O Pope, had I thy satire's darts
> To gie the rascals their deserts,
> I'd rip their rotten, hollow hearts,
>   An' tell aloud
> Their jugglin' hocus pocus arts
>   To cheat the crowd.

The champion of the worth of the ordinary man ('A Man's a Man for a' that') also thought fit to write this (though some devotees may not wish to be so reminded):

> However respectable, Individuals in all ages have been, I have ever looked on Mankind in the lump to be nothing better than a foolish, headstrong, credulous, unthinking Mob; and their universal belief has ever had extremely little weight with me (*Letters*, I, 349).

How understandable was Byron's reaction on reading the letters of Burns: 'What an antithetical mind!'[6]

Accounting for Burns's enduring popularity, Edwin Morgan comments in his essay:

> He was what he claimed to be, a man of independent mind; and yet this strongly marked, strongly individual character — that's the realism if you like — 'I, Rob, am here' — was able to join many people together, across classes and across countries, still does so in fact — and that's the strangeness. He will always be discussed, because there's no one quite like him.

While explaining Burns's attraction, this paradox also points to the price paid. Granted that there is something in Burns for everyone and that he is quoted more often than any other poet, some of his lines having become commonplaces in our everyday speech, yet the danger is that our satisfaction with the familiar Burns may blind us to his richness and diversity. For every hundred readers who know 'Tam o' Shanter' there is perhaps one who has read 'Death and Doctor Hornbook'; the egalitarian sentiments of 'For a' that and a' that' are cited the world over, but Burns's song, 'The Slave's Lament', is rarely heard. The selectiveness of memory can distort, a point well made by Thomas Crawford in relation to 'To a Louse':

> The first four lines of the eighth and last stanza, which extract a general truth from [the] concrete situation, have become proverbial throughout the English-speaking world, but perhaps because of their implicit criticism of sanctimoniousness the two concluding lines are seldom quoted:

> > O wad some Power the giftie gie us
> > To see oursels as ithers see us!
> > It wad frae monie a blunder free us,
> > An' foolish notion:
> > What airs in dress an' gait wad lea'e us,
> > An' ev'n devotion![7]

To neglect these last two lines is to misread one of Burns's subtlest poems. The episode takes place in church and the speaker is a member of the congregation whose attention has strayed from the sermon. Addressing the louse enables him to feast his eyes upon the attractive young lady whose face and bonnet it is intent on ascending. The speaker's words form an alternative sermon: specific example and observation lead to generalised truth. It is Jenny who exemplifies 'airs in dress an' gait', but the speaker himself, with his airs in devotion, is encompassed within the irony of the last line. Thus Jenny, Lunardi, and the speaker all exemplify the folly of human 'airs'.

Both popular appreciation and academic study of Burns have been coloured by the fact that Burns rapidly became a mythological figure, an icon. The effect of both myth and icon is to simplify or reduce to the level of the easily assimilated. By virtue of their very nature and function myth and icon foster acceptance rather than investigation or challenge. Within his own lifetime Burns had become a figurehead to a nation. On the streets of Dumfries, as news of his death spread, the question asked, as Carol McGuirk notes, was 'Who will be our poet now?' Since the Union of 1707 Scots had felt the need to prove their right to cultural partnership with England. In Burns they found their great poet. As compensation for the loss of nation-hood, Burns, allegedly epitomising Scottish characteristics, became a focus for national pride. Having invested so much in Burns, Scots felt (and continue to feel) entitled to a regular return and on their terms.

Four of the essays deal with aspects of precisely this issue: how Burns has been represented, used, and — at worst — abused. In a comprehensive survey of nineteenth-century editing practices, G. Ross Roy shows how editing could readily become a form of censorship whereby Burns's corpus might be 'cleansed' of moral impurities. Thus Currie replaced 'sodomy' in Burns's 'down-right sodomy of the soul' with 'prostitution', believing the substitute term less likely to offend. Currie was, in Roy's words, 'preparing an edition which would appeal to a broad general public'; hence he, like Thomson, portrayed 'a pure, if one is not to say, emasculated poet' (for instance, Currie omitted any mention of Burns's connection with *The Merry Muses of Caledonia*). Professor Roy's essay demonstrates very clearly that in presenting Burns in a particular light editors say something about themselves; editing here emerges as self-revelation.

In *A Literary History of Scotland* (1903) J.H. Millar observed that 'national partiality has been a complicating element in Burns criticism to an extent incredible to those unacquainted with the collective vanity which animates the more impulsive section of the nation'.[8] Citing William Power's claim that 'the partisan way of looking at Burns was . . . fatal to a true appreciation of his writings', Andrew Noble delineates the political and cultural aspects of the 'partiality'. Noting the radical nature of Burns's politics and the problem which that, together with Burns's class and ethnicity, presented to the Scottish establishment, Noble accounts for the poignant irony that 'Scottish culture . . . from the early nineteenth century manipulated Burns into an icon of the very values he detested'.

In 'Burns and Nostalgia' Carol McGuirk designates Burns 'the only poet of classic stature ever to emerge from the British peasant class'. As such, he deserves to be seen for what he is.

How ironic, but also how inevitable, that he should have been so subject to nostalgic representation. Noting that many of Burns's class found it necessary to emigrate, McGuirk comments, 'In the decades following Burns's death, nostalgia resulted inevitably from his being perceived as the final articulate voice of a dying social class and an ancient country swallowed whole by Greater Britain (on which the sun never set)'. Burns came to symbolise a Scotland that was no more. Paradoxically, the world reduced to the Scottish village was to have worldwide appeal. The road that was to take Scottish literature to the Kailyard was already mapped out. The imagery characteristic of the Burns myth — the plough, the thistle, the cottage, and the sensitive poet — idealises and distorts the real Burns. As McGuirk points out, of the various portraits it is only Reid's that gives any indication of Burns's essential humour. Carol McGuirk argues convincingly that the icon became increasingly detached from Burns's body of work. No other writer has been subjected to such intense mythologising, but McGuirk makes a suggestive comparison between Burns's iconic function and that of Elvis Presley in contemporary American society.

Donny O'Rourke's essay, 'Burns on the Box', deals with a further dimension of the mythologising process. By its very nature the visual image specifies and defines. Here there would seem to be far less potential for 'the pleasures of creative construction' which McGuirk sees as integral to nostalgia. The synthetic function of the creative memory of the reader is replaced by the effect created jointly by writer, actor, cameraman, and director. Film by its nature tends to demystify. The larger-than-life figure, the enigma, the super-hero — each by being given flesh and bones is reduced to the particular and the merely human. For some people mention of God evokes the features of George Burns; for others, his namesake Robert will forever be John Cairney. Film-makers, as O'Rourke shows, have been faced with the choice of perpetuating the myth courtesy of kitsch or attempting to penetrate to the reality.

It was almost certainly the scale and intensity of the Burns myth rather than Burns's poetry that shaped the response of Scottish writers to him. Carol McGuirk remarks that 'Scott,

Stevenson, MacDiarmid — all had to repudiate Burns in order to replace his mythic Scotland with one of their own imagining' (and Edwin Muir could be added to the list). It might be suggested, in passing, that the Scotlands which these writers imagined were not entirely without their own mythic elements. The point is, however, that MacDiarmid, in the words of Edwin Morgan, 'was doing the classic thing of attacking the old to make way for the new, kicking out the father, killing the king'. The deed is now history, and Morgan's essay reflects one Scottish writer's capacity for humane and balanced appraisal of Burns. For Morgan, 'as a writer, as a poet, you're more concerned with reacting in broad terms, with accepting or rejecting, with celebrating or absorbing the qualities that attract you in another poet'. Appropriately for a poet whose own work is characterised by an acute sense of the sound, the shape, and the feel of words, Morgan responds directly to the texture of Burns's language across its wide range, from the trenchant concision of satiric protest to the powerful and hauntingly evocative images such as the 'craz'd banes' in 'Epistle to Davie, a Brother Poet' and these mystical lines in the song, 'Open the door to me Oh': 'The wan moon sets behind the white wave, And time is setting on me, Oh'. As salutary counter to the reductive effects of the myth, Morgan identifies as essential qualities of Burns the emotional flux within poems ('the ability to switch between pathos and comedy, a broad, life-giving, therapeutic comedy'), and the range of his moods, tones, and voices.

In demonstrating the range of voices of which Burns was capable, Edwin Morgan cites instances of his mastery of direct address ('Ha! whare ye gaun, ye crowlan ferlie!'; 'O ye wha are sae guid yoursel,/Sae pious and sae holy'; 'Wee, sleeket, cowran, tim'rous beastie'). In this respect the English poet with whom Burns stands comparison is John Donne, but whereas in Donne's case expertise in dramatic poetry coincided with the full flowering of drama itself, in Scotland clerical disapproval denied poets the support of a flourishing dramatic tradition. Though Burns toyed with writing a play and did compose the cantata, 'The Jolly Beggars' ('Love and Liberty'), his considerable dramatic talent was channelled principally into the range of voices and personae of his poems. That Burns is an accomplished dramatic poet, expert in the creation of voices, cannot be over-stressed, because one effect of the cult has been, in quoting Burns out of context, to assume that he always speaks in his own voice. Plainly this is not the case in 'The Death and Dying Words of Poor Mailie' where the reader is addressed by a dying sheep; nor is Burns the Devil in 'Address of Beelzebub' or the 'auld farmer' in 'The Auld Farmer's New-Year-Morning Salutation to his Auld Mare, Maggie'. Some readers, though, may be startled by the suggestion that the late-night-revelling peasant who meets Death on his way home and narrates 'Death and Doctor Hornbook' is not necessarily Burns; nor is the public-bar philosopher who relates the 'tale' of 'Tam o' Shanter'. Devotees of the myth may not welcome the suggestion that Burns's tongue might be in his cheek in 'To a Haggis' and 'Scotch Drink'. For such readers Gilbert Burns's words are well worth citing:

> . . . every attentive reader of Burns's Works must have observed, that he frequently presents a caricature of his feelings, and even of his failings — a kind of mock-heroic account of himself and his opinions, which he never supposed could have been taken literally.[9]

'Holy Willie's Prayer' epitomises Burns's expertise in the ironic use of persona. Holy Willie reveals himself as both absurd in his bigotry and hypocrisy and awesome in his limitations. Without saying anything in his own voice Burns communicates his view of the creed which Holy Willie represents. Albeit that his irony is altogether more genial than Burns's, Iain Crichton Smith in his Murdo monologue demonstrates that the Scottish tradition of ironic self-revelation is alive and well and in good hands.

Burns's use of voice is one manifestation of the importance of the creative imagination to Burns. There is more than a grain of truth in Murdo's judgement on 'To a Mouse', that 'most great poets would not see in this tiny animal matter for speculation. But Rabbie Burns did. That is why he is our National Poet'. Burns excels in the imaginative transformation of the common-places of rural life. A simple-minded farmhand asked what to do about a sheep that had fallen over; the result was the masterly monologue, 'The Death and Dying Words of Poor Mailie'. Likewise, the fellowship of a collie and a retriever serves as springboard to an analysis of class divisions in society.

Two essays serve the important function of reminding us of the social reality out of which such poems developed. John Strawhorn points to the fact that Burns lived through a period of intense and rapid change, both economic and social. Burns, he notes, 'was typical of so many countrymen who ended their lives as townsmen'. Strawhorn details the ways in which economic developments effected change in social conditions, particularly in respect of housing, diet, and dress. However, the one constant, from the twelfth century to the twentieth, was the feudal system. The power of the landowners was manifested in the process of 'consolidation', of which the Burns family, as tenant-farmers, were themselves the unfortunate victims. Despite the pace of change the social order in Burns's time remained obdurately hierarchical, with the vast majority of the populace denied franchise. Christopher A. Whatley points to 'the inescapable fact that in eighteenth-century Scotland the route to personal security and social advancement depended to a large degree on patronage, and hence the goodwill of one's social superiors', a fact which had implications for Burns's prospects as both poet and exciseman. Whatley's essay identifies an ambivalence in Burns's attitude to labour: his 'radical empathy with the labouring poor' is beyond question (witness his comparison of Carron ironworks with 'the cave of Cyclops'),[10] yet in 'Bessy and Her Spinning Wheel' he idealises both the work and the situation of the spinner. Whatley identifies the limitations of historians' quest for solidarity in eighteenth-century Scotland in terms solely of class and ideology; account must also be taken of occupation, gender, religious sympathy, and community.

One of the particular features of Scottish parishes was the accessibility of education. If Presbyterianism was inimical to the creative arts, it nonetheless encouraged the establishment of schools (a typically Scottish paradox). John Strawhorn notes that by the year of the Scottish Education Act of 1696, half of Ayrshire's parishes had schools and in the course of the eighteenth century all the others followed suit. Here was one of the bases of the momentum towards enlightenment. Burns, whose education, at least in the formal sense, was sporadic but was pursued with vigour, was very much a product of that momentum. His poems and letters resonate sensitivity to change in local, national, and international contexts. It is salutary to compare Burns's letters with Micah Balwhidder's account in *Annals of the Parish* of Ayrshire life in the years 1760–1810. Ironically distanced from his annalist, Galt, by showing the latter's incapacity in the face of change, might be said to be pleading the cause of open-mindedness and breadth of vision of precisely the kind that Burns exemplified.

Two of the essays here engage with the cultural, intellectual, and educational influences on Burns. In 'Burns as Sassenach Poet' R.D.S. Jack challenges vigorously the Scottish tendency to introversion and parochialism and shows the limitations of the narrowly nationalist reading of Burns, which assumes that he is necessarily most successful when he writes in vernacular Scots. By using Pope and Wordsworth, Professor Jack 'isolates in each case the perversions and diminutions perpetuated by those who see the English poets as "sassenach" threats to Burns's Scottishness'. Jack substantiates his claim that Burns, like Ramsay and the late-medieval Makars, 'thought of language in terms of hierarchically arranged and linguistically distinguished styles', and he proves conclusively the influence of John Murdoch's teaching in making of Burns 'an unrepentant rhetorician'. In accelerating the critical momentum established by David Daiches and developed by Thomas Crawford in *Burns: A Study of the Poems and Songs* (1960) and Carol McGuirk in *Robert Burns and the Sentimental Era* (1985), Jack's essay exemplifies the value of reading Burns in terms of cultural relationships and interactions, in short, the importance of looking out and beyond — as Burns did. Jack's contention, 'if one thinks in terms of Scots and Sassenachs in the realms of the imagination, one is going, necessarily, to misjudge and, simply, to miss out', has implications for Scottish literary study far beyond Burns.

My own contribution identifies some of the ways in which Burns's extensive reading helped shape his poetry. 'Tam o'

Shanter' is presented as the triumphant synthesis of a range of diverse cultural strains — the folk-tale of supernatural encounter; the expressive vernacular of the Makars; its revival in Ramsay and Fergusson; the comic-epic as exemplified in Fielding's *Tom Jones*; and the experiments by Fielding, and by Sterne in *Tristram Shandy*, in the use of unreliable narrators. In the play of relationships which is integral to 'Tam o' Shanter' I see not just a literary, but also a personal, psychological dimension.

If Burns is indeed a sophisticated literary artist, how did he come to masquerade as the untutored ploughman-poet? The explanation lies in the desire of Scots to be in the vanguard of the reaction against Reason and the concomitant desire for a return to Nature. Hume wrote on 8 October 1754 to John Wilkes:

> If your time had permitted, you shoud have gone into the Highlands. You woud there have seen human Nature in the Golden Age, or rather, indeed, in the Silver.[11]

If Scots could but find amongst their number the Noble Savage as poet, then they would achieve prominence on the world stage and solve the crisis of identity by which they had been bedevilled since the Union of 1707. Enter Burns.

Collectively, these essays offer an antidote to Burns the 'Heaven-taught Ploughman' on whom, in the words of Murdo, 'the divine afflatus descended'. Here, rather, in his multiplicity of selves, he is revealed as essentially modern. Transmitted through poetic forms, the chameleon talent found expression in imaginative literature of the highest order. That same gift, however, was one of the factors in making his own life, especially latterly, so problematic. Though Burns's intellectual horizons were far-reaching and extensive, he never left Scotland. Carol McGuirk, noting that Burns's poems and songs immortalise the minutiae of rural life, observes, 'That the poet himself was driven nearly to insanity by the narrowness of parish-life is one of the ironies of literary history'. Perhaps the assumption of voices offered both relief and release. Burns's situation in such a community was an ambivalent one. His incisive wit, in both poetry and conversation, soon established him as a local celebrity and an object of suspicion. David Sillar recalled, 'His social disposition easily procured him acquaintance; but a certain satirical seasoning, with which he and all poetical geniuses are in some degree influenced, while it set the rustic circle in a roar, was not unaccompanied by its kindred attendant — suspicious fear'.[12] Analogy might be drawn with the uproarious laughter of the unscathed majority at the discomfort of the unfortunate victim of the alternative comedian: such laughter is tinged with both relief at escaping such treatment and apprehension that one may be the next target. The nature of his talent provides the satirist with his own cordon sanitaire; in my essay I suggest that Burns was increasingly aware of this fact. His 'first ambition', as he defined it to Moore, was 'to please my Compeers, the rustic Inmates of the Hamlet' (*Letters*, I, 88). It is a measure of his poetic achievement that he found means of both fulfilling this aim and expressing his own intellectual interests. Thus, many of his poems can be read on two levels — the communal and the individual.

Edwin Morgan writes of the 'real pathos of [Burns's] situation — a man of genius born a peasant'. If Ayrshire parish life exercised constraints, the celebrity which the Edinburgh literati bestowed upon him was something of a poisoned chalice. Burns seems to have played the man of feeling with enthusiasm, but if the Poet as Noble Savage provided him with a role on the national stage, it also proved to be an additional source of pressure. As the letters testify, life as a totem took its toll. The Dumfries period, too, exacerbated the sense of alienation, Burns's choice of career proving problematic in respect of not only the tension between his political sympathies and professional responsibilities but also his personal relations; excisemen, as Chris Whatley notes, were hate-objects particularly in the south-west of Scotland.

In view of these various factors it is understandable that, as Edwin Morgan indicates, 'there was a vulnerability just under the surface, which sometimes broke through'. Some of the letters reveal a deeply troubled spirit, aware of personal entrapment, internal division, and — above all — the impossibility of integrating the multiple selves or relating them to a psychological core. As early as 19 December 1787 he was writing,

My worst enemy is *Moimême.* I lie so miserably open to the inroads
and incursions of a mischievous, light-armed, well-mounted
banditti, under the banners of imagination, whim, caprice, and
passion; and the heavy armed veteran regulars of wisdom,
prudence and fore-thought, move so very, very slow, that I am
almost in a state of perpetual warfare, and alas! frequent defeat.
There are just two creatures that I would envy, a horse in his wild
state traversing the forests of Asia, or an oyster on some of the
desart shores of Europe. The one has not a wish without
enjoyment, the other has neither wish nor fear (*Letters*, I, 185).

Early in 1790 he was writing from Ellisland, 'My nerves are in a
damnable State. — I feel that horrid hypochondria pervading
every atom of both body & Soul. — This Farm has undone my
enjoyment of myself' (*Letters*, II, 3); that last phrase is particularly
telling psychologically. By late 1791 he was writing to Ainslie of
'my hell within, and all around me' (*Letters*, II, 121).

Despite the characteristic verve of much of the poetry, the
habitual spirited emphasis on conviviality, and the recurrent
echoes of a 'rumbustious Scotland' (Chris Whatley's term), there
is pervasive evidence of another Burns, a Burns, as Edwin
Morgan sees him, 'more strange, more mysterious, more
secret'. For this Burns, the transformative power of the imagination functioned as compensation and means of escape. But, as
the recurrent identification with the Devil may well suggest, it
also offered a means of externalising inner conflict.

In the opinion of Andrew Lang, writing in 1906:

The life of Robert Burns has been written so often, the history of
his career has been so intensely scrutinised, his poetry has passed
under the eyes of critics so numerous and so distinguished, that to
say about him what is both new and true is perhaps impossible.[13]

It is the wish of contributors to this volume that that view may
be disproved.

It had been the hope of the editor to be able to include the
paper, which Murdo was privileged to hear, on 'Burns and the
Silicon Chip', but the identity of its author is proving tiresomely
elusive. However, efforts in that direction continue . . .

Notes

1. The exception — and a most welcome addition — is the essay by Donald A. Low.
2. J. DeLancey Ferguson (ed.), *The Letters of Robert Burns*; 2nd edn., ed. G. Ross Roy (Oxford, 1985), II, 29–31.
3. Donald A. Low (ed.), *Robert Burns: The Critical Heritage* (London & Boston, 1974), 208.
4. *Ibid.*, 102.
5. James Kinsley (ed.), *The Poems and Songs of Robert Burns* (Oxford, 1968), III, 1538.
6. Low (ed.), *Burns: Critical Heritage*, 258.
7. Thomas Crawford, *Burns: A Study of the Poems and Songs* (2nd edn., repr. Edinburgh, 1978), 155.
8. J.H. Millar, *A Literary History of Scotland* (London, 1903), 409.
9. Low (ed.), *Burns: Critical Heritage*, 271.
10. Kinsley (ed.), *Poems and Songs*, III, 1242.
11. J.Y.T. Grieg, *The Letters of David Hume* (Oxford, 1969), I, 195.
12. Robert Chambers (ed.), *The Life and Works of Robert Burns*, rev. William Wallace, 4 vols (Edinburgh & London, 1896), I, 68–9.
13. Andrew Lang (intro.), *Poems and Songs of Robert Burns* (London, 1904), XIX.

1

A Poet's Response to Burns

Edwin Morgan

When I was asked to contribute 'A poet's response to Burns' I realised that I had not previously published anything on Burns and had, as it were, to start from scratch and try to sort out my feelings about him. If I haven't published essays or books on Burns, it wasn't because I didn't like his work — I do like it a lot — but either for accidental reasons or because I didn't feel the need to make any literary-critical response. Everything about Burns's background in society, the times he lived in, the influences on his writing — all that was interesting and useful — but the poetry itself has such clarity, and obviously gives so much enjoyment without having to make a laboured case for it, that I had not felt moved in the past to submit it to deep analysis. Perhaps this was wrong, since there are now so many different critical methods available that even apparently clear, simple and direct poems can be made to yield secrets — even non-existent secrets — to deconstruction. But as a writer, as a poet, one is more concerned with reacting in broad terms, with accepting or rejecting, with celebrating or absorbing in oneself the qualities that attract one in another poet. Of course, between any poet today and Burns there stands the figure of Hugh MacDiarmid, who published a good deal about Burns, in both verse and prose, and mainly though not entirely critical — critical especially of Burns's influence on nineteenth-century poets, for which the man himself can hardly be blamed, but critical too of Burns for not being Scottish enough ('Burns betrayed the movement Ramsay and Fergusson began'), and he quotes with favour T.S. Eliot's definition of Burns as 'a decadent representative of a great alien tradition', alien, that is, to English. Well, MacDiarmid of course was doing the classic thing of attacking the old to make way for the new, kicking out the father, killing the king. He had his own ideas, his own different

sort of poetry, to establish. Now that both Burns and MacDiarmid are a part of history, there is not the same need to take
sides — indeed there are many similarities between them —
and a young poet today could admire and learn from Burns
without looking through MacDiarmid-tinted spectacles. A 1986
pamphlet of new poems in Scots by three young poets, Robert
Crawford, W.N. Herbert, and David Kinloch, was called *Severe
Burns*, a pun which certainly brings Burns back, but also suggests
some necessary cauterisation of current literary attitudes.

So an active response to Burns is still on the cards. The force of
Burns's writing has not disappeared; nor has the force of the
man. I find in my own experience that with Burns (as with
Byron) it is extremely difficult to separate the man and the
writer. This might seem to be playing into the hands of the
idolators, the Burns Culters, whose interest in literature and
literary values may be slight. But we have to remember that what
was, in effect, a cult of Burns had begun in his own lifetime. The
impact he made on those who met him was extraordinary, and
the social and intellectual range of characters who paid tribute to
his personality, within the short period of his life and fame, is
astonishing. Dugald Stewart, Professor of Moral Philosophy at
Edinburgh University, wrote of him:

> His manners were . . . simple, manly, and independent; strongly
> expressive of conscious genius and worth; but without any thing
> that indicated forwardness, arrogance, or vanity. He took his share
> in conversation, but not more than belonged to him; and listened
> with apparent attention and deference, on subjects where his want
> of education deprived him of the means of information. If there
> had been a little more of gentleness and accommodation in his
> temper, he would, I think, have been still more interesting; but he
> had been accustomed to give law in the circle of his ordinary
> acquaintance; and his dread of any thing approaching to meanness
> or servility, rendered his manner somewhat decided and hard.
> Nothing, perhaps, was more remarkable among his various
> attainments, than the fluency, and precision, and originality of
> his language . . . more particularly as he aimed at purity in his turn
> of expression, and avoided more successfully than most Scotch-
> men, the peculiarities of Scottish phraseology.[1]

The interest of that last sentence is twofold, in that it bears out the oneness of the man in having clear articulation of speech as well as clear articulation of verse, and also it reminds us how bilingual, and convincingly bilingual, he must have been — a fact that in any case seemed obvious from the free and racy English of his letters. Dugald Stewart went on to make another valuable point:

> Among the poets whom I have happened to know, I have been struck, in more than one instance, with the unaccountable disparity between their general talents, and the occasional inspirations of their more favoured moments. But all the faculties of Burns's mind were, as far as I could judge, equally vigorous; and his predilection for poetry was rather the result of his own enthusiastic and impassioned temper, than of a genius exclusively adapted to that species of composition. From his conversation I should have pronounced him to be fitted to excel in whatever walk of ambition he had chosen to exert his abilities.[2]

This is very far from any idea of the child of nature or the heaven-taught ploughman, and from the later Burns Cult's efforts to play down his intellectual qualities. Stewart saw, I'm sure rightly, that the poetry came from feeling, from a passionate temperament, but underneath there was the solid sense of a mind at work, a stance, a confidence that indeed rubs off on the reader. I find this very attractive.

Walter Scott, also, was impressed by Burns's general intellectual assurance:

> His person was strong and robust; his manner . . . a sort of dignified plainness and simplicity . . . I think his countenance was more massive than it looks in any of the portraits . . . Among the men who were the most learned of their time and country, he expressed himself with perfect firmness.[3]

It is perhaps worth underlining what Scott says in his second sentence, in view of the popularity of the idealising and feminising Nasmyth portrait, by adding that other contemporary references to Burns's looks included terms such as 'coarse', 'rough', and even 'black countenance' — none of which derogated from his magnetic appeal (to both men and women), but perhaps that appeal was nearer Heathcliff than Bonnie Prince Charlie. And Scott, like Dugald Stewart, saw that there was also in Burns something that made a great contrast to his plain simple mental firmness. He goes on to say:

> There was a strong expression of sense and shrewdness in all his lineaments; the eye alone, I think, indicated the poetical character and temperament. It was large and of a dark cast, and glowed (I say literally *glowed*) when he spoke with feeling or interest. I never saw such another eye in a human head, though I have seen the most distinguished men in my time.

Maybe that glowing eye warns us that we should not push the intellectual case too far. Burns himself never joined, in any real sense, the Edinburgh literati; it was, as he said, a new world which he enjoyed visiting, but his aims lay elsewhere. He makes this clear in a letter to his friend Mrs Dunlop in March 1787 (that is, after the Kilmarnock edition of his poems in 1786):

> I have made some small alterations in what I before had printed. — I have the advice of some very judicious friends among the Literati here, but with them I sometimes find it necessary to claim the privilege of thinking for myself . . . The appelation (*sic*) of, a Scotch Bard, is by far my highest pride; to continue to deserve it is my most exalted ambition. — Scottish scenes, and Scottish story are the themes I could wish to sing.[4]

This emphasis on the Scottishness, the nativeness, of his aims and ambitions, is linked with the less intellectual, the more emotional side of his nature — with the part of him that admired Henry Mackenzie's *The Man of Feeling* ('next to the Bible'), Macpherson's *Ossian*, James Thomson's *The Seasons*, and William Falconer's *The Shipwreck*. Falconer (1732–69) was a seaman who published a long poem about a shipwreck, only to be drowned himself when he was still in his thirties. Burns wrote about his death in a letter to Mrs Dunlop in January 1790:

> Falconer, the unfortunate Author of the Shipwreck, that glorious Poem which you so much admire, is no more. — After weathering that dreadful catastrophe he so feelingly describes in

his Poem, and after weathering many hard gales of Fortune, he
went to the bottom with the Aurora frigate! I forget what part of
Scotland had the honor of giving him birth, but he was the son of
obscurity & misfortune.[5]

We know from different witnesses that Burns was easily moved,
easily touched, by certain subjects or in certain circumstances,
and particularly in circumstances relating to the precariousness of
life or of fame — this despite his confidence, his consciousness
of his genius. There was a vulnerability just under the surface,
which sometimes broke through. Walter Scott recalled an
incident in Edinburgh, when as a boy of fifteen he first saw
Burns, at a literary gathering:

> The only thing I remember which was remarkable in Burns'
> manner, was the effect produced upon him by a print of Bunbury's
> [H.W. Bunbury, 1750–1811], representing a soldier lying dead on
> the snow, his dog sitting in misery on the one side, on the other his
> widow, with a child in her arms. Those lines were written
> beneath, —

> Cold on Canadian hills, or Minden's plain,
> Perhaps that parent wept her soldier slain;
> Bent o'er her babe, her eye dissolved in dew,
> The big drops, mingling with the milk he drew,
> Gave the sad presage of his future years,
> The child of misery baptized in tears.

> Burns seemed much affected by the print, or rather the ideas which
> it suggested to his mind. He actually shed tears. He asked whose
> the lines were, and it chanced that nobody but myself remembered
> that they occur in a half-forgotten poem of Langhorne's, called by
> the unpromising title of 'The Justice of the Peace'. I whispered my
> information to a friend present, who mentioned it to Burns, who
> rewarded me with a look and a word, which, though of mere
> civility, I then received and still recollect with very great pleasure.[6]

Burns was moved by the early death of the soldier in the picture,
or by the drowning of William Falconer, as also by the early
death of the poet Robert Fergusson, all examples of youth and
promise suddenly snuffed out. I do not think this is sentimen-

tality (though there may be moments in his poetry when he goes perilously near sentimentality). It was partly an age of sentiment, the age of Henry Mackenzie and Laurence Sterne, and it was a time when men were not ashamed to weep in public — people were obviously not embarrassed in the room where the incident Scott describes took place. But Falconer and Bunbury and Langhorne and Fergusson all made Burns think of his own life, which he often talked about in terms of physical hardship, or poverty, or sheer unluckiness. In his letters he refers again and again to the baleful or damned star he was born under, and he had moods of intense depression and melancholy. It may have been psychology, but it was certainly social conditions, going back to his boyhood: poor farms; a tyrannical factor; back-breaking work in the open which doubtless gave him his weatherbeaten 'black countenance'. 'This kind of life,' he wrote, 'the chearless gloom of a hermit with the unceasing moil of a galley-slave, brought me to my sixteenth year.'[7] But in the same letter (the long autobiographical letter of August 1787, to Dr John Moore) he has the interesting comment on his love poetry, that under the conditions he describes, love becomes one of the major values, love is the opposite of work, work is hell, love is heaven. He places his love poems within their social context. When he began farming for himself, he seemed to be dogged by bad luck and never really made a go of it; nor did he much enjoy his later work as a 'poor damned rascally gauger' in the excise. At the age of thirty-five, he wrote in a letter to Mrs Dunlop on New Year's Day 1795: 'Very lately I was a boy; but t'other day I was a young man; & I already begin to feel the rigid fibre & stiffening joints of Old Age coming fast o'er my frame.'[8] And a year after that, in 1796, he was dead. He died at the same age of thirty-seven as the sailor-poet William Falconer, thereby fulfilling his own fears and forebodings.

Yet the other side of Burns was always there, what his friend Maria Riddell called the *vivida vis animi*, 'vivid energy of soul', the high spirits, the humour and wit and fun, the sheer enjoyment of life which comes bubbling up in his letters even when least expected. A good example of this madcap, inventive, quicksilver Burns occurs in a long letter to Mrs Dunlop in December 1788:

Page the twelfth! 'tis absolutely unconscionable! If Miss Georgina McKay is still at Dunlop, I beg you will make her my Compliments, & request her in my name to sing you a song at the close of every page, by way of dissipating Ennui; as David (who, by the by, was, baiting the Sex, no bad Prototype of Miss Mc——, for he was not only fam'd for his musical talents, but was also 'ruddy & well-favor'd, & more comely than his breathren') playing on his harp chased the Evil Spirit out of Saul. — This Evil Spirit, I take it, was just, long-spun Sermons, & many-pag'd Epistles, & Birthday Poetry, & patience-vexing Memorials, Remonstrances, Dedications, Revolution-Addresses, &c.&c.&c. while David's harp, I suppose was, mystically speaking, Tristram Shandy, Laugh & be fat, Cauld kail in Aberdeen, Green grows the rashes, & the rest of that inspired & inspiring family.[9]

Burns seemed to those who met him to be more vigorously alive than most other people. It would be gratifying to think that this might be true of every creative person, yet if you compare Burns with someone like Wordsworth you see a difference — Wordsworth was disappointing to meet, he appeared aloof, wrapped up in himself, his whole life seemed to be inward, it was just as intense but it didn't show itself — whereas in Burns everything is outgoing, he shows his feelings, he sees no need to conceal, speaks his mind. From this point of view the growth of a cult, of a legend, is not really surprising, any more than it was surprising that the same thing happened with Byron. Both the positive values of love, humour, and poetry (or song) which he sets up in his writing against the hardship and misery and poverty of life, and the negative satirical protest which he makes against the bad and oppressive aspects of his society, rise quite naturally out of his experience. And that is the real pathos of Burns's situation, a man of genius born a peasant — conscious of his talent, proud of his 'independent mind', but agonised by the deficiencies in himself and in his society. This is what makes 'To a Mouse' such a moving poem. The wild panic of the fieldmouse turned out of its nest reminds him instantly of the precariousness of human happiness and plans, but the worst thing of all is not the precariousness but the consciousness of it, which the mouse does not have:

> Still, thou art blest, compar'd wi' me!
> The present only toucheth thee:
> But Och! I backward cast my e'e,
>   On prospects drear!
> An' forward, tho' I canna see,
>   I guess an' fear!

That kind of pathos, and the ability to switch between pathos and comedy (both ways), a broad, life-giving, therapeutic comedy, are what I respond to most strongly in Burns. I also find very congenial his dramatic sense, his habit of direct address, which goes with his outgoing personality — in poems such as 'To a Mouse', 'Address to the Deil', 'Address to the Unco Guid', 'Holy Willie's Prayer', 'To a Louse', 'Address of Beelzebub to the President of the Highland Society', his many 'Epistles' to various friends, and many of the songs. Each address is different, and although you do sense a personality behind them all, you also hear a multiplicity of voices. You may hear them on the page with the inner ear, but the surest way to begin admiring the range of Burns's dramatic projection is to read his opening lines aloud and discover the exact tone he has devised for each: the intimate surprised concern of 'Wee, sleeket, cowran, tim'rous beastie . . .'; the grim but unabashed button-holing of 'O thou, whatever title suit thee! Auld Hornie, Satan, Nick, or Clootie . . .' the sardonic fingerwagging of 'O ye wha are sae guid yoursel, Sae pious and sae holy . . .'; the unctuous self-assurance of 'O thou that in the heavens does dwell! . . .'; the subject-matching impudence of 'Ha! whare ye gaun, ye crowlan ferlie! . . .', the totally ruthless irony of 'Long life, My lord, an' health be yours, Unskaith'd by hunger'd Highlan Boors! . . .'

I've always thought that his racy, unbuttoned, freewheeling verse Epistles show this dramatic aspect of Burns very attractively. They are humorous, yet serious too. They often claim to be careless and spontaneous, and perhaps they were, but it is a spontaneousness, like Byron's, that shows a mastery of rhyme and rhythm nevertheless — the practised hand at work. One of the best is the 'second Epistle to John Lapraik', local minor poet and farmer in Ayrshire, written in 1785. The poem is full of

characters and voices. Burns addresses himself, he addresses
Lapraik, he addresses God, the Muse addresses Burns, Burns
addresses her, the State addresses the populace, Fortune is
personified, a city gent appears, a feudal thane appears . . . it's
a good example of that *vivida vis animi* that Maria Riddell spoke
about:

> . . . Sae I gat paper in a blink,
> An' down gaed stumpie in the ink:
> Quoth I, 'Before I sleep a wink,
>   I vow I'll close it;
> An' if ye winna mak it clink,
>   By Jove, I'll prose it!' . . .
>
> My worthy friend, ne'er grudge an' carp,
> Tho' Fortune use you hard an' sharp;
> Come, kittle up your moorlan harp
>   Wi' gleesome touch!
> Ne'er mind how Fortune waft an' warp;
>   She's but a bitch.
>
> She's gien me mony a jirt an' fleg,
> Sin' I could striddle owre a rig;
> But, by the Lord, tho' I should beg
>   Wi' lyart pow,
> I'll laugh, an' sing, an' shake my leg,
>   As lang's I dow!
>
> Now comes the sax an' twentieth simmer,
> I've seen the bud upo' the timmer,
> Still persecuted by the limmer
>   Frae year to year;
> But yet, despite the kittle kimmer,
>   I, Rob, am here.
>
> Do ye envy the city-gent,
> Behint a kist to lie an' sklent,
> Or purse-proud, big wi' cent per cent,
>   An' muckle wame,
> In some bit brugh to represent
>   A bailie's name?

Or is't the paughty. feudal thane,
Wi' ruffl'd sark an' glancin cane,
Wha thinks himsel nae sheep-shank bane,
      But lordly stalks,
While caps an' bonnets aff are taen,
      As by he walks?

'O Thou wha gies us each guid gift!
Gie me o' wit an' sense a lift,
Then turn me, if Thou please, adrift,
      Thro' Scotland wide;
Wi' cits nor lairds I wadna shift,
      In a' their pride!'

Were this the charter of our state,
'On pain o' hell be rich an' great,'
Damnation then would be our fate,
      Beyond remead;
But, thanks to Heav'n, that's no the gate
      We learn our creed . . .

But there is another Burns, not the extrovert Burns of these Epistles and similar poems, but something more strange, more mysterious, more secret, often associated with images or settings of twilight or darkness, not so much a matter of whole poems as of a few lines which reverberate in your mind and make you wonder where the impact came from — these also I find very powerful and haunting, almost at the opposite end of the spectrum from his dancing bouncy vigorous verse, the verse of the ranting dog, as he called himself. This is something very different. I am thinking of lines like

To lye in kilns and barns at e'en,
When banes are craz'd, and bluid is thin
           ('Epistle to Davie, a Brother Poet')

Within the poem, these two lines are like a change of key in music; there's a sudden grimness which is both vivid and yet tantalising; perhaps the word *kilns* has a certain horror about it, even though it is only a place where homeless people might go to get warm; and the idea of the *crazed bones* has a range of possible meanings, some of which seem to link back to the kilns, others towards old age or madness or both. And this part of the poem sticks in your mind long after you read the rest of it, which tries to soften the blow and tell you (rather as Wordsworth would tell you) that it is possible to be shelterless and yet content.

Another of these haunting moments in Burns is in the song 'The Lea-Rig', and again it is nocturnal:

> At midnight hour, in mirkest glen,
>   I'd rove and ne'er be irie O,
> If thro' that glen I gaed to thee,
>   My ain kind Dearie O.

All the eeriness of the countryside at night, with a kind of darkness you never find in towns or villages, seems to be in these lines, which also hold suggestions right back to the ballads and to medieval Scottish poetry. The suggestiveness is complex, and yet the lines themselves, with their rhyme and rhythm and alliteration, are instantly memorable — unforgettable if you like.

And a last example, also from a song, 'Open the door to me Oh', which is on a traditional theme of the lover pleading for the woman to open her door, which she refuses to do till the end of the poem, when it is too late, and the lover lies frozen to death outside. This too is a night-piece. The two outstanding lines have often been quoted, and they have become almost a classic example of the unexplained powers of poetry:

> The wan moon sets behind the white wave,
>   And time is setting with me, Oh.

The action of the poem takes place in the open countryside at night, on a plain, and there is no explanation of the *white wave*, though it might presumably be some sea in the distance, but if so, it is only there in these two words, and plays no other part in the poem. It is almost as if the two lines suddenly moved the poem out into another world, a cold beautiful but sinister world where everything is about to come to an end, including time itself. I imagine Hugh MacDiarmid must have remembered the lines, which seem to be echoed in some of the cosmic poems in his early volume *Sangschaw*.

So I see Burns not only as a storyteller, not only as a social commentator, not only as a songwriter, not only as an entertainer, but also as the possessor of imagination, bodying forth the forms of things unknown. If imagination, as Blake thought, is the one thing that really makes a poet, Burns had it; and his combination of realism and strangeness is a great gift. I come back finally to the man. He was what he claimed to be, a man of independent mind; and yet this strongly marked, strongly individual character — that's the realism, if you like — 'I, Rob, am here' — was able to join many people together, across classes and across countries, still does so, in fact — and that is the strangeness. He will always be discussed, because there is no one quite like him.

Notes

1. W.L. Renwick (ed.), *Burns As Others Saw Him* (Edinburgh, 1959), 11–12.
2. Renwick, *op. cit.*, 13–14.
3. Renwick, *op. cit.*, 24.
4. J. DeLancey Ferguson (ed.), *The Letters of Robert Burns*; 2nd edn., ed. G. Ross Roy (Oxford, 1985), I, 100–1.
5. *Letters*, II, 6–7.
6. Renwick, *op. cit.*, 23–4.
7. *Letters*, I, 137.
8. *Letters*, II,333.
9. *Letters*, I, 343.

2
Everyday Life in Burns's Ayrshire

John Strawhorn

The years from 1759 till 1796 produced a number of great economic and social changes which transformed Scotland and had their effect on the life and career of Robert Burns. He was born in the rural society of auld Ayrshire which in many ways had remained unchanged for generations; before his death many innovations were creating a modern urban industrial way of life. One thing, however, persisted throughout Burns's lifetime, which affected every generation from the twelfth century till the early years of the twentieth. The feudal system instituted by David I and the kings who followed him awarded control of the land and its occupants to warlords whose successors continued as landlords to dominate life in this county as elsewhere.

The Landlords[1]

In the twelfth century, to assert royal authority over an unruly southwest, the kings of Scots awarded the de Morville family the district of Cunninghame on the north side of the River Irvine. Kyle, which lay between the Rivers Irvine and Doon, was divided, part being granted to Walter Fitzalan, progenitor of the royal Stewarts, part retained in crown possession. Carrick, south of the Doon, was given to a lord of Galloway from whom was descended Robert Bruce. These ancient divisions retained their significance in the eighteenth century. Burns in an early song announced that 'My father was a farmer upon the Carrick border'. Alloway was just a few yards from that border on the River Doon. So he could identify himself as 'There was a lad was born in Kyle'. More precisely his birthplace was in King's Kyle, and afterwards he could mark his move to Tarbolton and Mauchline in a third song, 'When first I came to Stewart Kyle'. He opened his Kilmarnock edition with that local scene: 'Twas in that place of Scotland's isle, That bears the name o' auld king Coil'. In so doing he showed he was familiar with the local legend of Old King Cole as mythical founder of Kyle. In his Commonplace Book for the year 1785 the twenty-six-year-old Robert Burns exhibited a remarkable acquaintance with Ayrshire local history: 'the ancient Bailieries of Carrick, Kyle, and Cunningham, famous both in ancient and modern times for a gallant, and warlike race of inhabitants; a country where civil, and particularly religious liberty have ever found their first support, and their last asylum; a country, the birthplace of many famous Philosophers, Soldiers, and Statesmen, and the scene of many important events recorded in Scottish History, particularly a great many of the actions of the glorious Wallace, the saviour of his country'. This sense of tradition inspired him to compose 'The Vision'. In that long and ambitious poem Burns reiterated his tribute to 'His country's saviour', and showed an intimate knowledge of family history by praising also the 'Chief of Sark', who was John Wallace, fifth laird of Craigie, who in 1448 won a battle at Sark near the Solway. In his first letter to Mrs Dunlop (15 Nov. 1786) he described William Wallace as 'your illustrious Ancestor'[2]; she was not really a direct descendant, but both were of the family of Richard Wallace who in the twelfth century had been granted lands in Kyle by Walter Fitzalan. Burns could not be expected to know the genealogical background of all the other landed families of Kyle, but in 'The Vision' he did supply biographical details of those who then possessed its seventeen principal estates. He was aware that Kyle was a district 'where once the Campbells, chiefs of fame, Held ruling power'. James de Loudoun had received from Richard de Morville an estate in Cunninghame which was inherited by the Craufurds, then the Campbells, who were elevated to the peerage in 1633. Sir Matthew Campbell of Loudoun had in 1566 acquired the lands of Mauchline, including Mossgiel.[3]

In the middle of the eighteenth century Ayrshire contained eight earldoms: Loudoun, Glencairn, Eglinton, and Glasgow in Cunninghame; Stair, Dumfries, and Dundonald in Kyle; Cassillis in Carrick. The earls of Loudoun, Eglinton, Dumfries, and

Cassillis held the largest estates, and together with a hundred other considerable lairds they owned and controlled Ayrshire. Then, as before and later, whatever one's business, one was dependent upon the landowners — whether one wanted to rent a farm, make a living as a tradesman, take up a profession, or gain recognition as a poet. In each parish it was the principal landowner who appointed the minister and with the other landowners maintained the school. The county landowners assessed and collected the land tax, provided police and prisons, built roads and bridges, and elected the county member of parliament.

In 1759 there were ninety-seven freeholders in Ayrshire who possessed the right to vote. That number increased to 224 in 1787 by including a number of nominal and fictitious voters who had been enfranchised by greater landowners consigning parts of their estates to nominees. The principle was that only those who owned a considerable portion of the country might participate in running the country's affairs; that was regarded as natural law. The numerous bonnet lairds who owned only their own farm had no vote, nor of course had any tenant farmer. Choice of a member of parliament was made by freeholders making public declaration at an assembly within Ayr tolbooth, but in fact the winner was usually known in advance. In practice choice of an Ayrshire MP was managed by the earls who as peers had no vote but were able by agreement or superior influence to persuade sufficient freeholders to support one candidate. In 1759 the MP for Ayrshire was James Campbell of Rowallan (later 5th Earl of Loudoun), followed in 1761 by Archibald Montgomerie of Minnoch (later 11th Earl of Eglinton), in 1768 by David Kennedy of Newark (later 10th Earl of Cassillis), in 1774 by Sir Adam Fergusson of Kilkerran (when the Dumfries/Glencairn bloc defeated a Cassillis/Eglinton/Loudoun alliance), in 1784 by Hugh Montgomerie of Coilsfield (later 12th Earl of Eglinton). Similarly, the choice of an MP for Ayr Burghs, made by five commissioners representing the royal burghs of Ayr, Irvine, Rothesay, Inveraray, and Campbeltown, was dictated by the earls. As for Kilmarnock, although it was the largest burgh in the county by 1792, not one person in the town was entitled to a parliamentary vote. Though lacking a franchise, Robert Burns exhibited interest in parliamentary politics. In 'The Author's Earnest Cry and Prayer to the Scotch Representatives in the House of Commons', he listed the candidates campaigning in 1786 for the Ayrshire seat: 'Sodger Hugh' Montgomerie of Coilsfield and James Boswell of Auchinleck; they would 'like Montgomerie fight, Or gab like Boswell' and had as their rival the 'aith-detesting, chaste Kilkerran'. In 1788 the 'Fête Champètre' repeated that choice between 'a Man-o'-law, Or will we send a Sodger, Or him wha led o'er Scotland a', The meikle Ursa Major?' The decision, Burns realised, depended on who could 'court a noble Lord, Or buy a score o' Lairds, man'. Later in Dumfriesshire Burns would contribute 'The Five Carlins' to the Dumfries Burghs contest of 1789 and the 'The Heron Ballads' for the Stewartry of Kirkcudbright seat in 1795; but he never had a vote.[4]

The regime dominated by the landlords was one of wide social divisions. At the top of the Ayrshire pyramid of wealth was the Earl of Eglinton with an annual income of £20,000 from his rents; at the bottom were the poor of Mauchline parish, subsisting on less than £3 yearly from the kirk session, even less well off than some of the itinerant beggars who frequented Poosie Nansie's. In between were substantial lairds such as James Boswell of Auchinleck on £1000 a year; and lesser lairds considered very comfortable on incomes over £200 a year. There were in Ayr, Irvine, and Kilmarnock some merchants and bankers who were doing well enough to infiltrate the ranks of the gentry by setting themselves up in country mansions. Parish ministers were well off: Daddy Auld of Mauchline had a stipend of £100 and nearly as much from his glebe. The rector of Ayr Academy, established in 1796, was passing rich at £80, plus fees: much more than the average Ayrshire parish schoolmaster's annual income of about £30, which John Wilson in Tarbolton supplemented by serving also as village apothecary and earning the nickname of Dr Hornbook. Handloom weavers in good years could earn £25, about the same as other craftsmen; and it is now evident that coalminers could make as much, even though nominally serfs until 1799. Ploughmen in 1780 got £8 a year plus their keep; farm labourers less. Some tenant farmers might earn up to £100 a year, but only if they could rent a big farm, if the land was improved, if they had capital to stock it, and if harvests were good. Most earned much less, and many failed to survive — such as William Burnes at Lochlea. His son, an equally competent farmer, would sensibly abandon Ellisland for a more promising career in the excise, beginning at £50 a year, and taking in double that by 1792. Such extreme differentials remained unchanged throughout Burns's lifetime, a period when so many other things were changing.[5]

The landowners were the principal promoters of the changes which historians later would call the Agricultural and Industrial Revolutions. Their agrarian improvements transformed what was essentially subsistence farming into commercial farming concentrating on serving an expanding market. Massive investment in farms resulted in improved productivity, and inflated rents could be charged to tenants. Increased output of wool, flax, and hides contributed towards extended manufacture of cloth and shoes for export. We should remember how Burns became involved in the linen trade, growing flax at Lochlea and working in the heckling shop at Irvine. The farms also provided food products to sell to the growing urban population. In 1755 about 75 per cent of Ayrshire's 59,000 inhabitants lived in the countryside; forty years later the population had increased to 73,500 — 53 per cent of them living in towns and villages. Robert Burns was himself typical of so many countrymen who ended their life as townsmen. The 'Cotter's Saturday Night' was an appropriate tribute to a disappearing class who on the farms were being replaced by wage-earning employees.[6]

Not all landowners were successful. David McLure of Shawood had to press his tenant William Burnes in Lochlea because he was himself on the verge of bankruptcy.[7] Sir John Whitefoord of Ballochmyle was also ruined by the Ayr Bank crash of 1772. His vacant estate was taken by an incomer with money to invest, Claud Alexander, who had made his fortune in India and beside Ballochmyle set up the Catrine Cotton Works in 1787. Two local earldoms were extinguished: Kilmarnock by attainder in 1747 when the Jacobite earl was executed; Glencairn following financial losses and failure of issue in 1796. Their lands were among those which in 1786 and following years were purchased for the rich heiress Henrietta Scott, whose husband was elevated to a dukedom and developed the resources of the great Portland estate.

Economic developments spawned changes in social conditions — changes, for example in housing, in diet, and in dress.

Housing[8]

In the middle of the eighteenth century the landed proprietors lived in tower-houses which had most of them been constructed in the fifteenth and sixteenth centuries. These had replaced earlier wooden dwellings, and were designed to combine defence with a measure of improved comfort. But despite fine furniture and rich tapestries, they must have been cold, draughty, and smelly places. Some of the lairds had town houses in the royal burghs of Ayr and Irvine, where the wealthier burgesses had also stone-built dwellings dating from the sixteenth century.

Most of the people lived in settlements dispersed throughout the countryside, where each group of tenants in a cluster of cottages shared in runrig cultivation of their unenclosed farm. Older dwellings were quite primitive, having low walls of turf, and cupples, which were timber rafters stretching from the ground to form a V-shaped roof, covered with thatch. When tenants moved, they might remove the cupples and use them to rebuild their cottage elsewhere. The cottars and labourers who were employed by the tenant farmers seem to have lived in even more primitive huts: there is mention in sixteenth-century Alloway records of 'ane hous of ane cuppill'.[9] By the eighteenth century the traditional cottage was a but-and-ben, its low walls built of stone or clay, the rafters still sometimes rising from the floor, the roof still thatched. Within, there was a dirt floor, with a peat fire in the centre, the smoke escaping through a hole in the roof. 'There lanely, by the ingle-cheek,/I sat and ey'd the spewing reek,/That fill'd, wi hoast-provoking smeek,/The auld clay biggin;/And heard the restless rattons squeak/About the riggin.' That 'auld clay biggin' which Burns described in 'The Vision' was probably Lochlea. The furnishings would comprise a table, forms and stools to sit upon, a girnel to store meal, a dresser to keep everything else. In the built-in beds, a layer of straw was covered with a linen sheet, the bolsters were filled with chaff, and there were woollen blankets and patchwork coverlets. This was the ben; the animals were wintered in the other apartment, called the but, which was separated from the living quarters by a lobby, the throughgang, or sometimes by a hallan, which was just a low partition. In 'The Cotter's Saturday Night' that humble family had only one cow, 'That 'yont the hallan snugly chows her cood'. Craftsmen in the towns and villages had similar accommodation, with their workshop in the but, like Souter Johnie who plied the shoemaking trade in his cottage at Kirkoswald.

In the second half of the eighteenth century the successful lairds invested their wealth in construction of new mansion houses. In Ayrshire William Adam and his famous sons designed such houses as Culzean, Dalquharran, Dumfries House, Auchincruive, and possibly Auchinleck and Ballochmyle. Some, such as Auchinleck, were built on a new site, most like Culzean incorporated the older tower-house. Stonemasons were kept busy, like James Armour of Mauchline, whose father before him had apparently been involved in building several mansions.

As the eighteenth century advanced, but-and-ben cottages with improved features were built. Some had an extra living room (the spense), upstairs attics, slated roofs, glazed windows instead of shutters, fireplaces set in the gable and provided with chimney vents, and flagstones on the floor. Additional furnishings included Kilmarnock-made carpets (which Burns first encountered at Adamhill farm), chairs, a mirror (the looking glass), and a clock (such as Clockie Brown of Mauchline made). At Alloway the house William Burnes built in 1757 had its spense, in which his son Robert was born. At Mossgiel there were attic apartments, in one of which some of his best poems were written down.

This is the period when many of our present farmhouses were created, often on new sites. Aiton in his Agricultural Report noted that 'Mr Fairly and others began between the years 1770 and 1780 to rebuild the farm houses on their estates' and described the plan most commonly adopted as 'a dwelling house, of two or three rooms in length, with garrets above, and the offices in a transverse direction on each side, forming a court open on one side'. In 1786 James Boswell began rebuilding, according to this plan, ten farmhouses on his Auchinleck estate. On one typical farm, Turnerhill, in 1787 he spent £22 planting 6,200 thorns purchased from Samsons of Kilmarnock, to form hedges between nine newly enclosed fields; in 1788 he built a two-roomed dwelling house costing £31; in 1790 he added a stable, byre, barn, shed, and dairy, the provision of these offices costing £58, the most expensive part of his investment.[10]

In the growing towns and villages similar but-and-bens were built to provide accommodation for handloom weavers and other craftsmen. Additional two-storey tenements were provided for those who did not work at home. In the Back Causeway at Mauchline, Burns in 1787 rented from a local tailor, Archibald Meikle, an upstairs single-end where he set up house with Jean Armour. Later in Dumfries he could afford less cramped housing for his family.

Food[11]

In the eighteenth century oatmeal was the basis of everyday diet in Scotland, and until recently it has been assumed that it was always so. It now appears that until the fifteenth century meat and dairy products were the principal elements, in the sixteenth century came a dramatic change, and by the eighteenth century these had become rarities, to be displaced by a grain-based diet. This diet, based upon what could be produced locally, was common to all classes. James Boswell's father recalled that, as a child in the 1720s, his meals consisted of porridge for breakfast, eggs with kail for the midday dinner, bread and butter for the afternoon meal called 'four hours', and bread and milk for supper.[12] For lesser folk bread was a luxury, because little wheat could be grown in Ayrshire, and only big houses had ovens.

The principal local crop was oats, so oatmeal was the main constituent of everyday diet, as porridge at two of the three daily meals and as an ingredient in brose, bannocks, sowens, and haggis. Bear (or bere), a coarse barley, was the only other grain crop; kail, peas, and beans were the common vegetables. So the menu could be extended with barley bannocks and with broth, which was served three or four times weekly. Home-brewed ale was the common drink. Milk was scarce, for the traditional black cattle had a limited yield and were dry three months in the year. Most milk was converted into cheese for winter use. The 'weel-hain'd kebbuck' of 'The Cotter's Saturday Night' was a special treat to supplement the supper of porridge, which was (surprisingly, for it was November) served with milk, that 'soupe their only Hawkie does afford'. If cheese was a treat, meat was a luxury that few could afford. Gilbert Burns recalled that at Mount Oliphant, 'For several years butcher's meat was a stranger in the house'. Marts, beasts killed off around Martinmas, might be salted for preservation, and cooked in the broth to provide boiling beef. Fish, however, were sometimes plentiful. Herrings and salmon appeared regularly on the menu of Ayr Poorshouse, whose superintendent was that Adam Campbell who earlier in 1765 had been briefly Robert Burns's first teacher at Alloway.[13] Poultry and eggs were produced on the farms, but seem mainly to have been required as kane, that part of the rent paid in kind. In 'The Twa Dogs' it was lamented that 'Our Laird gets in his racked rents. His coals, his kane, an' a' his stents'.

Depending upon what they themselves produced, the farm folk suffered dreadfully when crops failed. The disastrous harvest of 1782 was a final blow to William Burnes at Lochlea, and his son wrote (to James Burness, 21 June 1783) that 'this country has been, and still is decaying very fast'.[14] In fact, new items of diet were being introduced, and increased cultivation of potatoes would make a major contribution to the standard of living.

Robert Burns was never inspired to write a poem about potatoes, but they were the subject of three efforts by his rival Tarbolton versifier Alexander Tait.[15] He thus addressed them: 'Hail, mighty progeny of dung, From mony a sappy midden sprung'; and continued their praise with 'I get tatties to breakfast wi butter, At dinner I eat them wi sap, I get tatties wi syboes to supper, At night then I sleep like a tap'. Like potatoes, turnips by the end of the century were increasingly cultivated. These provided good fodder for the new breed of Ayrshire dairy cattle, which by the early nineteenth century were giving sufficient milk to increase marketing of Dunlop cheese, and producing additional dung to improve the yield of grain crops.

A notable eighteenth century innovation was the drinking of tea. James Boswell's father remembered that in the 1720s it was consumed in his Auchinleck home only when there were guests, who might thus be impressed. There was a prejudice against tea since it was often included among smuggled cargoes. This persuaded the members of Kilmarnock town council in 1744 to 'moderate and discourage the drinking of tea in our several familys', and a group of Dundonald farmers to denounce 'that foreign and consumptive luxury called tea . . . and leave the enjoyment of it altogether to those who can afford to be weak, indolent, and useless'.[16]

John Galt in *Annals of the Parish* had the fictitious Rev. Micah Balwhidder record the practice in his Ayrshire parish in 1761: 'Before this year the drinking of tea was little known in the parish saving among a few of the heritors houses on a sabbath evening; but now it became very rife; yet the commoner sort did not like to let it be known that they were taking to the new luxury, especially the elderly women who for that reason had tea drinking parties in outhouses and by places and they made their tea for common in the pint stoup, for very few of them had cups and saucers. Well do I remember one night in harvest in this very year, as I was taking my twilight daunder aneath the hedge along the backside of Thomas Thorl's yard, meditating on the goodness of providence and looking at the sheaves in the field I heard Thomas Thorl's wife and two three other old women in the inside of the hedge. They were at their tea and no doubt had a wee lacing of brandy in it and were cracking away like pea guns. But I gave them a sign by a loud hoast that providence sees all; and I heard them like guilty creatures whispering and gathering up their pots and cowering away hame'. Twenty years later when he took his wife to Edinburgh for the General Assembly, 'Mrs Balwhidder bought her silver teapot, and other ornamental articles; but this was not done as she assured me in a vain spirit of bravery which I could not have abided but because it was wellknown that tea draws better in a silver pot and drinks better in a china cup then out of any other kind of cup or teapot'.

Galt also noticed another new item of diet when honey was supplemented by imported sugar. This found mention in *Annals of the Parish*, for the year 1787: 'I should not forget to mark a new luxury that got in at this time. By the opening of new roads and the traffic thereon with carts and carriers and our young men that were sailors going upon the Clyde and sailing to Jamaica and the West Indies heaps of sugar and coffee beans were brought home while many among the kailstocks and cabbages of their yards had planted groset and berry bushes; which two things happening together the fashion to make jam and jelly, which hitherto had been only known in the kitchens of the gentry, came to be introduced into the village. It was found that jelly was an excellent medicine for a sore throat and jam a remedy as good as London candy for a cough or a cold or a shortness of breath. It occasioned great fasherie to Mrs Balwhidder for there was no end of borrowing of her brass pan, till Mrs Toddy of the Crosskeys bought one, which saved ours'.

A generation later, William Aiton criticised pedlars at the fairs who sold 'these abominable mixtures, they call Gibralter-rock, Black-man, London-candy, etc.' But he approved of everyday diet. Porridge remained the principal breakfast dish; dinner was usually broth followed by potatoes and meat; at supper there might be porridge again or what he termed 'champed potatoes . . . beaten with butter and milk'. He concluded that 'the food and mode of living of the superior ranks, in the county of Ayr, are not inferior to those of the same station in any part of Britain; and those of the farmers, with their servants and labourers, are more comfortable, than what are enjoyed by those of their rank in any other part of Scotland'.[17]

Dress[18]

'A Man's a Man for a' that', Burns proclaimed in song, 'What though on hamely fare we dine, Wear hoddin grey, and a' that'. As with food, dress depended on local materials, with cloth made from wool or linen, and leather from hides. The country gentry and burgh merchants had imported cloth for their best clothes, which might continue in use for several generations, as testified by wills and testaments bequeathing garments. Everyday wear was much plainer, even if adorned with pieces of foreign lace for gala occasions.

In the mid-eighteenth century, older women dressed themselves in long gowns of drugget, locally made woollen cloth in stripes of different colours. Younger lasses wore a closely-fitting shorter gown called a jupp. Outdoors, the older women covered their heads with a mutch, a close cap of linen or flannel. On the way to church or market all had a cloak of grey duffel cloth, or sometimes a treasured red one of finer imported material. Men wore breeches, jackets, bonnets, and plaids of hoddin grey, coarse undyed woollen cloth. If they could afford it, they would have items of finer quality dyed true blue. So Tam O' Shanter at market day in Ayr wore his 'guid blue bonnet'. Men's shirts and the underwear of both sexes were made of coarse linen called harn. The dress of young boys was not unlike that of their sisters, having a garment with a closely-fitting sleeved top and hanging loose like a kilt.

Everyday attire was often badly-fitting, made by itinerant tailors who travelled from farm to farm making up garments. The same was true of footwear. Lasses often went barefoot, and in 'The Holy Fair' even those decked in 'silks an' scarlets' came 'skelpan barefit' and only donned their shoes when nearing the church. Men wore plain, strong, shoes. Only a few could afford boots, which were kept for riding. Such riding boots were worn in 1787 by Burns, who then wore quite fashionable costume, if we can rely on Charles Hardie's painting of Burns in Edinburgh, executed a century later.

Clothing was revolutionised in the later eighteenth century by importation of exotic fibres. Silk weaving was introduced into a number of Ayrshire parishes, principally in north Ayrshire. But the more important innovation was cotton. Claud Alexander of Ballochmyle, whose sister Wilhelmina was celebrated by Burns as 'The Bonnie Lass', set up at Catrine in 1787 one of the great cotton-spinning works which supplied yarn to handloom weavers. Before the end of the century the manufacture of cotton materials was Ayrshire's principal trade, for export and for home sales. Cotton came into common use, to supplement wool and linen. It was plentiful enough to become cheap, it could be more comfortable to wear, it was simpler to wash, and replacement was easier. It contributed to improved health and the declining death rate which was augmenting the population in Burns's latter years.

In the *Statistical Account* of the 1790s, the parish minister of Symington wrote of the changes in dress he had observed:

'Young women of the middle and even of the lower ranks would now blush to be seen in the blue cloaks, red plaids, and plain caps which only 20 years ago adorned their sex; Nay even the scarlet mantle which was a badge of distinction among the daughters of the farmers is now despised; and the silk worms of the East must be pillaged to deck the heads and shoulders of our milkmaids. The bonnet makers of Kilmarnock no longer find demand for their manufactures from the servant men and labourers; but hats are worn both by men and boys of all ranks. Our young men are not to be seen at church or market in a coat of their mothers spinning but must dress themselves in English broadcloths, fashionable cotton stripes, and fine linen. Every stripling must have a watch in his pocket, whereas only 40 years ago there were but three in the parish.'

The Rev. William Auld in the last year of his long life similarly reminisced about Mauchline:

'The manner of living and dress is much altered from what it was 50 years ago. At that period there were only two or three families in this parish who made use of tea daily; now it is done by at least one half of the parish and almost the whole use it occasionally. At that period good twopenny strong ale and home spirits were in vogue but now even people in the middling and lower stations of life deal much in foreign spirits, rum punch, and wine. As to dress about 50 years ago there were few females who wore scarlets or silks. But now nothing is more common than silk caps and silk cloaks; and women in a middling station are as fine as ladies of quality were formerly. The like change may be observed in the dress of the male sex, though perhaps not to the same extent.'

New fashions in dress were becoming commonplace. David Sillar recalled how in Tarbolton about the years 1780 Robert Burns attracted his attention: 'He wore the only tied hair in the parish; and in the church, his plaid, which was of a particular colour . . . he wrapped in a particular manner round his shoulders'. Sillar indicated that apart from other things, 'his exterior made such a magical influence on my curiosity, as made me particularly solicitous of his acquaintance'.[19] A further sample of fashion history may be added. In October 1785 the Italian, Vincent Lunardi, visited Edinburgh and made an ascent in his hot-air balloon. A balloon-shaped Lunardi bonnet became the latest city fashion, and within two months it was being worn in Mauchline. For then Burns wrote 'To a Louse' depicting that insect crawling to 'the vera tapmost, towerin height, O' Miss's bonnet', which he defined as a 'fine Lunardi'. So rapidly did fashions spread, like so many other things, in that age of change.

Opportunities[20]

An age of change was also one of opportunity. It is not surprising that the eighteenth century brought fame to Ayrshire lairds such as James Boswell of Auchinleck and John Loudon McAdam of Sauchrie. What is unusual is that the late eighteenth century brought new opportunities to more humble men. For this, credit must go to the system of parish schools developed since the sixteenth century. A series of acts of the Scots parliament in the seventeenth century culminated in the 1696 Education Act. At that date about half of Ayrshire's parishes had acquired schools; in the eighteenth century all the rest were supplied. There is evidence of kirk sessions also supporting private adventure schools, as at Beith and Stewarton; and where local facilities were lacking, there are examples of groups of parents combining to hire teachers for their children, at Colmonell, Sorn, and Auchinleck, as well as at Alloway — so great was enthusiasm for education. The new reading public in the eighteenth century was catered for by bookshops in Ayr, Irvine, Beith, and Kilmarnock, where John Wilson also had his printing press; there were subscription libraries in Ayr (1762) and Kilmarnock (1797); and some travelling chapmen dealt in books.

Availability of schooling and access to books provided opportunities for able children of what were then called 'the lower orders'. William Murdoch (1754–1839), son of the miller at Lugar, learned technical expertise from his gifted father, with formal schooling at Cumnock, and went south to become a noted inventor, pioneering steam locomotion, and perfecting coal-gas illumination in 1792. James Boswell, then visiting Murdoch at Redruth in Cornwall, snobbishly noted in his journal, 'It was a curious sensation to me to find a tenant's son in so good a state'.[21] Another native of Ayrshire, John Galt (1779–1839), son of a sea captain, was a delicate child; in Irvine he had private lessons from Benjamin Maul, a teacher whose enthusiasm for Scottish literature must have contributed to Galt's eventual success as a novelist.[22] And of course eighteenth-century Ayrshire's greatest product was Robert Burns, who had the benefit of schooling at Alloway, Dalrymple, Kirkoswald, and in Ayr burgh school. He had access to a wide range of books. And he took advantage of another new local opportunity. He enjoyed — and so has the world — the fortunate circumstance that Ayrshire's first printing press was set up in 1780, which made possible the Kilmarnock Edition of 1786.

Notes

1. For Ayrshire's landed families, see James Paterson, *History of the County of Ayr*, 2 vols., 1847, 1852, 5 vols. 1863–6 (later cited as Paterson); William Robertson, *Ayrshire, Its History and Historic Families*, Vol. 2, 1908; J.T.Ward, 'Ayrshire Landed Estates', *Ayrshire Collections*, Ayrshire Archaeological & Natural History Society (AANHS), Vol. 8, 1969; John Strawhorn, *Ayrshire: The*

Story of a County, 1975; *The Statistical Account of Scotland* 1791–9, ed. Sir John Sinclair, Ayrshire items reprinted as Vol. VI, 1982 (cited as *OSA Ayrshire*); and especially *Ayrshire at the Time of Burns* (cited as *ATB*), ed. John Strawhorn, AANHS, 1959.

2. *Letters*, I, 62.

3. *The Poems and Songs of Robert Burns*, ed. James Kinsley, 3 vols., 1968 (cited as Kinsley) with Commonplace Book quoted in Vol. 3, p. 1070. Burns noticed in 'The Vision' declining influence of the Campbells of Loudoun. They had been hereditary sheriffs of Ayr until 1747; later Burns learned that on 28 April 1786 the 5th Earl of Loudoun 'shot himself out of sheer heart-break at some mortifications he suffered, owing to the deranged state of his finances' (quoted Kinsley, Vol. 3, 1268). Thereafter Mossgiel was sold to Claud Alexander of Ballochmyle.

4. For freeholders and elections, see *ATB*, 100–13; Frank Brady, *Boswell's Political Career*, 1965, and also Frank Brady, *James Boswell: The Later Years*, 92–5; for Ayr Burghs elections, John Strawhorn, *History of Ayr*, 1989 (cited as *Ayr*), 88, 90.

5. Figures derived from *OSA Ayrshire* and from sources listed in Introduction by John Strawhorn, viii–xv. For Burns's non-literary career, John Strawhorn, 'Farming in 18th Century Ayrshire', *Ayrshire Collections*, AANHS, Vol. 3, 1955, and the briefer Gavin Sprott, *Robert Burns, Farmer*, 1990; Graham Smith, *Robert Burns the Exciseman*, 1989.

6. John Strawhorn, 'Industry and Commerce in 18th Century Ayrshire', *Ayrshire Collections*, AANHS, vol. 4, 1958; *ATB*, 150–72, 247–8; *OSA Ayrshire*, viii.

7. For McLure, John Strawhorn, 'The Litigation at Lochlea', *Burns Chronicle*, 1985.

8. John Mitchell, 'Memories of Ayrshire about 1780' (cited as Mitchell) in *Miscellany of the Scottish History Society*, Vol. 6, 1939, 256–62, 267–8; William Aiton, *General View of the Agriculture of the County of Ayr*, 1811 (cited as Aiton), 106–33.

9. Margaret Sanderson, *Scottish Rural Society in the Sixteenth Century*, 1982, 8.

10. Quotations from Aiton, 115, 116; Auchinleck material from a forthcoming Yale Research Edition, *Correspondence of James Boswell with his Estate Overseers*, ed. Nellie P. Hankins & John Strawhorn.

11. Mitchell, 271–2, 278–80; Aiton, 533–5, 653–6; A. Gibson & T.C. Smout, 'Scottish food and Scottish history', in *Scottish Society*. ed. R.A. Houston & I.D. Whyte, 1989.

12. Unpublished Auchinleck Memoirs, MS Yale C 338.7.

13. Minute Book of Ayr Poorshouse in Carnegie Library, Ayr, quoted in *Ayr*, 123, 124; for Campbell, Gilbert Burns in James Currie, *The Life of Robert Burns*, 1800, 59. His name was Adam Campbell, not William as erroneously given elsewhere.

14. *Letters*, I, 19.

15. Alexander Tait, *Poems and Songs*, 1790.

16. Quotations from Paterson, 1866 edn., Vol. 3. ii, 393; J.H. Gillespie, *Dundonald*, Vol. 1, 1939, 139.

17. Quotations from Aiton, 574, 653, 655.

18. Mitchell, 262–7; *OSA Ayrshire*, esp. 642–3 (Symington), 449 (Mauchline).

19. *The Life and Works of Robert Burns*, ed. Robert Chambers & William Wallace, 4 vols., 1896, Vol. 1, 68.

20. William Boyd, *Education in Ayrshire Through Seven Centuries*, 1961; Mitchell, 272–6; Careen S. Gardner, *Printing in Ayr and Kilmarnock*, AANHS, 1976.

21. Marlies K. Danziger and Frank Brady, *Boswell: The Great Biographer*, 1789–1795, 1989, 174, 178; John Griffiths, *The Third Man: life and times of William Murdoch*, 1992.

22. John Strawhorn, *History of Irvine*, 1985, 92, 93, 100.

'The Immortal Memory'

3
Burns and Nostalgia

Carol McGuirk

'[Burns's] life was a failure until he died. Ever since it has been a marvelous success.'

Revd Henry Ward Beecher, Centenary Oration,
New York City, 1859

Nostalgia may be defined as our impulse to preserve in memory select details only of what is lost in the course of historical, social and personal change. Unlike grief, nostalgia can be pleasurable, perhaps because (based as it is on selective perception) nostalgia is quite capable of 'commemorating' losses that never, historically speaking, occurred. Nostalgia's backward glance offers even the most unimaginative among us the pleasures of creative construction: we all are free to redesign the past, and most of us do. Though a memory-art like poetry or history, nostalgia, unlike history, deals in synthetic (because wishfully edited) memories. And unlike poetry, with its strong emotion recollected in tranquillity, nostalgia retroactively creates an emotion around events or people taken more or less for granted prior to the moment of nostalgic recovery.

The link between nostalgia and Robert Burns may already be clear. His seemingly inextricable entanglement with nostalgic reminiscence is suggested even by the traditional toast to 'The Immortal Memory' at Burns-Night celebrations. By comparison with such possible variants as 'The Immortal Bard' or 'Rabbie, God Bless Him!' the traditional wording metonymically displaces the poet with 'memory' itself, insisting (appropriately enough) on the interactive relationship of poets to posterity but also inviting the selectivity and wishful thinking of nostalgia. And while no poet survives without some capacity for retrospective re-animation, Keats and Milton and even Shakespeare, in their respective linguistic afterlives, have never

been subjected to anything like the degree of wishful recon-
struction that characterises the Robert Burns who lives on in
collective memory — 'immortal' to be sure, yet improbably
stylised.

Multiple personae, each of them recogisably 'Robert Burns',
are toasted and 'remembered' each 25 January: the poet of 'The
Cotter's Saturday Night', but also the poet of 'Holy Willie's
Prayer' and 'Adam Armour's Prayer'. One reveller is thinking of
'Dear Christless Bobie' the Dumfries revolutionary; another of
poor doomed Robin with his 'habits of skinless sensibility',
writing tender songs for Jessie Lewars on his deathbed. Some are
pledging (with covert envy) dangerous 'Rab Mossgiel', striding
into Mauchline on the hunt for 'proper young belles'. '[Burns]
wore the only tied hair in the parish', remembered David Sillar
in prosperous middle-age, 'and . . . his plaid . . . was of a
particular colour, I think *fillemot*'. (Sillar was the only surviving
friend who remembered a man of fashion as well as feeling.)
Invoking the 'immortal memory', in short, is like placing a
conference call: a dozen poets answer.

These multiple and often contradictory images of Burns that
the selectivity of nostalgic memory makes possible are the subject
of this essay. The Burnsiana to be discussed here — material held
by the Mitchell Library in Glasgow and by the G. Ross Roy
Collection of the Thomas Cooper Library (University of South
Carolina) — consists of prose and verse tributes to the poet by his
admirers and visual images of Burns in portraits and illustrations of
his writings. Most of this material dates from the nineteenth
century and particularly the period around 1859, the centenary of
the poet's birth, and the point at which the transformation of
Burns from controversial literary celebrity into 'immortal memory' seems to have been completed. Burnsiana (by which is
meant materials whose focus is predominantly anecdotal or
nostalgic rather than critical) merits examination because it is
important in understanding the evolution and persistence of the
Burns myth. If most of this material falls into the realm of folklore
rather than critical commentary, that realm is hardly alien to
Robert Burns and moreover has received almost no critical
attention. Indeed, despite or perhaps because of its tendency

to vehement excess, nineteenth-century Burnsiana retains a vitality and interest hard to recover from the nineteenth-century academic discourse on Burns: such estimable and indefatigable scholars as Robert Chambers, Scott Douglas, and William Wallace nonetheless are hard-going reading today, especially since concise summaries of (and extensions to) their findings are available through James Kinsley's Clarendon edition of the poet's poems and songs (1968) and DeLancey Ferguson's and G. Ross Roy's Clarendon edition of his letters (1985). Finally, the popular commentary on Burns contains insights of continuing importance. The Victorians read Burns's songs with a more intelligent sympathy than we moderns do, as concluding discussion of illustrations to 'Scots Wha Hae', 'The Soldier's Return' and 'Auld Lang Syne' will demonstrate.

Class nostalgia was a strong element in the early reception of Burns's writings. The only poet of classic stature ever to emerge from the British peasant class, Burns himself emphasises his social class in the Preface to the Edinburgh edition of *Poems, Chiefly in the Scottish Dialect* (1787): 'The Poetic Genius of my Country found me as the Prophetic Bard Elijah did Elisha; at the plough, and threw her inspiring mantle over me'. It is not surprising to find early reviewers and illustrators embroidering on Burns's own hint. Indeed, in an influential early review of the Kilmarnock edition (1786), the sentimental novelist Henry Mackenzie even anticipated Burns's stance as Scotia's chosen prophet, at once founding Burns scholarship and falling into class-nostalgia when he hailed Burns in December 1786 as 'this Heaven-taught ploughman' — a compliment distinctly left-handed in its implication that divine intervention alone could account for literary excellence emerging from such an unlikely quarter as the farming community.[1]

In two illustrations of Burns's Preface to the Edinburgh edition — one clearly based on the other yet revising its images — we see two conflicting interpretations of Burns's self-portrait as Elisha. Figure 1, almost certainly the earlier, is bound into a unique multi-volume scrapbook (its binding stamped with the leisurely title *Burnsiana Gleanings*) in the Mitchell Library, Glasgow. The picture, engraved probably

between 1825–40, may be one of the 'German prints' of Burns
whose inaccuracies are reported to have irritated surviving
friends of the poet during the 1830s; a slight variant (with an
unwheeled plough) was signed H. Melville and included in
some issues of Allan Cunningham's edition of Burns (1834;
many subsequent reissues).[2] The picture captures, in its magnificent ineptitude, the inherent contradictions in what was a still-
evolving myth. On the one hand is the lofty background: the
seedy-looking, bird- or bat-infested tower suggestive of Gothi-
cism, but also the baroque sheltering Muse, whose blank gaze is
derived from Burns's account of Coila in 'The Vision' ('Her *eye*,
ev'n turn'd on empty space/Beam'd keen with *Honour*' [ll. 59–
60]) but whose descending pose and elegant pointed foot derive
from Tiepolo. The heroically attired poet, not exactly dressed
for a hard night's ploughing (the scene occurs, apparently, at
dusk) is the point where realism meets fantasy. For the details in
front of the posturing bard are homely — the enormous farming implement to the left, the tiny ponies and rat-faced dog to
the right. The overgrowth in the foreground suggests that this
particular field needs weeding as well as ploughing. As in
nostalgia itself, the eye travels front to back, back to front,
negotiating the distance between concrete detail and a pleasantly
hazy generality. The poet himself is appropriately positioned at
the clashing and equivocal mid-ground.

   Figure 2 (unlike 1, which is apparently a steel-plate engraving)
is a woodcut. Almost certainly based upon the first, it revises to
improve coherence by playing up the sentimental details and
eliminating the clashing 'heroic' and 'realistic' elements. The
woodcut is to be found in several nineteenth-century *Works*;
that reprinted here is from the 'Self-Interpreting' edition of
Burns published in Philadelphia in 1886. (The well-worn
impression suggests, however, that 1886 is a late printing.[3])
Figure 2 harmonises the clashing elements in the earlier
portrayal: the midnight *penseroso* of 1 becomes a sensitive rustic
by daylight, and the ruined tower becomes the farmhouse at
Lochlie or Mossgiel. Finally, that distractingly toothy harrow is
transformed into a less obtrusive thistle. The stones, weeds, and
alien-collie-from-hell of the foreground in Figure 1 have been

Figure 1

deleted, and the poet no longer stands behind an incongruously wheeled plough. There is still heroic panache in the poet's gesture of removing his bonnet out of respect for the descending poetic Genius of Scotland, but she is now closer to his own level, less decisively 'above' and 'beyond' the poet. This second rendering, more confident yet less compelling than the first, shows the settling of the myth into today's most familiar iconographic conventions. As posterity learned the Burns myth, it became easier to 'remember' its characteristic imagery: the plough, the thistle, the cottage, and the sensitive poet himself in Figure 2 are all clearly being *repeated*, not (as in Figure 1) laboriously conceived and invented. By the time of the woodcut, Victoria and Albert had made rural Scotland fashionable — another possible reason why the rustic images seem to come more easily to the later artist.

A historical footnote to Burns's Elisha-at-the-plough self-representation comes down to us in an anecdote from August 1844, when a crowded outdoor reception was held on the banks of the Doon to honour the surviving legitimate sons of Burns upon the return (after years of service in India) of Lieutenant-Colonel James Glencairn Burns, youngest of the three. The poet's sons listened, it is likely, with some embarrassment as John

Figure 2

Wilson ('Christopher North' of *Blackwood's Magazine*) held forth
for over an hour, providing what might be called the Tory line
on Burns in a speech that angered many present in its focus on
the poet's so-called reckless immorality.[4] In his response to
Wilson, however, the eldest son Robert meekly overlooked the
provocation and, poignantly enough, used the poet's own
imagery to distance the 'sons of Burns' from their father's
problematic legend:

> I am sure the sons of Burns feel all they ought on an occasion so
> gratifying. . . . Wherever they have gone they have found a
> reception prepared for them by the genius and fame of their father,
> and under the providence of God, they owe to the admirers of his
> genius all that they have and what competencies they now enjoy.
> We have no claim to attention individually; we are all aware that
> genius, and more particularly poetic genius, is not hereditary —
> and in this case the mantle of Elijah has not descended upon
> Elisha.[5]

In 1844, Robert Burns the Younger was estranged from his wife
and living with another woman whom he could never marry.
He had retired on a small pension, having failed to receive any
promotion from the menial clerkship to which he had been
appointed by a patron during his youth, and he had struggled for
many years with a disastrous addiction to gaming. At fifty-seven,
he lacked either the energy or the spirit to challenge John
Wilson; in fact, tired of mythology, he seems rather relieved to
announce that he at any rate is no Elisha. By 1844, a life at the
receiving end of patronage has taught the sons of Burns that they
cannot afford the luxury of their touchy father's chief constituent
elements: 'pride and passion'.[6]

One can only imagine the scene at the Doon if the ghost of
the poet himself could somehow have been there to respond to
Wilson. People were afraid to attack Burns during his life: his
rebuttals were fearsome. But as William Nichol wrote bitterly to
John Lewars a month after Burns's death:

> the encomiums passed upon [Burns], both in the Scotch and
> English newspapers, are mingled with reproaches of the most
> indelicate and cruel Nature. But stupidity and idiocy rejoice when

a great and immortal genius falls; and they pour forth their
invidious reflections without reserve, well knowing that the dead
Lion from whose presence they formerly scudded away with
terror, and at whose voice they trembled though every nerve, can
devour no more.[7]

Figure 3 is the Burns image with which we are most familiar,
the cliché of clichés. It captures the gentle, tender poet of 'To
a Mouse' and 'Mary Morison' — the Burns canonised by the
Victorians — but it offers no hint of Burns's capacity for
bawdry or the anarchic glee of 'Love and Liberty'. This is
only a 'Heaven-taught ploughman'. The picture is based on the
ubiquitous portrait by Alexander Nasmyth, taken from the life
in 1787; this version (from a turn-of-the-century postcard)
further idealises what was already an idealising portrayal by
Nasmyth. For, despite its strong influence on all subsequent
representations of Burns, Nasmyth's portrait was never considered to be a good likeness: the painter's specialty was
landscape, not portraiture. (Nasmyth, who formed a friendship with the poet, considered the picture so faulty that he
refused William Creech's offer of payment, eventually giving it
to Jean Armour Burns during her widowhood.) Nasmyth's
Burns is slight, slender, and genteel: the portrait does not bear
out Burns's own account of himself (in 'Elegy on Robert
Ruisseaux') as 'wight and stark' (stout and strong). Sir Walter
Scott, who as a boy once spoke briefly to Burns, remembered
the poet's countenance as 'more massive' than that rendered in
the portraits, and recalled that Burns's large, dark, flashing eye
'alone indicated the poetical temperament'.[8] Other contemporary accounts of Burns record a mouth habitually pursed and
a pronounced 'ploughman's stoop', or round-shouldered
appearance.[9] (Though Burns was never a ploughman in the
sense of a day-labourer, he did, as eldest son in his family,
work from childhood as chief labourer on his elderly father's
farm — and the years of hard manual labour showed in his
physique.) In the case of this postcard image, an original
gentrification of the poet's appearance by Nasmyth is even
further sweetened. The Nasmyth (like its numerous descen-

dants) depicts Frances Dunlop's tame 'Robert Burns', to be sure — but not Willie Nichols' lion.

Figure 4, not a picture of Burns himself, illustrates the persistence of the Nasmyth image. This is a photograph of the poet's great-granddaughter, Jean Armour Burns Brown, a descendant of Robert Burns the Younger. The picture appeared in *The Burns Chronicle* in 1939, two years after Miss Brown's death. Let me dispel any suspicion that Jean Brown habitually cross-dressed to impersonate her distinguished ancestor.[10] This is a photographer's trick — Miss Brown's face has been super-imposed on a reproduction of the Nasmyth portrait to test the truth of what was often alleged of her during her lifetime — that she was the descendant who most closely resembled the poet. In truth, almost anyone blended into the Nasmyth representation — Napoleon, Elvis Presley, Mary Pickford — would work as well as Jean Brown, because the original image is itself so vague. The picture, at any rate, reminds us of how powerful

Figure 3

the Nasmyth portrait continues to be in perpetuating notions of a nostalgic, softened, sentimentalized and in this case literally feminised Robert Burns. Figure 5, a picture of Jean Brown in adolescence, shows that she was a striking Victorian beauty. Whether or not she resembled her great-grandfather, she did have large, deep-set dark eyes and a pronounced overbite.

Figure 6 provides a Zen exercise: what if Robert Burns looked like this? This unsigned portrait has sometimes been said to be the 'lost' Raeburn portrait of Burns mentioned once in a letter of Raeburn's to Cadell and Davies but never traced.[11] It is 50 in by 40 in.; the label reads 'Robert Burns born 1759, died 1796'. The biggest problem with the portrait, owned by the Lady Stair's House Museum at Edinburgh, is that the sitter has blue eyes. The short jacket (almost a Spencer) worn by the sitter was not fashionable until the early nineteenth century: the earliest reference — in a sporting journal — is from 1796 [*Oxford English Dictionary*]), another reason the picture could not have

Figure 4

been done from the life. (Burns died at thirty-seven in 1796, but looked — as may be seen in the Alexander Reid miniature done from the life when Burns was thirty-six — older than his years, more like a man of fifty.) This, however, is clearly a portrait of a very young man. No details of this picture's whereabouts exist before 1870 — though the Reid miniature of Burns, now accepted as authentic and on display in the Scottish National Portrait Gallery in Edinburgh, is of similarly sketchy provenance.

Figure 5

Favourable elements in terms of authenticity are that this painter has rendered the poet (though he is still improbably slight) with a stooping posture. The sitter's watch fob is decorated with several masonic charms, and the inkwell in the corner is resting on what appears to be an unbound copy of the Edinburgh edition of *Poems, Chiefly in the Scottish Dialect*. And the upper lip of the sitter has the distinctive curl that the poet's brother Gilbert once mentioned as a peculiarity of his brother's countenance that Nasmyth had not captured.[12] (We see a similar pursing of the mouth in the John Miers silhouette Burns had made in November 1787 and in the older Burns rendered in Reid's profile miniature.)

The most generous assessment of this portrait would be that it was done from memory in the first decade of the nineteenth century (hence the shortwaisted coat) by a painter who had seen Burns and was trying to recapture the image. This theory requires, however, that we accept the idea that a professional artist (this is a

Figure 6

competent portrait) could forget the colour of the poet's eyes, which by consensus were Burns's most distinctive feature. So almost certainly this picture was painted by a mid-nineteenth-century artist hoping to impose on posterity. I did not include the picture to argue for its authenticity but to raise consciousness about the vacuous imagery with which Burns is typically portrayed. At least this painter's 'Robert Burns' looks intelligent and moody — major elements in the poet's personality of which Nasmyth's famous picture offers no hint. (Ill and prematurely aged as Burns appears in the Reid miniature, Reid's remains the only image of the poet that in any way conveys his humour — there is a mirthful, mocking cast to the poet's face in the Reid.)

Figure 7 returns us to the Nasmyth image. Here, in an engraving by Edmonstone and Mitchell from the 1830s, is an illustration of the episode in Burns's life about which he was himself most persistently nostalgic — his betrothal (?) to the (virginal? dissolute?) Mary (Margaret?) Campbell and her sudden death (from typhus? post-partum fever?) some six months later.[13] (Here nostalgia cannot but be selective: the poet's own accounts are hysterically intense yet oblique, and his sister and friends provide conflicting information.) This artist's Burns is deliciously plump, a fatter Nasmyth. Indeed, the engraver is so attracted by the Nasmyth countenance that he infuses something of its sweet vagueness into Highland Mary as well as the poet. The Scottish landscape in the background, however, with its banks and braes, shows sensitivity to Burns's minute descriptions of the countryside in his poems and songs about Mary.

Figure 8 is the frontispiece of the unauthorised pamphlet publication of Burns's folk-cantata, which commentators from Thomas Carlyle to Matthew Arnold to Walt Whitman have called his masterwork. Thomas Stewart, the pamphlet's co-publisher, was nephew of Burns's crony John Richmond (from whose hands Stewart probably received the manuscript); and it was almost certainly Stewart who imposed the title this pamphlet bears, 'The Jolly Beggars'. For both surviving holograph manu-scripts are titled 'Love and Liberty', echoing Alexander Pope's 'Eloisa to Abelard' ('Oh, happy state! When Souls each other draw,/When love is liberty, and Nature law'). Evidently, Stewart felt 'Love and Liberty' to be too subtle a title for his pamphlet's target-audience of jovial males. For Figure 8's rare pre-1800 attempt to sum up Burns pictorially — though dated 1800, the pamphlet appeared in 1799 — wholly rejects Nasmyth's genteel poet.[14] The artist has included a cloven-footed satyr on the right-hand side of the monument to the poet, which reproduces the Nasmyth Burns in bas-relief. The bare-breasted Muse that flanks the other side holds a wickedly smiling mask in one hand, dangling a laurel wreath in the other. Finally, a very large flying herald (a pubescent putto?) seems in imminent danger of crash-landing into the monument but is diligently trumpeting the name of Burns. The bas-relief on the bottom of the monument, under the relief of Burns, depicts Pan with his pipes. This is the only 'pagan', 'neoclassical' rendering of Burns that I know of in early illustrations. The artist (W. Weir) probably puts in all the visual clues to the then-shocking content of 'Love and Liberty' to titillate reader interest and increase the sales of the cantata, but

Figure 7

whatever his motive, his rendering shows artistic independence from the emerging consensus that the visual portrayal of Burns should be predominantly sweet rather than saucy.

Figure 9 also predates the full conventionalisation of images of Burns: it is the title-page engraving for the 'Dove's English Classics' edition of James Currie's *Life and Works of Burns* (1808).[15] Fishing with the arm extended at the angle depicted here must have been intensely painful. The picture illustrates a passage from Dr Currie's biography, describing two travellers who came upon Burns one day: 'On a rock that projected into the stream, they saw a man employed in angling, of a singular appearance. He had a cap made of a fox's skin on his head, a loose greatcoat fixed round him with a belt, from which depended an enormous Highland broadsword. It was Burns' (202). Here, Burns is partly a rustic swain in the manner that by 1808 was becoming traditional, but also partly a noble savage, combining elements of nostalgic pastoral with elements of Davy

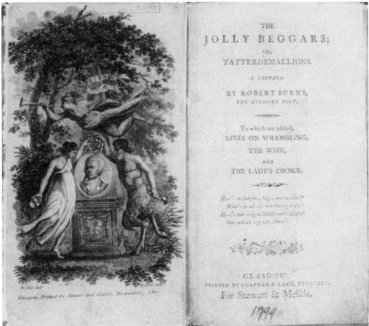

Figure 8

Crockett primitivism. Incidentally, Jean Armour Burns, who submitted quietly to so many of Currie's inaccurate and tendentious statements about her late husband, for some reason drew the line at this innocuous anecdote. The poet's abhorrence of blood sports, she indignantly declared, extended to angling, and the travellers must have mistaken someone else for her husband.

Figure 10, frontispiece of the 'Dove's English Classics' edition, likewise illustrates an incident described in Currie's biography. The poet, not paying much attention to the guidance of his diminutive steed during a violent thunderstorm, relaxes in the saddle, arms quietly folded, in a poetic reverie inspired by the weather. (Though it is unlikely that the poet ever did ride out in this mood of profound reverie, any such habit would account for the frequent riding injuries and fractured limbs generally blamed by his biographers on his broken-winded old horse.) The other person in the picture is John Syme, the source for the anecdote.

Figure 9

Syme was collector of stamp revenues for Dumfries and a close friend of Burns's; eventually he served as an executor of the poet's will. In the picture, Syme is protecting his expensive hat (Burns is wearing a cloth tam) and looking appalled at the poet's capacity to wool-gather in the middle of such a storm. The artist's message is clear: Burns may have been a great poet, but he did not have the sense to come in out of the rain.[16]

Yet this is, as is characteristic of nostalgia, a highly selective interpretation of Syme's journal-notation, made during the poet's lifetime: the illustrator selects only the first part of the anecdote for portrayal, editing out Syme's comic conclusion:

> I took him the moor-road, where savage and desolate regions extended wide around. The sky was sympathetic with the wretchedness of the soil; it became lowering and dark. The hollow winds sighed, the lightnings gleamed, the thunder rolled.[17] The poet enjoyed the awful scene — he spoke not a word, but seemed wrapt in meditation. In a little while the rain began to fall;

Figure 10

it poured in floods upon us. . . . *Oh, oh 'twas foul.* We got utterly wet; and to revenge ourselves, Burns insisted at Gatehouse on our getting utterly drunk.[18]

The anecdote suggests (and other contemporary evidence bears out) that it was John Syme himself, not Robert Burns, who was inclined to scenic raptures. (DeLancey Ferguson sums him up in *Pride and Passion* as 'rhapsodic and absent-minded . . . the sort who could set off on a long-planned hunting trip and find on arriving at his destination that he had forgotten his dogs'.[19] The illustrator here has confused the anecdote-maker with his subject.

Moving from the charming to the macabre, Figure 11 shows the excesses of nineteenth-century bardolatry at their most florid, though at least this rendering of Burns avoids the sweet nostalgia of the Nasmyth images. This engraving of the poet's skull by W. & A.K. Johnson is dated 30 April 1834; it is from a plaster cast made in 1834. The poet's coffin was opened at least twice — once on the night before his widow's funeral in 1834 (Jean was buried on 1 April) and once much earlier, on 19 September 1815, when the remains of the poet and two of his sons were moved from their original burial place in a grave in St Michael's Churchyard to the vault under the newly com-pleted mausoleum.[20] During the later of these intrusions, a plaster cast of the poet's skull was made; the skull was then inserted in a small separate wooden box filled with saltpetre as a preservative and returned to the coffin. The nineteenth-century's fascination with details of physical decay, which rivals that of the Elizabethans, was not restricted to Burns's mortal remains. Still, there is a remarkably grisly particularity in the accounts of the disinterments.

John McDiarmid, a witness to the earlier exhumation of 1815, reports that when the coffin was opened, the poet's body appeared intact, but then collapsed upon being disturbed:

There lay the remains of the great poet, to all appearances entire, retaining various traces of recent vitality, or, to speak more correctly, exhibiting the features of one who had recently sunk into the sleep of death. The forehead struck everyone as beautifully arched, if not so high as might be reasonably supposed, while the scalp was rather thickly covered with hair, and the teeth perfectly firm and white . . . But the scene, however imposing, was brief; for the instant the workmen inserted a shell beneath the original wooden coffin, the head separated from the trunk, and the whole body, with the exception of the bones, crumbled into dust.[21]

By 1834, reports Archibald Blacklock (a surgeon present when the poet's coffin was opened again the night before Jean's funeral), only bones remained:

The cranial bones were perfect in every respect, if we except a little erosion of their external table, and firmly held together by their sutures; even the delicate bones of the orbits, with the trifling exception of the *os unguis* in the left, were sound . . . Some small portions of black hair, with a very few gray hairs intermixed, were observed while detaching some extraneous matter from the occiput. Indeed, nothing could exceed the high state of preservation in which we found the bones of the cranium, or offer what has been so long desiderated by phrenologists — a correct model of our immortal poet's head: and in order to accomplish this in the most accurate and satisfactory manner, every

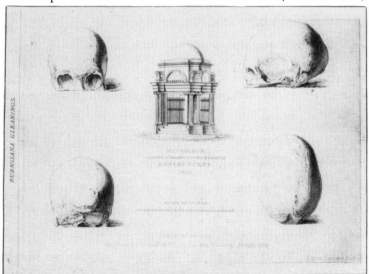

Figure 11

particle of sand, or other foreign body, was carefully washed off, and the plaster of Paris applied with all the tact and accuracy of an experienced artist. The cast is admirably taken, and cannot fail to prove high [*sic*] interesting to phrenologists and others.[22]

John McDiarmid's earlier testimony (1815) is strikingly similar to scenes occurring near the conclusion of James Hogg's *The Private Memoirs and Confessions of a Justified Sinner* (1824) — two contradictory accounts (the plurals in Hogg's title are apt) of the disinterment of Robert Wringhim, the Justified Sinner of the title, a suicide who has been buried for over a century. The report of the first exhumation, said in the novel to have occurred in 1823, includes an account of a witness actually pinching the cheek of the miraculously preserved body:

> Behold the body came up into a sitting posture, with a broad blue bonnet on its head, and its plaid all around it, a fresh as that day it was laid in! . . . The features were all so plain, that an acquaintance might easily have known him . . . He had fine yellow hair, about nine inches long, but not a hair of it could they pull out till they cut part of it off with a knife. They also cut off some portions of his clothes . . . distributing them among their acquaintances to keep as natural curiosities (375).[23]

The account of a second exhumation that concludes the novel (written by an 'editor' allegedly 'correcting' the details provided in the first account) is as follows:

> I will describe everything as I saw it before four respectable witnesses . . . A number of the bones came up separately . . . At length great loads of coarse clothing, blanketing, plaiding, etc., appeared; we tried to lift these regularly up, and on doing so, part of a skeleton came up, but no flesh, save a little that was hanging in dark flitters about the spine; it was merely the appearance of flesh without the substance. The head was wanting; and I being very anxious to possess the skull, the search was renewed. We first found a part of the scalp, with the long hair firm on it, which, on being cleaned, is neither black nor fair, but of a darkish dusk . . . Soon afterwards we found the skull, but it was not complete. A spade had damaged it, and one of the temple quarters was missing. I am no phrenologist, not knowing one organ from another, but I

thought the skull of that wretched man no study. If it was
remarkable for anything, it was for a smooth, almost perfect
rotundity, with only a little protuberance above the vent of the ear
. . . All the limbs from the loins to the toes, seemed perfect and
entire, but they could not bear the handling. Before we got them
returned again into the grave they were all shaken into pieces
except the thighs, which retained a kind of flabby form. (383-5)

Did the disinterment of 1815, described in McDiarmid's
account, exert some influence on Hogg's conclusion? Was
Hogg present, or did he know some witness of it, perhaps
McDiarmid himself? (If this is the same John McDiarmid who
later befriended the poet's son Robert, referred to in a late-
nineteenth-century anecdote as having been in 1847 'the able
proprietor and editor of the *Dumfries and Galloway Courier*', it is
very likely Hogg was acquainted with him.[24]) In short, is there,
in the back of James Hogg's peculiar mind, some oblique
analogy being made between the 'Scots Mummy' and 'The
Immortal Memory'?[25]

The coincidence of first names — the sinner is named
Robert Wringhim — is not in itself significant. It is the other
correspondences that raise suspicion: the similar emphasis on
manipulations of a long-dead corpse by curiosity-seekers, the
witnesses' testimony on the body's apparent state of preservation, the dissolution of the corpse upon being moved, the
exhumers' inadvertent decapitation of the remains, even the
insistence on the roundness of the forehead and the distribution of hair and relics as souvenirs and keepsakes. Hogg's
description (in 1829) of an incident that had occurred in 1812
provides a further tantalising hint. Hogg was present that year
when the poet's brother Gilbert and a group of Burns's
surviving friends visited the widow of the coach and sign-
painter Peter Taylor in order to view a long-forgotten
impromptu portrait of Burns that her late husband (who
had been friendly with the poet) had done in May 1787.
Mrs Taylor had been treasuring the picture in secret, Hogg
reports, but had finally communicated its existence to the
poet's family: 'In a little neat house up one stair in West
Register Street we found . . . Mrs Taylor, a decent widow-

lady, past middle life . . . Taking a key out of a private drawer
she opened the upper leaf of a clothes press. From that she
took a little box, and from that she took a portrait of Burns
carefully rolled up in silver paper. Mr Gray first exclaimed,
"Glorious! glorious! Burns, every inch!"'[26]

Yet Peter Taylor's portrait of Burns — it now hangs in the
Scottish National Portrait Gallery in Edinburgh — is painted on
a wooden panel. Unlike a canvas, it could never have been
'rolled up' or 'unrolled' in the manner at least implied here.
(Hogg might be referring to the unwrapping of the silver paper,
not the picture.) In either case, the anecdote emphasises the
gradual revelation (through many layers of disclosure) of a dead
man's long-forgotten image. The key is fetched from a 'private
drawer'; it opens a locked portion of Mrs Taylor's clothes press,
producing a 'small box' (the picture is indeed quite small at 8 in.
by 8 ½ in.) and finally a layer of silver paper: all this precedes
the 'glorious' disclosure of the dead poet's face.

Hogg's details delay, in order to dramatise, the moment of
discovery. A similar insistence on a hidden document's long
concealment and painstakingly gradual disclosure may be seen in
Hogg's novel, when Robert Wringhim's narrative — which
conflicts with that provided by a moralising 'editor' — is found
in the suicide's grave during the second exhumation, 'rolled up'
tightly inside the tobacco pouch of the corpse. For over a
century Robert Wringhim's 'private memoir' has been hidden
while buried with its author but it finally comes to light. In one
sense, the Sinner's case is enviable compared to Burns's: at least
he retains control over his text after his death — and this despite
the indifference and even hostility of an invasive posterity prone
to misreading. James Hogg not only compiled a (mediocre)
edition of the works of Burns but succeeded Burns as Poet
Laureate of Edinburgh's Canongate Masonic Lodge. His dark
portrait of Calvinism in *The Private Memoirs and Confessions of a
Justified Sinner* seems to incorporate some echo of the life — and
posthumous mythification — of a fellow peasant, vernacular
poet and critic of 'Auld Licht' Calvinism.

The purpose of these four views of Burns's skull was to supply
the insatiable curiosity of phrenologists. George Combe (1788–

1858), the most famous phrenologist of his day, worked from the .plaster cast of 1834 to write the major (though by no means the only) treatise on 'The Phrenological Development of Robert Burns' (1859).[27] The bumps on the exhumed skull prove beyond doubt, says Combe, that Burns was a highly creative individual, possibly even a professional writer. They also 'prove' an amorous nature and self-destructive impulses. The cast of the skull had one practical use: Charles Calverley, the sculptor who designed the Burns statue in Albany, New York, used it to justify the unusually broad and massive head of his 'Robert Burns'.

To move ahead one generation — to *Punch*'s cartoon of 1859 alluding to the 25 January centenary of the poet's birth in figure 12 — is to see the myth's full integration into Victorian popular culture. The Burns cult itself is so well-established as to be incidental to the humour. The apparent target is instead Queen Victoria's infatuation with all things Scottish, but especially her head gillie at Balmoral, John Brown, who in the cartoon 'entertains' his royal 'friend' on Burns Night (25 January) with disastrous results: the exploding haggis seems to be generating a great deal of smoke as well as shrapnel.[28] As 'Brown' is among the most common of Scottish names (it was the maiden-name of the poet's mother and the surname of one line of his direct descendants), it could be that some generic and anonymous expatriate 'Brown' is meant, entertaining on Burns Night in London. Yet the singular noun — 'friend', not 'friends' — and the broad back of the lady in the foreground, not to mention the corona of white flowers in her hair, suggest a more pointed reference to Queen Victoria and her Scottish favourite. John Brown was first mentioned in a journal entry of Victoria's on 11 September 1849; originally assigned to Prince Albert, Brown had replaced John Macdonald as the Queen's chief gillie in 1858. Victoria was not widowed until 1861 and widespread public criticism of her emotional dependency on Brown dates from the later 1860s.[29] But this cartoon suggests that already there were whispers.

On 22 January 1859, *Punch*, in a parody of 'Charge of the Light Brigade', had commented on the unexpectedly brisk competition for the Burns Centenary Ode Prize offered by the Crystal Palace Company. More than 600 entries had been received, and the parody commiserates with the overwhelmed panel of judges:

> Rhymesters to right of them,
> Rhymesters to left of them,
> Rhymesters behind them,
>   Volleyed and thundered,
> Stormed at with shout and yell,
> They that had given the bell,
> Pale on the judgment seat,
> Wished themselves off again,
> Ere they had dared to sell
> Thirty score bards save one,
>   Out of six hundred!
>
> Honour to BURNS! and gold,
> Fifty broad pieces told,
> To him the prize shall hold,
>   One of six hundred!

GRAND BURNS' FESTIVAL. BROWN ENTERTAINS HIS FRIEND WI' A HAGGIS!

Figure 12

Punch's feminist correspondent, Thalestris Hardlines, responded to the parody on 5 February (her letter is printed under the 'Brown' cartoon) correcting the pronoun in the poem's second last line, for in the event the winner of the Centenary competition, announced on 25 January, was a woman, Isabella (Isa) Craig Knox. Hardlines concludes her heavily italicised letter with reference to a major component of the now well-established Burns myth: 'I feel *doubly* the *triumph* of our sex, in that it has been won in doing honour to a *bard*, who, whatever his *errors* and *imprudences*, had a proper *esteem* for *woman*'.[54]

Any perusal of the numbers of *Punch* for 1859 shows that by the Centenary year, British popular culture was permeated with the familiar aspects of the Burns myth as it has come down to us. Robert Burns was in at least two senses the Elvis Presley of the nineteenth century: in the strong component of class-nostalgia in the foundation of his cult and in the way his icon, even during his life but increasingly after his death, was so often detached from his actual body of work. And if Burns was their Elvis, Scotland was (with Switzerland) the Victorians' theme park, their Disney World. Where did Stanley go after finding Livingstone, upon his triumphant return from Africa? He went to Alloway, to wait upon the Misses Begg, the poet's nieces.

A minority only of the Victorians who fashioned images of Burns for popular consumption were reading the poet's works and not only 'remembering' an icon; and those speech-makers and illustrators saw Burns's songs as his most important texts. In one American Burns-Night oration delivered in 1859, David Coddington, a Democrat swinging towards support of Lincoln in those months of crisis, gives — for all his plummy, epideictic style — impressive testimony to the idealising power of Burns's lyrics, especially in the contexts of human rights and social reform:

> [Burns's lyric poetry] relieves truth from all sordid and conventional restraints, by applying the universal law of appreciation to every form of excellence . . . reducing the gold mine to its proper level in the landscape, and elevating the . . . humblest effort of duty, to kindred communion with the grandest achievement . . . The poetry of Burns is simply the steps of a poor plain man keeping time to the richest music of the human soul,

where obscure joys and uninteresting troubles are sublimed into universal beauties. Every trivial circumstance in his path seems strung with the strings of a harp, so melodiously do ordinary facts play about him . . . Washington's sword has cut away the outer impediment, Jefferson's pen framed the outer charter, and as long only as such spirits as Robert Burns' shall follow in their path, . . . so long will humanity be hopeful, reform possible, and freedom safe.[30]

A similarly fervent evocation of Burns in a time of crisis may be seen in Figure 13, a poster from the General Election of 1880. Gladstone had emerged from semi-retirement to challenge the incumbent Prime Minister Disraeli, incensed at his old adversary's favouritism towards the Turks in the war between Russia and Turkey: in Gladstone's eyes, Disraeli's policies had condoned the massacre by the Turks of over 12,000 unarmed Christian peasants in Bulgaria. The poster also addresses Disraeli's guidance through Parliament of an unpopular law that gave Queen Victoria the right to style herself 'Empress of India'. Gladstone's campaign poster summons up the ghosts of Wallace and the Nasmyth Burns under a banner marked Liberty. 'Scots Wha Hae', in rewritten form, is printed on the bottom:

> Scots whose sires wi' Wallace bled,
>   Scots to truth and justice wed,
> Prepare for a servile bed,
>   Or a victory!
>
> Now's the day and now's the hour,
> See the front o' battle lour,
> See advance proud jingo's power,
>   Chains and slavery!

The caption reads: 'Gentlemen of Midlothia, the spirits of Burns and Wallace stand by my side, and we appeal to you to be jealous of liberties bequeathed to you by your forefathers and to hand them down to your children unsullied and untarnished by the withering hand of Imperialism and Tyranny'. The tiny figure of Disraeli is depicted wearing ermine and an imperial crown, as he cries havoc and lets loose the dogs of war — as the caption reads. Gladstone, by contrast, is depicted as taller, simply dressed and addressing a crowd of voters — clearly a bigger man on higher moral ground. The additional touch of the ghosts suggests which candidate the patriots of Scottish history would have supported at this time of crisis. Seventy-one-year-old Gladstone won this election, unseating Disraeli — who died in 1881 — one last time.

Figure 14, frontispiece to *The Soldier's Return* (a handsome large-format book illustrating Burns's song of that title), offers a visual interpretation of Burns's many songs criticising the post-Culloden British policy of recruiting the remaining male Highlanders into Scottish regiments of the regular army.[31] The title of John Faed's picture is *The Horrors of War*. The young widow has just received news of the death of her soldier husband — a medal has fallen out of the letter and lies, disregarded, on the table. The bereaved Highland madonna holds her sleeping youngest child, while her own mother

Figure 13

consoles a slightly older toddler. The contrast between the bare
furnishings of the cottage and the lush beauty of the human faces
and human forms captures contrasts typical of Burns — especially in his songs about the impact of foreign wars upon
survivors at home. (The grief and anxiety of women left alone
to rear small children with insufficient resources is also empha-
sized in 'Logan Water'.) 'The Soldier's Return' was a favourite
text for Victorian illustrators, probably because it has a happy
ending and the 'plot' lends itself to dramatisation: the returning
soldier comes back to claim a sweetheart who gave him up for
lost so long ago that at first she does not recognise him. John
Faed has chosen in his frontispiece, however, to offer a
composite reading of Burns's anti-war sentiments in a picture
that forms a dark foreground for the happier events dramatised
later in his book of illustrations.

I conclude with an illustration of that most nostalgic of Burns's
songs, 'Auld Lang Syne', from a picture book in the same series

Figure 14

as *The Soldier's Return*. The painter, George Harvey, emphasises something that modern commentators often miss: 'Auld Lang Syne' is one of Burns's elegies for displaced Highlanders. In this picture, the two boys, years before their separation, pick daisies together in what is unmistakably a Highland landscape: the boys wear kilts. All Harvey's illustrations for this song assume that Burns is dramatising the chance reunion of two exiled Jacobites, or at any rate two reluctant emigrants. For as Burns's lyrics emphasise, the two men have been separated not only by time but by extended exile — 'braid' seas and 'weary' wanderings.[32]

Harvey's illustration suggests one conclusion to be drawn from the study of Burns and nostalgia: the poet's entwinement with faulty, half-effaced memories has much to do with the Highland clearances and also with the economic exile experienced by so many Scots — Lowlander and Highlander — between 1745 and 1900. Within a generation of the poet's death, many of his own class — Scotland's peasantry — had

Figure 15

emigrated to North America or (like two of the poet's three surviving legitimate sons) to eastern outposts of the British Empire. Most of those who remained in Britain left the land for industrial work, or for merchant trading in Liverpool or Glasgow that bound the remaining Scots (almost as firmly as if they had emigrated) to a global and colonial economy. 'Scottishness' was no longer a matter of daily identity; it required the selective effort of memory called 'nostalgia'. In the decades following Burns's death, nostalgia resulted inevitably from his being perceived as the final articulate voice of a dying social class (the tenantry) and an ancient country swallowed whole by Greater Britain (on which the sun now never set). What was left to the Scots was the picturesque: tourism and Balmoral, Scott and Burns. But unlike the heroic fiction of Scott, the poems and songs of Burns emphasise the small world of parish gossip and the most intimate details of Scottish landscape — the birds, the flowers, the riverbanks. That the poet himself was driven nearly to insanity by the narrowness of parish life is one of the ironies of literary history: the Scots in exile wished to remember, in the kind of detail Burns supplies, this vanished rural world. (Burns prepared the Kilmarnock edition itself in 1786 under the pressure of the same impulse to remember: he probably booked passage for Jamaica during the same month that he determined to publish a book of his poems.)

It was not by force of personality (and hardly by feats of womanising) that Burns imposed himself on popular consciousness during the nineteenth century. It was through his idealising portrait of a 'Scotland' that he remembered for the tens of thousands of people who shared his social class and historical dilemma though not his poetic genius. Robert Burns 'remembered' Scotland on behalf of all its uncounted nineteenth-century exiles — the economic exiles who worked in London offices as well as those who sailed for the new colonies in the Far East or the new republics in North America. And in their turn, the Scots remembered Burns.

Burns's dialect also facilitated the development of this nostalgia bred by exile. He wrote in the language of a sovereign Scotland almost two hundred years after the Union of Crowns of

1603. In Burns's songs and poems, the dialect (like the subject matter) insists upon the separate and unique status and vocabulary of 'Scottishness', an emphasis congenial to a culture in exile. Much has been written about the universality of Burns, but that emphasis can be misleading. Burns's speakers are universal in that they are chosen from the largest group of human beings — those who can seldom afford to do as they wish. He dramatises the conflicts and joys of people who may only in one or two instances in their lives make an independent choice — of a suitor, of an occupation, of a political creed. But Burns's language is another matter — it is emphatically and even defiantly local. In their insistent and inherent 'Scottishness', Burns's dialect poems make themselves virtually untranslatable. Convert 'To a Mouse' into Latin and nothing is left:

> Eheu, parva nitedula, qualis nunc tremor implet
> Pectora! ne subito celeri te proripe cursu;
> Insectare te nollem rulla truculenta.[33]

Change 'Auld Lang Syne' into French and matters become more hopeless still:

> Doit-on negliger ses amis,
>   Outrager la tendress,
> De ceux qu'on cherissoit jadis,
>   Aux jour de la jeunesse?[34]

One of the few incidents that rings true in Allan Cunningham's unreliable *Life of Burns* (1834) is an anecdote he tells of the day Burns died — a question overheard on the streets of Dumfries: 'Who do you think will be our poet now?' But Burns is always Scotland's poet, for the 'Immortal Memory' is itself a recollection of a vanished Scotland (I would say a Scotland that never was — a selective and itself nostalgic construction of the poet's powerful imagination). The poems and songs of Burns recall a language, a class, and a place that for reasons determined by history and by Burns's own artistry cannot be found — let alone reappropriated — by later Scottish writers. (Scott, Stevenson, MacDiarmid — all had to repudiate Burns in order to replace his mythic Scotland with one of their own imagining.)

Contradictory icons of Burns will cease to multiply when the Scots settle on a single definition of their national identity and character. The nostalgic celebrations will stop when the Scots decide it is time to leave behind the mythically intact 'Scotland' that forms the backdrop of Burns's work, or when they find it possible to adopt English as a natural way of voicing feelings as well as thoughts. Given the reasons Burns is remembered by the Scots, the 'Immortal Memory' is likely to be toasted for many years to come.

Notes

1. Henry Mackenzie, *The Lounger* 97 (9 Dec. 1786), in Donald A. Low, *Robert Burns: the Critical Heritage* (London, 1974), 67–70. In using the phrase 'Heaven-taught', Mackenzie echoes 'The Minstrel' by James Beattie:

   > Then grieve not, thou, to whom th' indulgent Muse
   > Vouchsafes a portion of celestial fire;
   > Nor blame the partial Fates, if they refuse
   > Th' imperial banquet, and the rich attire.
   > Know thine own worth, and reverence the lyre.
   > Wilt thou debase the heart which God refined?
   > No; let thy heaven-taught soul to heaven aspire,
   > To fancy, freedom, harmony resign'd;
   > Ambition's grovelling crew forever left behind.
   >   *The Minstrel, in Two Books, With Some Other Poems*
   >   (London; 1784), 4.

2. A sculptural mural by Turnerelli depicting the same scene of Coila throwing her mantle over Burns adorns the poet's mausoleum in Dumfries.

3. *The Complete Works of Burns* [Self-Interpreting] (Philadelphia; 1886), VI, 285.

4. 'I shall speak reverently of Burns's character in hearing of his sons; but not even in their hearing must I forget what is due always to established judgment of the everlasting right. Like all other mortal beings, he had his faults — great even in the eyes of men — grievous in the eyes of Heaven. Never are they to be thought of without sorrow, were it but for the misery with which he himself

repented them.' 'Speech at the Burns Festival', from John Wilson, *Essays Critical and Imaginative* (Edinburgh, 1856), III, 213.

5. Quoted in *Speeches and Essays* (Washington, DC: Jean Armour Burns Club, 1908), 9.

6. Letter to Agnes M'Lehose ('Clarinda'), 28 Dec. 1787. *The Letters of Robert Burns*, eds. Ferguson and Roy (Oxford, 1985), I, 189–90. Incidentally, the other Robert Burns the Younger — the poet's illegitimate son by Jenny Clow (who refused to surrender her infant to Burns) prospered more in obscurity than the 'Robert' brought up in the glare of publicity. The assiduous new biography of Burns by James Mackay has traced this forgotten child: 'Jenny's little son Robert Burns survived, became a prosperous merchant, and married well . . . [H]e named his own elder son Robert and told him who his grandfather was' (425). Robert III (grandson of Jenny Clow and Burns) led an adventurous life, reports Mackay, emigrating to Borneo and exposing the atrocities of 'the white rajah of Sarawak'; he married the daughter of a Kayan chief and was murdered in 1851 by pirates. 'Descendants of the poet, through Robert Burns III, are believed to live in Sabah to this day.' *RB: A Biography of Robert Burns* by James Mackay (Edinburgh, 1992), 425–6.

7. *Ibid.*, 646. Nichol's eighteenth-century hyper-punctuation — a comma every other word — has been silently corrected. William Nichol was the choleric Master of Classics at the High School of Edinburgh — a man who, like Burns, had raised himself from humble beginnings through a combination of extraordinary talent and hard work. Burns named one of his sons after Nichol.

8. 'His person was strong and robust: his manners rustic, not clownish; a sort of dignified plainness and simplicity . . . His features are represented in Mr Nasmyth's picture, but to me it conveys the idea that they are diminished as if seen in perspective. I think his countenance was more massive . . . I would have taken the poet . . . for a very sagacious country farmer of the old Scotch school . . . There was a strong expression of sense and shrewdness in all his lineaments; the eye alone, I think, indicated the poetic character and temperament. It was large, and of a dark cast, and glowed (I say literally *glowed*) when he spoke with feeling or interest. I never saw such another eye in a human head, though I

have seen the most distinguished men of my time.' Sir Walter
Scott, quoted in Donald Low, *Burns: The Critical Heritage*, 261–2.

9. Mackay, *Burns*, 54.

10. The obituary account accompanying this photograph does note
that Jean Brown once acted the role of the poet's mother in a
drama based on Burns's life and wore on stage several articles from
his wardrobe. The trick photograph (by H. J. Rennie of
Blairgowrie) and accompanying obituary appeared in *The Burns
Chronicle*, 2nd Ser., Vol. 14 (1939), 116–17.

   Illustration 4a is taken from *Speeches and Essays*, cited above in
Note 5: the photograph faces p. 72.

11. For a more sympathetic account, see 'Is This Really Burns?' in *The
Burns Chronicle*, 3rd Ser., XVIII (1969), 8–10. The photograph
faces p. 8.

   Basil Skinner concludes his definitive study of the poet's
portraits with a dismissal of all legends of 'lost' Raeburns: 'I
have left until last any discussion of the bedevilled controversy that
links the names of Raeburn and Burns. That Raeburn reached
Edinburgh on his return from Italy in sufficient time to overlap
with Burns's visits to the city, there is no doubt, and the possibility
of finding a portrait of Scotland's greatest poet by her greatest
painter has been too strong a lure for enthusiastic and over-
optimistic collectors of more than one generation. On the other
hand, letters from Raeburn to Messrs Cadell and Davies, the
publishers in London, show that he did, in fact, paint a copy of
Nasmyth's bust portrait . . . The subsequent history of this [1803]
copy is not known, although engravings are on record that
associate the name of Raeburn with a portrait of the Nasmyth
type . . . No painting is . . . known today that can be identified,
even remotely, with the canvas referred to in 1803 to Messrs
Cadell. As far as an original Raeburn depiction of Burns is
concerned, various portraits of a more or less improbable nature
have appeared . . . but without exception these have proved to be
either reasonably credible Raeburns or pictures completely
unassociated with either poet or painter.' In *Burns: Authentic
Likenesses* (Edinburgh, 1963), 11–12.

12. Gilbert Burns, in a letter of 2 July 1821 to George Thomson,
mentions that his 'brother's lips showed a separation outward
when not speaking'. Edward Barrington Nash, *Robert Burns, An*

Address Upon the Portraiture of the Poet Delivered in the Royal Glasgow Institute for the Fine Arts, 29th September, 1896 (Paisley, 1896), 28.

13. James Mackay has established Margaret as 'Highland Mary's' probable first name. See his full discussion of the many enigmas that surround the story of Highland Mary in *Burns*, 196–227. It is, incidentally, characteristic of Burns to bestow slightly variant names on his song-heroines: 'Anna's' real name was Helen; 'Clarinda' and 'Nancy' were really Agnes; 'Chloris' was Jean Lorimer. Mary Morison (though she really existed) was a child when Burns appropriated her name, which suited his tune, in order to celebrate either Alison Begbie (according to Robert Chambers) or Eliza Gebbie (according to James Mackay, 83–90). Jean Armour is the exception: she is featured in relatively few of Burns's songs, but in those cases she usually is named directly, as in 'Of a' the airts'.

14. This is the rarest of the images printed for this essay: I am particularly grateful to the Mitchell Library for permission to publish it.

15. The painter is H. Corbauld; the engraver C. Heath. The passage being illustrated occurs in *The Life of Robert Burns, by Dr Currie, with his Correspondence and Fragments* (London, 1808), 202.

16. *Ibid.*, Frontispiece.

17. Perhaps unconsciously, Syme is echoing 'Tam o'Shanter' (11. 73–6).

18. The anecdote occurs on p. 102 of the Dove edition.

19. *Pride and Passion: Robert Burns*, by DeLancey Ferguson (New York, 1964), 125. This work, originally published by OUP in 1939, is, despite the passage of time, still the most readable and insightful biography of Burns. It should be supplemented, however, by reference to works such as Mackay's that document their findings: Ferguson did not use footnotes.

20. Cf. Mackay, p. 680.

21. John McDiarmid, 'St Michael's Churchyard, Disinterment of Burns', in *Sketches from Nature* (Dumfries 1830), cited in Mackay, 681. *The Catalogue of the Mitchell Library, Glasgow* (Glasgow, 1959) gives the place of publication as Edinburgh (p. 171; Mitchell Cat. No. 52548). Although some have assumed that McDiarmid is describing the second exhumation of 1834, Robert Chambers' appropriately titled essay 'A Posthumous History of Robert

Burns' verifies John McDiarmid as a witness in 1815. 'Self-
Interpreting Burns' [cf. Note 3], VI, 286.

22. Mackay, *Burns*, 681. Section 13 of the *Mitchell Library Catalogue* is
    devoted to phrenological studies of Burns — all based on
    examination of the cast of the skull or on the engraving (p. 92).

23. James Hogg. *The Private Memoirs and Confessions of a Justified Sinner.
    Written by Himself* (London, 1824).

24. John D. Ross, *Burnsiana: A Collection of Literary Odds and Ends
    Relating to Robert Burns* (Paisley and London, 1892–7), VI [1897],
    45.

25. 'A Scots Mummy' was the title of a letter describing an exhuma-
    tion that Hogg published in *Blackwood's Edinburgh Magazine* in
    August 1823, one year before the publication of *Memoirs of a
    Justified Sinner* (XIV, 188–90). Whether or not Hogg began his
    adventures in exhumation in 1815, he had certainly opened a
    suicide's grave by 1823, before writing his novel. See David
    Groves, 'James Hogg's *Confessions*: New Information'. *The Review
    of English Studies*, Vol. XL, No. 158 (May 1989), 240–2.

26. Barrington Nash, 9–10. Basil Skinner, discussing Hogg's anec-
    dote, notes that a large version of the same Burns portrait Hogg
    describes was produced on canvas by Taylor, copying the first.
    But the wooden panel is the original portrait, the one cherished
    by Peter Taylor's widow in 'a little box' (p. 14).

27. Mackay, *Burns*, 681, from *The Phrenological Development of Robert
    Burns*. Also in *Catalogue of the Mitchell Library* (No. 25630, p. 92).
    Another work by Combe, preserved in the Thomas Cooper
    Library, is *The Life of David Haggart*. In an appendix to this
    penitential narrative by a condemned murderer, Combe sum-
    marised his findings uncovered during an examination of Haggart
    shortly before his execution: 'a great self-esteem, a large comba-
    tiveness, a prodigious firmness, a great secretiveness, and a
    defective love of approbation'. *Life of David Haggart* (Edin-
    burgh; 1821), 159–60.

28. *Punch; or The London Charivari*, 5 Feb. 1859, 51.

29. See Tom Cullen's account of this scandal of the 1860s in *The
    Empress Brown: The Story of a Royal Friendship* (London, 1969).

30. David Coddington, 'Speech at Mozart Hall', *Speeches and Addresses*
    (New York, 1866), 7–8.

31. Painted by John Faed (RSA) and engraved by Henry Lemon. *The

Soldier's Return. Edinburgh, 1857. Caption: 'Mony a sweet babe fatherless,/ And mony a widow mourning'. One satire by Burns, the Postscript to 'The Author's Earnest Cry and Prayer', likewise attacks the British army's recruitment efforts among the poorest Scotsmen.

32. Painted by George Harvey (RSA) and engraved by Lumb Stocks. *Auld Lang Syne*. Edinburgh, 1859. Caption: 'We twa hae rin about the braes/An pu'd the gowans fine'.

   Gilbert Burns, the poet's brother, mentioned in a letter to Mrs Dunlop a story that suggests a source for 'Auld Lang Syne' in tales Burns's father told his children of his own painful separation from his brother Robert: 'I have often heard my father describe the anguish of mind he felt when he parted with his elder brother Robert on the top of a hill, on the confines of their native place [Kincardineshire], each going off his several way . . . and scarcely knowing whither he went.' Maurice Lindsay, *The Burns Encyclopedia* (New York, 1980), 399.

33. [James Graham], *Poems in English, Scotch and Latin* (Paisley, 1794), 131.

34. John D. Ross, comp., *A Little Book of Burns Lore* (Stirling, 1926), 43.

Acknowledgements

The research on which this essay is based was begun during Fall 1989, when a grant from the British Academy, combined with leave from Florida Atlantic University, allowed me to work at the Mitchell Library, Glasgow. The essay was greatly expanded in summer of 1993, when a W. Ormiston Roy Fellowship allowed me a summer's work at the Thomas Cooper Library of the University of South Carolina, with its rich holdings in Burns editions and Burnsiana, the G. Ross Roy Collection in Scottish Literature. For hospitality and assistance in South Carolina, I thank Patrick Scott and Roger Mortimer, Sandy Lovvorn, Jamie Hansen and Paul Schultz; and especially Ross, Lucie and Madeleine Roy. My semester in Scotland was made possible through the efforts of Andrew Noble and Simon Frith, and my research there was clarified and challenged by friendly debates with Kenneth Simpson, Andrew and Jennifer Noble, Margaret Elphinstone, my excellent students at the University of Strathclyde, and the helpful and knowledgeable staff at the Mitchell Library, especially John McGuire.

Illustrations 1, 7, 8, 9, 10, 11, 12, 13, 14, and 15 are published with the permission of the Mitchell Library. Illustrations 2 and 5 (from the G. Ross Roy Collection) appear with the permission of the Thomas Cooper Library, University of South Carolina. The Burns Federation (publisher of *The Burns Chronicle*) has authorized the publication of Illustration 4; and the Lady Stair House Museum has granted permission to publish Illustration 6.

Works Cited

Beattie, James. *The Minstrel in Two Books, With Some Other Poems.* London: C. Dilly, 1784.

Burns, Robert. *The Complete Works of Burns* [Self-Interpreting]. 6 Vols. Philadelphia: Gebbie, 1886.

Currie, James. *The Life of Robert Burns, by Dr Currie, with [Burns's] Correspondence and Fragments.* London: J. Dove, 1808.

Catalogue of the Mitchell Library. Glasgow: Corporation Public Libraries, 1959.

Coddington, David. *Speeches and Addresses.* New York: Appleton, 1866.

Cullen, Tom. *The Empress Brown: The Story of a Royal Friendship.* London: Bodley Head, 1969.

Faed, John [artist]. *The Soldier's Return.* Edinburgh: T. Constable, 1857.

Ferguson, J. DeLancey. *Pride and Passion: Robert Burns.* New York: Russell and Russell, 1964.

Ferguson, J. DeLancey and G. Ross Roy. *The Letters of Robert Burns.* 2 Vols. Oxford: Clarendon, 1985.

[Graham, James.] *Poems in English, Scotch and Latin.* Paisley: J. Neilson, 1794.

Groves, David. 'James Hogg's Confessions: New Information.' *The Review of English Studies.* XL. 158 (May 1989): 240–42.

[Haggart, David and George Combe.] *The Life of David Haggart, alias John Wilson, alias John Morison, alias Barney M'Coul, alias John M' Colgan, alias Daniel O'Brien, alias The Switcher.* Edinburgh: Tait, 1821.

Harvey, George [artist]. *Auld Lang Syne*. Edinburgh: T. Constable, 1859.

[Hogg, James.] *The Private Memoirs and Confessions of a Justified Sinner. Written by Himself*. London: Longmans *et al*, 1824.

'Is This Really Burns?' *The Burns Chronicle*. Third Series. XVIII (1969): 8–10.

Lindsay, Maurice. *The Burns Encyclopedia*. New York: St Martin's, 1980.

Low, Donald A. *Robert Burns: The Critical Heritage*. London: Routledge and Kegan Paul, 1974.

Mackay, James. *Burns: A Biography of Robert Burns*. Edinburgh: Mainstream, 1992.

Nash, Edward Barrington. *Robert Burns, An Address Upon the Portraiture of the Poet Delivered in the Royal Glasgow Institute for the Fine Arts*, 29th September, 1896. Paisley: A. Gardner, 1896.

'Obituary: Jean Armour Burns Brown.' *The Burns Chronicle*. Second Series. XIV (1939): 116–117.

Punch; or the London Charivari. The issues for 22 January 1859 and 5 February 1859.

Ross, John D. *A Little Book of Burns Lore*. Stirling: Eneas Mackay, 1926.

—————. *Burnsiana: A Collection of Literary Odds and Ends Pertaining to Burns*. 6 Vols. Paisley and London: Alexander Gardner, 1892–97.

Skinner, Basil. *Burns: Authentic Likenesses*. Edinburgh: Oliver and Boyd, 1963.

Speeches and Essays. Washington, DC: Jean Armour Burns Clubs, 1908.

Wilson, John ['Christopher North']. *Essays Critical and Imaginative*. 3 Vols. Edinburgh: Blackwood's, 1856.

4
Robert Burns: 'Heaven-taught ploughman'?

Kenneth Simpson

It was Henry Mackenzie who, in December 1786, wrote admiringly of Burns as 'this Heaven-taught ploughman'.[1] Within a few decades Scott was claiming, 'Burns . . . had an education not much worse than the sons of many gentlemen in Scotland'.[2] Scott's version is probably closer to the mark than Mackenzie's, but each had his reasons for forming a very specific conception of Burns, just as each had a specific conception of Scotland (and the two are closely interrelated).

Mackenzie's essay in *The Lounger* was headed 'Surprising Effects of Original Genius, exemplified in the Poetical Productions of Robert Burns, An Ayrshire Ploughman'. Mackenzie, whose values epitomise the polite taste of the Edinburgh literati, laments Burns's use of 'provincial dialect' as a 'bar . . . to his fame' but notes enthusiastically 'with what uncommon penetration and sagacity this Heaven-taught ploughman, from his humble and unlettered station, has looked upon men and manners'. Mackenzie's enthusiasm is symptomatic of the desire of Scottish writers and thinkers that Scotland should lead the response to Rousseau's plea for a return to Nature on the grounds that Reason had failed man by creating a corrupt social order. Heaven's greatest gift is the values of the heart; heaven teaches natural benevolence. 'Heaven-taught' is used by Burns himself with reference to Robert Fergusson as a term of the highest praise. In 'Ode for General Washington's Birthday' Burns addresses Scotland in these terms:

> Thee, Caledonia, thy wild heaths among,
> Famed for the martial deed, the heaven-taught song,
>   To thee, I turn with swimming eyes.
>   Where is that soul of Freedom fled?
> Immingled with the mighty Dead!
> Beneath that hallowed turf where Wallace lies!

Freedom is lost, but the 'heaven-taught song' endures.

It is strikingly paradoxical — and somehow typically Scottish — that while the work of the Scottish philosophers, essentially secular in its bias, was placing man at the centre of human investigation, at the same time Scottish poets were to be seen as the recipients of divine inspiration. Scottish intellectuals, intent on proving Scotland's right to cultural partnership with England, were determined to show that Scotland was in the vanguard of taste. With a strong religious tradition and sublime landscape, Scotland seemed a plausible breeding-ground for the noble savage as poet. Michael Bruce, a prime contender, had died young, while James Macpherson's undeniably massive achievement had been shown to be a forgery. The Ayrshire ploughman-poet fitted the bill perfectly. Burns was recruited to the cause of establishing Scottish pre-eminence in the vogues of noble savagery and sensibility. He enlisted readily and helped perpetuate the myth, presenting himself as follows in the Preface to his Commonplace Book:

> As he was but little indebted to scholastic education, and bred at a plough-tail, his performances must be strongly tinctured with his unpolished, rustic way of life; but as I believe, they are really his own, it may be some entertainment to a curious observer of human-nature to see how a ploughman thinks, and feels, under the pressure of Love, Ambition, Anxiety, Grief with the like cares and passions, which, however diversified by the Modes, and Manners of life, operate pretty much alike I believe, in all the Species.[3]

It is ironic that Burns's prose is often at its most formal when he is claiming in letters to his social superiors that he is an uneducated peasant. In fact these letters prove that he was a master of voice and persona. Yet the belief persisted that Burns always wrote about himself and his own experience and was incapable of anything as sophisticated as the invention of personae. His first editor, James Currie, was adamant that 'if fiction be . . . the soul of poetry, no one had ever less pretensions to the name of poet than Burns . . . the subjects on which he has written are seldom, if ever, imaginary'.[4] With help from the poet himself, the image of the untutored rustic was firmly established. It has bedevilled Burns criticism ever since.

Yet the reality was altogether different. Commenting on the work of a fellow poet, Burns challenged the description of Truth as 'the soul of every song that's nobly great', offering instead, 'Fiction is the soul of many a song that's nobly great'.[5] As one who numbered himself among 'the harum-scarum Sons of Imagination and Whim'[6], he upheld the importance of the imagination. His social life was characterised by inventiveness and self-drama, so much so that Maria Riddell pronounced him unequalled in 'the sorcery of fascinating conversation'.[7]

If Burns was indeed 'this Heaven-taught ploughman', then the Almighty's school was indeed a good school. Burns is revealed in both poems and letters as an alert observer of events in the wider world. The French king and queen are labelled 'a perjured Blockhead & an unprincipled Prostitute'.[8] Of events across the Atlantic he writes:

> I will not, I cannot, enter into the merits of the cause; but I dare say, the American Congress, in 1776, will be allowed to have been as able and as enlightened, and, a whole empire will say, as honest, as the English Convention in 1688; and that the fourth of July will be as sacred to their posterity as the fifth of November is to us.[9]

A week later he was writing to Mrs Dunlop:

> Is it not remarkable, odiously remarkable, that tho' manners are more civilized, & the rights of mankind better understood, by an Augustan Century's improvement, yet in this very reign of heavenly Hanoverianism, and almost in this very year, an empire beyond the Atlantic has had its REVOLUTION too, & for the very same maladministration & legislative misdemeanors in the illustrious and sapientipotent Family of H—— as was complained of in the 'tyrannical & bloody house of Stuart'.[10]

Developments in the sciences interested him also. In one letter he writes of the soil structure of Ellisland in terms which indicate some awareness of James Hutton's infant geology, and Mrs Dunlop discusses with him experiments in chemistry and natural physics. Mrs Dunlop sends for his appraisal some poems she has written in French. They debate the respective merits of

Dryden's Virgil and Pope's Homer ('I suspect the translators would have suited better had Pope and Dryden exchanged authors',[11] comments Mrs Dunlop). She sends him Ariosto and Tasso, only to remark ruefully, 'I fear you have not liked Tasso'.[12]

Burns's own letters are replete with evidence of his range of reading. To Moore he writes:

> I know very well, the novelty of my character has by far the greatest share in the learned and polite notice I have lately got; and in a language where Pope and Churchill have raised the laugh, and Shenstone and Gray drawn the tear; where Thomson and Beattie have painted the landskip, and Littleton and Collins described the heart; I am not vain enough to hope for distinguished Poetic fame.[13]

What he termed 'the history of MYSELF' which he sent to Moore has references to Addison, Pope, Shakespeare, 'Tull and Dickson on Agriculture, The Pantheon, Locke's Essay on the human understanding, Stackhouse's history of the Bible, Justice's British Gardiner's directory, Boyle's lectures, Allan Ramsay's works, Taylor's scripture doctrine of original sin, a select collection of English songs, Hervey's meditations . . . Thomson's and Shenstone's works . . . Sterne and Mackenzie — Tristram Shandy and the Man of Feeling were my bosom favorites'.[14] The letters are testimony to the range and quality of Burns's education. That education helped shape both the man and the poet.

Burns wrote to Mrs Dunlop, 'I cannot for the soul of me resist an impulse of any thing like Wit'.[15] His reading helped him to give free play to such impulses. At regular social gatherings in a fairly close community the play of wit was a useful outlet for his considerable intelligence. His wide reading also introduced an element of stability and it was a source of values. It had a more practical function, too, as this remark to Mrs Dunlop suggests:

> Do you know, I pick up favorite quotations, and store them in my mind as ready armour, offensive, or defensive, amid the struggle of this turbulent existence. Of these is one, a very favorite one, from Thomson's Alfred —

> Attach thee firmly to the virtuous deeds
> And offices of life: to life itself,
> With all its vain and transient joys, sit loose'.[16]

(He had already quoted these lines in a letter to her two years earlier.) As 'Sylvander' he writes to Mrs McLehose's 'Clarinda':

> The only *unity* (a sad word with Poets and Critics!) in my ideas is CLARINDA. There my heart 'reigns and revels' —
>
> > 'What art thou Love! whence are those charms,
> >   That thus thou bear'st an universal rule!
> > For thee the soldier quits his arms,
> >   The king turns slave, the wise man fool.
> >
> > In vain we chase thee from the field,
> >   And with cool thoughts resist thy yoke:
> > Next tide of blood, Alas! we yield;
> >   And all those high resolves are broke!'
>
> I like to have quotations ready for every occasion. They give one's ideas so pat, and save one the trouble of finding expression adequate to one's feelings.[17]

(If he was truly devoted to 'Clarinda', wouldn't he have taken the trouble? Or wouldn't he at least have found something better than those lines of turgid cliché from an anonymous song in *The Hive* (1724)? This suggests that the Sylvander/Clarinda correspondence involved a considerable degree of posing and play.) The letter continues:

> I think it is one of the greatest pleasures attending a Poetic genius, that we can give our woes, cares, joys, loves &c. an embodied form in verse, which, to me, is ever immediate ease.

Emotions need to be expressed. Having a stock of quotations readily speeds the process and brings ease. Poetry is here functioning essentially as catharsis.

On a deeper level, Burns found in literature the means of clearly identifying and expressing values and attitudes which he personally held. Nationalism is a case in point. Burns had to be circumspect as to the expression of nationalist views. Here the work of Ramsay and Fergusson was to provide useful precedent.

One of the foremost indications of the ingenuity of the poets of the eighteenth-century vernacular revival is in the metaphors which they find to communicate their nationalism. 'Base foreign fashions have intervened', claims the speaker in Ramsay's 'Tartana'. How better to assert the national cultural identity than by attacking foreign tastes and trends? Music provides a fertile source. Take these stanzas from Ramsay's 'An Elegy on Patie Birnie':

> After ilk tune he took a sowp,
> And bann'd wi' birr the corky cowp
> That to the Papists' country scowp,
>   To lear 'ha, ha's,
> Frae chiels that sing hap, stap, and lowp,
>   Wanting the b — s.
>
> That beardless capons are na men,
> We by their fozie springs might ken,
> But ours, he said, could vigour len'
>   To men o' wier,
> And gar them stout to battle sten
>   Withoutten fear.

The identification of culture with heroism here is significant. Fergusson's celebration of the New Year holidays, 'The Daft Days', includes this:

> Fiddlers, your pins in temper fix,
> And roset weel your fiddlesticks;
> But banish vile Italian tricks
>   From out your *quorum*;
> Nor *fortes* wi' *pianos* mix —
>   Gie's *Tullochgorum*.
>
> For nought can cheer the heart sae weel,
> As can a canty Highland reel;
> It even vivifies the heel
>   To skip and dance:
> Lifeless is he wha canna feel
>   Its influence.

In these poems are two of the precedents for the favourable comparison of Scottish melodies with Italian in stanza 13 of 'The Cotter's Saturday Night':

> They chant their artless notes in simple guise;
>   They tune their hearts, by far the noblest aim:
> Perhaps *Dundee's* wild-warbling measures rise,
>   Or plaintive *Martyrs*, worthy of the name;
> Or noble *Elgin* beets the heaven-ward flame,
>   The sweetest far of Scotia's holy lays:
> Compar'd with these, *Italian trills* are tame;
>   The tickl'd ears no heart-felt raptures raise;
> Nae unison hae they, with our Creator's praise.

Sometimes Burns's nationalism surfaces in the most unexpected ways. The witches in 'Tam o' Shanter' have travelled the world: their collection of trophies includes 'Five tomahawks, wi' blue red-rusted/ Five scymitars, wi' murder crusted'. But when it comes to music and dance they are patriots to the core:

> Warlocks and witches in a dance:
> Nae cotillion, brent new frae France,
> But hornpipes, jigs, strathspeys, and reels,
> Put life and mettle in their heels.

Food offers another metaphor for nationalism. Behind the humorous flyting bluster of 'Address to a Haggis' a serious claim is being made for Scottish values. Again Fergusson ('my elder brother in the Muse', Burns called him) was almost certainly the inspiration with his poem, 'To the Principal and Professors of the University of St Andrews, on their superb treat to Dr Samuel Johnson'. Fergusson claims that the university regents have spared no expense to treat Dr Johnson to all sorts of foreign delicacies. Had he been in charge, Fergusson would have provided a quite different menu:

> *Imprimis*, then, a haggis fat,
> Weel tottled in a seything pat,
> Wi' spice and ingans weel ca'd through,
> Had helped to gust the stirrah's mou',
> And placed itself in trencher clean
> Before the gilpy's glowrin een.

> *Secundo*, then, a gude sheep's head,
> Whase hide was singit, never flea'd,
> And four black trotters cled wi' girsle,
> Bedown his throat had learn'd to hirsle.
> What think ye, niest, o' gude fat brose,
> To clag his ribs? a dainty dose!
> And white and bluidy puddings routh,
> To gar the Doctor skirl, 'O Drouth!'.

Fergusson goes on to infer that Scottish writing, like Scottish cuisine, is lively, and natural, and praiseworthy. The poem develops into a moving plea to the Scottish people: be true and natural Scots, for the alternative is a gloomy one — the demise of Scottish culture:

> Devall then, Sirs, and never send
> For daintiths to regale a friend;
> Or, like a torch at baith ends burning
> Your house'll soon grow mirk and mourning'.

There is a subtle irony in Fergusson's making claims for the vigour of the native Scottish literary tradition by means of techniques which epitomise it at its most expressive. Similarly, in 'Elegy on the Death of Scots Music' his expressive use of standard Habbie for serious purposes shows that despite the ostensible lament Scottish cultural forms are alive and well.

Authority is almost certainly inimical to the Scottish character; hence the vigour of Ramsay's and Fergusson's reaction against the unquestioning adoption of classical and neo-classical forms, modes, and rules. But there is also a sense in which Scottish poets of the vernacular revival compensate for the loss of political independence by asserting their cultural independence through the innovative use of classical poetic forms to render distinctly Scottish material. Here is the start of Ramsay's 'Elegy on Lucky Wood':

> O Canongate! poor eldritch hole,
> What loss, what crosses thou dost thole!
> London and death gar thee look drole,
>   And hing thy head:
> Wow, but thou hast e'en a cauld coal
>   To blaw indeed.

Burns's 'Tam Samson's Elegy' has its antecedents in Ramsay's mock-elegies. But Burns could achieve moving and original effect within the conventional elegiac mode, as the very fine 'Elegy on Captain Matthew Henderson' shows.

Another important respect in which Burns was influenced by the earlier poets of the vernacular revival is in the interplay of Scots and formal English. To employ both the vernacular and standard English within the one poem was a risky undertaking. The perfect modulation of the tongues was not always achieved, and sometimes the ultimate effect was not the intended one. Here is the start of Ramsay's pastoral eclogue, 'Richy and Sandy on the Death of Mr Addison':

Richy
What gars thee look sae dowf, dear Sandy, say?
Cheer up, dull fellow, take thy reed and play
'My apron deary', or some wanton tune:
Be merry, lad, an' keep thy heart aboon.

Sandy
Na, na, it winna do; leave me to mane:
This aught days twice o'er tell'd I'll whistle nane.

Richy
Wow, man, that's unco' sad! Is't that yer jo
Has ta'en the strunt? Or has some bogle-bo,
Glowrin frae 'mang auld wa's, gi'en ye a fleg?
Or has some dauted wedder broke his leg?

Sandy
Naething like that, sic troubles eith were borne:
What's bogles, wedders, or what Mausy's scorn?
Our loss is meikle mair, and past remead:
Adie, that played and sang sae sweet, is dead!

Richy
Dead! says't thou? — Oh, haud up my heart, O Pan!
Ye gods, what laids ye lay on feckless man!

Ramsay is making a genuine attempt to claim vernacular Scots' right to a place in British literature; but it doesn't quite succeed. Burns, too, could unwittingly achieve a comic effect by the incongruous use of formal English. One suspects that he might wish to revise these lines from 'Epistle to Davie, a Brother Poet':

> It lightens, it brightens,
> The tenebrific scene,
> To meet with, and greet with
> My Davie or my Jean!

The makars had employed the juxtaposing of Scots idiom and formal English for reductive effect. It is the ideal means for deflating pomposity and pretension. In Fergusson, Burns encountered the clashing of tongues for comic and reductive effect. Typical is the conclusion of 'The Daft Days':

> Let mirth abound, let social cheer
> Invest the dawning of the year;
> Let blithesome Innocence appear,
>   To crown our joy:
> Nor envy wi' sarcastic sneer,
>   Our bliss destroy.

> And thou, great god of *Aqua-vitae*!
> Wha says the empire o' this city,
> Whan fou we're sometimes capernoity,
>   Be thou prepared
> To hedge us frae that black banditti,
>   The City-Guard.

Similarly, Burns is expert at undermining pretension by the strategic use of vernacular Scots as, for instance, in stanza 6 of 'Address to the Unco Guid':

> Ye high, exalted, virtuous Dames,
>   Ty'd up in godly laces,
> Before ye gie poor Frailty names,
>   Suppose a change o' cases;
> A dear-lov'd lad, convenience snug,
>   A treacherous inclination —
> But, let me whisper i' your lug,
>   Ye're aiblins nae temptation.

Burns's bilingualism was set to serve a range of purposes, personal as well as literary. Revealingly, after one of his visits to Edinburgh Burns wrote in exaggeratedly sustained vernacular to William Nicol, master of the High School of Edinburgh. The expressive Scots idiom seems to convey a sense of release; writing the letter has had a cathartic effect on its author.

The linguistic and cultural duality in Burns reflects in part the respective influences of his parents. Through Agnes Brown of Kirkoswald Burns had access to the native oral tradition. William Burnes, with his emphasis on the importance of both reading and correctly pronouncing English, saw clearly where the future lay.

In the English authors whom Burns read avidly there was a further rich source of personae. To varying degrees these personae corresponded with, and gave voice to, aspects of his own personality. In Pope and the *Spectator* essays Burns found the voice of the observer. To Murdoch he wrote, 'I seem to be one sent into the world, to see, and observe . . . the joy of my heart is to "Study men, their manners, and their ways"'.[18] This was a useful stance for the satirist. But for a satirist of Burns's skill and vehemence (he wrote on one occasion of 'the bloodhounds of Satire'[19]), living in a tight-knit community, one of the effects was, as David Sillar noted, to prompt 'suspicious fear'[20] among his neighbours and hence a progressive distancing of the poet from his community. The voice of the detached observer comes to challenge that of the exuberant participant for primacy of place in both Burns's poems and his letters. There are a number of letters in which Burns rails at the mob or fashionable society (including one to Peter Hill in which he clearly distinguishes the two Edinburghs). Here he protests to Mrs Dunlop:

> However respectable, Individuals in all ages have been, I have ever looked on Mankind in the lump to be nothing better than a foolish, headstrong, credulous, unthinking mob; and their universal belief has ever had extremely little weight with me.[21]

That voice is remarkably similar to that of the elderly misanthrope, Matt Bramble, in Smollett's *Humphry Clinker*. Six months earlier, Burns had written to Hill, 'I want Smollett's novels, for the sake of his incomparable humour. I already have *Roderick Random* and *Humphry Clinker*.'[22]

To one of 'the harum-scarum sons of Imagination and Whim' the lure of Sterne's *Tristram Shandy* was strong. Plainly the Shandean voice struck a chord with Burns's desire to present himself as a whimsically independent spirit. Here is part of one of the letters first published in G. Ross Roy's revised edition of the *Letters* (1985):

> Writing Sense is so damn'd, dry, hide-bound a business, I am determined never more to have anything to do with it. — I have such an aversion to right line and method, that when I can't get over the hedges which bound the highway, I zig-zag across the road just to keep my hand in.[23]

In *Tristram Shandy* Burns encountered Sterne's amused demonstration in terms of fictional practice of Locke's views on understanding, association, and identity. It is evident that the flux of the human mind and the ways in which we associate fascinated Burns, and a letter to Mrs Dunlop in which he tells of the appeal which 'The Vision of Mirza' in the *Spectator* had for him traces the caprices of individual association to a spiritual source — the Soul.[24] One of Burns's greatest achievements was — out of personal need — to shape the verse-epistle into a medium for communicating mental flux. 'The self-dramatisations of the epistles', says Thomas Crawford, 'express a mind in motion, giving itself over at different times to *conflicting* principles and feelings; they mirror that mind as it grappled with a complex world. In order to body it forth, Burns had to be, in himself, and not simply in play, both Calvinist and anti-Calvinist, both fornicator and champion of chastity, both Jacobite and Jacobin, both local and national, both British and European, both anarchist and sober calculator, both philistine and anti-philistine'.[25] A mode and a form had been found that were capable of rendering complexity, even multiplicity, of self.

Of the qualities essential to the personality of the poet, Burns habitually identifies open-heartedness as the foremost. Gavin Hamilton's brother is complimented as having 'a heart that might adorn the breast of a Poet'[26]: and to Josiah Walker Burns writes, 'You know from experience the bedlam warmth of a poet's heart'[27]. Rousseau had claimed that our ancestors were naturally benign and that it was rationalist civilisation that had corrupted man, and in *Tristram Shandy* Sterne had offered man's capacity for benign emotion as a positive good. Here Burns was to find endorsement of his own belief in the values of the heart. To Murdoch he writes, on 15 January 1783:

> My favorite authors are of the sentimental kind, such as Shenstone, particularly his Elegies, Thomson, Man of feeling, a book I prize next to the Bible, Man of the World, Sterne, especially his Sentimental journey, Macpherson's Ossian, etc. these are the glorious models after which I endeavour to form my conduct[28].

Before his twenty-fourth birthday Burns has found in literature models for his behaviour as well as his writing. In Mackenzie was more than endorsement of the values of the heart: there was also the recommendation that one practise benevolence, it being not only beneficial for the victim to have relief from suffering but also rewarding for the benefactor to contemplate himself in that role. In *The Man of Feeling* the 'self-approving joy' of the age of sensibility raises its refined head. Thus in 'To a Mountain Daisy' Burns could employ the sentimental rhetoric which Pope some seventy years earlier had used in 'Elegy to the Memory of an Unfortunate Lady'; Burns employs it to address a flower whose stem he has severed. The Edinburgh literati found Burns exemplifying what for them was a prime requisite of the peasant-poet, pathetic struggle, and they were able to view him with benevolent condescension, rather in the manner of Burns's speaker's response to the mountain daisy. Burns paid a price for his participation in polite Edinburgh's sentimental games: in Carol McGuirk's terms it was a 'chronic anxiety'.[29]

There is one other highly significant source of endorsement of the values of the heart. Sending Moore his impressions of *Zeluco*, Burns commented, 'Original strokes, that strongly depict the human heart, is your and Fielding's province, beyond any other Novellist, I have ever perused'.[30] Moore was being complimented; Fielding's influence was very real. David Daiches has noted that Burns, 'like Fielding's Tom Jones, believed in the doctrine of the good heart and held that kindness, generosity of spirit, and fellow feeling were the central virtues'.[31] Could it be that Burns modelled some of his conduct on that of Fielding's romantic hero, Tom Jones? In their relations with women each maintains a clear distinction between idealised love and sexual needs. His passions aroused by thinking of his beloved Sophia, Tom leaps into the bushes with the first woman he encounters, who happens to be Molly Seagrim, fresh from a day's manure-spreading in the fields. Similarly Burns writes a typically stylised and formal letter to 'Clarinda' in the course of which he makes reference to his having fathered a child to the maid, Jenny Clow.[32]

In terms of literary technique Fielding's influence on Burns was considerable. Both Fielding and Burns relished their abilities as stylists. One of Fielding's aims in *Tom Jones* was to check by parody the excesses of popular romance. As a consequence Tom and Sophia are at times required to act and speak like the hero and heroine of that genre (for example, the chance meeting of the lovers at the corner of the canal where previously Tom risked drowning to save Sophia's little bird). Such passages must surely have been at the back of Burns's mind when he wrote this to Wilhelmina Alexander of Ballochmyle:

The Scenery was nearly taken from real life; though I dare say, Madam, you do n't recollect it: for I believe you scarcely noticed the poetic Reveur, as he wandered by you. — I had roved out as Chance directed, on the favorite haunts of my Muse, the banks of Ayr; to view Nature in all the gayety of the vernal year. —

The Sun was flaming o'er the distant, western hills; not a breath stirred the crimson opening blossom, or the verdant spreading leaf.

'Twas a golden moment for a poetic heart. — I listened the feathered Warblers, pouring their harmony on every hand, with a congenial, kindred regard; and frequently turned out of my path lest I should disturb their little songs, or frighten them to another station. — 'Surely,' said I to myself, 'he must be a wretch indeed, who, regardless of your harmonious endeavours to please him, can eye your elusive flights, to discover your secret recesses, and rob you of all the property Nature gives you; your dearest comforts, your helpless, little Nestlings.'

Even the hoary Hawthorn twig that shot across the way, what

heart, at such a time, but must have been interested in its welfare, and wished it to be preserved from the rudely browsing Cattle, or the withering eastern Blast?

Such was the scene, and such the hour, when in a corner of my Prospect I spyed one of the finest pieces of Nature's workmanship that ever crowned a poetic Landskip; those visionary Bards excepted who hold commerce with aerial Beings. —

Had CALUMNY & VILLAINY taken my walk, they had, at that moment, sworn eternal peace with such an Object. —[33]

It is inconceivable that Burns, as an accomplished mimic and master–ironist, did not realise that what he was offering here was the posturings of romance.

One of the main elements in Fielding's *Tom Jones* is the comic–epic. Ordinary, even mundane, experience is presented with the elaborate formality appropriate to the classical heroic mode. In Ramsay and Fergusson Burns found that inflation and reduction were integral to the Scottish poetic tradition. Fielding, writing in a different tradition and a different genre, sanctioned the technique further. Two traditions met, the common ground being the clash of manner and matter, or formal and idiomatic language, or generalisation and detail. One episode in *Tom Jones* finds the narrator following Mr Allworthy to the top of a hill to watch the sunrise. If there is anything finer in nature, he suggests, it can only be that which Mr Allworthy represents — a being replete with benevolence. Mr Allworthy has to descend because his sister rings the breakfast-bell — from the sublime to the mundane, but doubly so because the narrator is now concerned about how to get the reader safely back down the hill of his elaborate prose without breaking his neck. Compare the following extract from a letter of Burns to Thomson in which a lengthy passage in the grand manner reaches a climax, only to be undermined:

> Do you think that the sober, gin-horse routine of existence could inspire a man with life, & love, & joy — could fire him with enthusiasm, or melt him with pathos, equal to the genius of your

Book? — No! No!!! — Whenever I want to be more than ordinary *in song*; to be in some degree equal to your diviner airs; do you imagine I fast & pray for the celestial emanation? — Tout au contraire! I have a glorious recipe, the very one that for his own use was invented by the Divinity of Healing & Poesy when erst he piped to the flocks of Admetus. — I put myself in a regimen of admiring a fine woman; & in proportion to the adorability of her charms, in proportion are you delighted with my verses.

The lightning of her eye is the godhead of Parnassus, & the witchery of her smile the divinity of Helicon!

To descend to the business with which I began; if you like my idea of — 'when she cam ben she bobbit' — the following stanzas of mine, altered a little from what they were formerly when set to another air, may perhaps do instead of worse stanzas.[34]

Also noteworthy is a wonderfully, almost manically, exuberant letter to Cunningham in which Burns plainly relishes his expertise in the grand manner for comic effect. It includes, 'I feel, I feel the presence of Supernatural assistance! Circled in the embrace of my elbow-chair, my breast labors, like the bloated Sybil on her three-footed stool, & like her too, labors with Nonsense'.[35] Likewise, the account of the celebrations before sunrise at Ben Lomond is, simply, a *tour de force*.[36]

In the poems the reductive contrast of manner and matter is used to telling effect. For instance, this is part of the description of Moodie's preaching in 'The Holy Fair':

> Hear how he clears the points o' Faith
>   Wi' rattlin an' thumpin!
> Now meekly calm, now wild in wrath,
>   He's stampan, an' he's jumpan!
> His lengthen'd chin, his turn'd up snout,
>   His eldritch squeel an' gestures,
> O how they fire the heart devout,
>   Like cantharidian plaisters
>   On sic a day!

In 'Elegy on the Year 1788' international and local events are set on the one level, the former reduced, the latter inflated:

> The Spanish empire's tint a head,
> An' my auld teethless Bawtie's dead;
> The toolzie's teugh 'tween Pitt an' Fox,
> An' our gudewife's wee birdy cocks.

In 'Death and Dr Hornbook' the process of inflation and reduction informs the whole poem. Death? — He is a pathetic figure, in need of a comforting chat and struggling to retain the vestiges of his pride. Who is to be feared now? — The monstrously incompetent pharmacist, Dr Hornbook, who has made Death redundant.

It is in Burns's other great narrative poem, 'Tam o' Shanter', that the epic and comic–epic legacies are put to greatest effect:

> By this time he was cross the ford,
> Whare, in the snaw, the chapman smoor'd;
> And past the birks and meikle stane,
> Whare drunken Charlie brak's neck-bane;
> And thro' the whins, and by the cairn,
> Whare hunters fand the murder'd bairn;
> And near the thorn, aboon the well,
> Whare Mungo's mither hang'd hersel . . .
>
> Coffins stood round, like open presses,
> That shaw'd the dead in their last dresses;
> And, by some devilish cantraip slight,
> Each in its cauld hand held a light.
> By which heroic Tam was able
> To note upon the haly table,
> A murderer's banes, in gibbet-airns;
> Twa span-lang, wee, unchristen'd bairns;
> A thief, new-cutted frae a rape,
> Wi' his last gasp his gab did gape;
> Five tomahawks, wi' blude red-rusted;
> Five scymitars, wi' murder crusted;
> A garter, which a babe had strangled;
> A knife, a father's throat had mangled . . .

— What are these if not the epic catalogue set to the service of mock-Gothic horror? And the 'Heaven-taught ploughman' seems to have mastered the epic simile:

As bees bizz out wi' angry fyke,
When plundering herds assail their byke;
As open pussie's mortal foes,
When, pop! she starts before their nose;
As eager runs the market-crowd,
When 'Catch the thief!' resounds aloud:
So Maggie runs, the witches follow,
Wi' mony an eldritch skreech and hollow.

One effect of rendering ordinary beings by means of the machinery of epic is to endow them with representative significance. The elevating effect is most obvious in Fielding's *Tom Jones* in the mock-epic account of the battle in the graveyard between Molly and the villagers. The participants in the battle assume archetypal significance courtesy of the epic rhetoric which inflates and generalises; it becomes *the* village punch-up. Similarly Tam becomes mankind's representative; he is truly 'heroic Tam', and the account of his experiences has become the definitive version of man's encounter with the supernatural.

There is one other respect in which *Tom Jones* and 'Tam o' Shanter' may be compared. Fielding creates an identifiable narrator — identifiable in terms of personality and values. Urbane and witty, Fielding's narrator is also fallible and he certainly likes the sound of his own voice: scarce an episode passes that has not been prefaced by commentary from our ever-present guide. This pattern is repeated in 'Tam o' Shanter' — episode, commentary, episode, commentary. The narrator is eager to place his account of Tam's experiences in the context of universalising commentary, the fruits of his worldly wisdom:

Ah, gentle dames! it gars me greet,
To think how mony counsels sweet,
How mony lengthen'd sage advices,
The husband frae the wife despises!

Like Fielding's narrator in *Tom Jones*, the narrator of 'Tam o' Shanter' is capable of irony and self-irony ('But here my Muse her wing maun cour/ Sic flights as far beyond her power'). But as Fielding is not synonymous with the narrator of *Tom Jones* and so subjects his narrator to authorial irony, so Burns — who is equally not the narrator of 'Tam o' Shanter' — subjects his creation to authorial irony. 'Tam o' Shanter: A Tale' — the sub-title is deceptively simple, and deliberately so. It is a tale of what happens to Tam; it is also a tale of someone telling a tale. *Tom Jones* is as much an account of narrator-reader relations as a story of what happens to Tom and Sophia. Sterne's *Tristram Shandy* is about the narrator's desperate and largely futile attempt to give an account of his life and opinions, enlisting the reader's help when necessary.[37] Could it be that Burns's 'tale', traditionally regarded as the culmination of the folk-tradition, may be set alongside these sophisticated experiments in narration, where what happens is important, but how it is recounted is equally important? And could it be that in that play of relationships involving poet, narrator, and Tam there is some sort of resolution — albeit temporary — of the poet's problems of identity: multiplicity of identity finds a focus in that play of relationships; paradoxically, in the controlled flux of play lies the basis of stability? It might be added that Burns's obsessive and fluctuating relationship with the Devil (who is both 'that noble personage' and 'Auld Hangie . . . Auld Nickie-Ben') has a comparable function.

Burns lived in various worlds, sometimes simultaneously. The chameleon nature and the charismatic personality made this possible; and, by and large, the linguistic ability and stylistic expertise kept pace with the multiplicity of perspective (the point is perhaps most readily demonstrated by comparing 'Tam o' Shanter' with Burns's prose account to Grose[38] of largely the same material). Burns wrote to Moore, 'my first ambition was, and still my strongest wish is, to please my Compeers, the rustic Inmates of the Hamlet'.[39] In that sentence substance and style are plainly at loggerheads. In the preface to the Commonplace Book he observed, 'I was placed by Fortune among a class of men to whom my ideas would have been nonsense'. Some of Burns's finest poems are those in which he finds the means of communicating on various levels and to various audiences. 'To a Mouse' is both an address to a mouse and, as Thomas Crawford has suggested, a depiction of the plight of both the peasantry and the human race. Burns's 'compeers' may well have been amused by two dogs conversing, but 'The Twa Dogs', echoing Goldsmith and Crabbe and showing the influence of Adam Smith, is a poem about the political and social state of man in the eighteenth century. In 'The Auld Farmer's New-Year-Morning Salutation to his Auld Mare, Maggie' the 'rustic inmates' would hear a familiar voice — that of the peasant-farmer who gives an account of his hardships but stoically accepts his condition. Burns, ironically distanced, offers such a voice as a means of suggesting that men must begin to question their lot and challenge their condition; Enlightenment is meaningless unless it reaches such people also. 'Address to the Deil' would be immediately accessible to those versed in the folk-tradition and Presbyterianism. It is also, though less obviously, a poem about Burns trying to identify and reconcile conflicting elements within himself, elements in whose creation both the folk-tradition and Presbyterianism have played a significant part.

How could a man of acute intelligence and notable breadth and depth of knowledge countenance the reduction of himself to the stereotype of the 'Heaven-taught ploughman'? One answer is that he responded to market forces. Robert Anderson challenged Burns with being more learned than he would acknowledge, and this was the poet's response:

> It was . . . a part of the machinery, as he called it, of his poetical character to pass for an illiterate ploughman who wrote from pure inspiration. When I pointed out some evident traces of poetical imitation in his verses, privately, he readily acknowledged his obligations . . . but in company he would not suffer his pretensions to pure inspiration to be challenged, and it was seldom done where it might be supposed to affect the success of the subscription for his *Poems*.[40]

But he responded so successfully that there was no escape; having helped create the role, he was obliged to continue to play it. The range of reading, ready absorption of material, and talent for mimicry combined in Burns to produce a range of styles, modes, and personae which he used to great creative effect. Ultimately, however, these served more than a literary function: Burns became trapped behind the personae which he had so readily created.

If since 1707 Scots have been uncertain as to their identity, then it is understandable that they should worship a poet who had such a gift for creating voices and personae. But the poet himself paid a price.

Notes

1. *Lounger*, No. 97 (9 Dec. 1786); reprinted in Donald A. Low (ed.), *Robert Burns: The Critical Heritage* (London & Boston, 1974), 67–71.
2. Letter to Lord Byron, 6 Nov. 1813; reprinted in Low (ed.), *Burns: Critical Heritage*, 258.
3. *Robert Burns's Commonplace Book 1783–1785*, intro. David Daiches (London, 1965), 1.
4. 'Criticism on the writings of Burns', *The Works of Robert Burns, with an Account of his Life* (Liverpool, 1800), I, 267; reprinted in Low (ed.), *Burns: Critical Heritage*, 132.
5. *The Letters of Robert Burns*, ed. J. DeLancey Ferguson; 2nd edn., ed. G. Ross Roy (Oxford, 1985), I, 326.
6. *Letters*, I, 109
7. 'Character Sketch' by 'Candidior' (Maria Riddell), *Dumfries Journal*, Aug. 1796; reprinted Low (ed.), *Burns: Critical Heritage*, 102.
8. *Letters*, II, 334.
9. *Letters*, I, 334–5.
10. *Letters*, I, 337.
11. *Robert Burns and Mrs Dunlop: Correspondence*, ed. William Wallace (London, 1898), 60.
12. *Ibid.*, 65.
13. *Letters*, I, 88.
14. *Letters*, I, 138, 141.
15. *Letters*, I, 392.
16. *Letters*, II, 165.
17. *Letters*, I, 207.
18. *Letters*, I, 17.
19. *Letters*, I, 175.

20. *The Life and Works of Robert Burns*, ed. Robert Chambers, rev. William Wallace, 4 vols. (Edinburgh & London, 1896), I, 68–9.
21. *Letters*, I, 349.
22. *Letters*, I, 296.
23. *Letters*, I, 131.
24. *Letters*, I, 348.
25. Thomas Crawford, *Burns: A Study of the Poems and Songs* (2nd edn., reprinted Edinburgh, 1978), 104.
26. *Letters*, I, 152.
27. *Letters*, I, 155.
28. *Letters*, I, 17.
29. Carol McGuirk, *Robert Burns and the Sentimental Era* (Athens, Georgia, 1985), 77
30. *Letters*, II, 74.
31. David Daiches, *God and the Poets* (Oxford, 1984), 144.
32. *Letters*, II, 122.
33. *Letters*, I, 63–4.
34. *Letters*, II, 315–16.
35. *Letters*, II, 146.
36. *Letters*, I, 124–5.
37. For a fuller account of Sterne's influence on Burns, see Kenneth Simpson, *The Protean Scot: The Crisis of Identity in Eighteenth-Century Scottish Literature* (Aberdeen, 1988), ch. 8.
38. *Letters*, II, 29–31.
39. *Letters*, I, 88.
40. Robert Anderson to James Currie, 28 Sept. 1799, printed in *Burns Chronicle*, 1925, 12; cited Crawford, *Burns*, 198–9, n. 20.

5

Burns: Work, Kirk and Community in Later Eighteenth-Century Scotland

Christopher A. Whatley

Readers of Burns have benefited immensely from the labours of those who have attempted to place his life and poetry within the context of Scottish social history in the later eighteenth century.[1] The quality of much of this work has been such that it can reasonably be objected that yet another essay on Burns's historical background is unnecessary.

Yet eighteenth-century Scotland is now portrayed by historians rather differently than was the case twenty or even ten years ago. The Scotland of Christopher Smout's seminal and still unsurpassed *History of the Scottish People* (1969), which has been intensively mined by literary critics and others who wish to understand Burns in his economic and social context, is not quite the same place in the early 1990s as it was in the late 1960s. Large parts of it would be almost unrecognisable to those whose familiarity with the period derived from Henry Grey Graham's widely read *Social Life of Scotland in the Eighteenth Century* (1899), which coloured the views of even the innovative Smout. New shafts have been sunk, and fresh insights and the results of detailed research projects have both refined and provided challenges to older views.[2] In short, the Scottish past has been, and is still in the process of being, re-made.[3] This essay attempts to locate and comprehend some of Burns's poetry in this changing historical landscape.

There is a sense in which Burns stands out quite starkly against the backcloth of the older, 'traditional', view of a tightly controlled and calm Scottish society. He can be portrayed as a Romantic rebel, an angry, fiery, and passionate radical, exceptional amongst what have been described by Professor Smout as the 'uninflammable' Scots.[4] On the other hand, some literary scholars have been inclined to pay little attention to the social context of Burns's poetry and instead to interpret it principally by reference to poetic traditions and even in psycho-biographical terms. There can be no objection to this. The myth of the 'Heaven-taught ploughman' has been dismissed; Burns was well-read and self-consciously a poet, and as has recently been emphasised, an enigmatic and highly complex individual whose various poetic personae did not necessarily reflect his views when stripped of their self-dramatised garb.[5] It is, however, a matter of interpretative balance. Although sight should not be lost of what have convincingly been described as his 'striking poetic ambitions'[6] — and achievements — neither should the specific social and cultural context in which Burns lived and wrote, especially as the historiographical advances referred to above can, it is argued here, enhance our understanding of his work. With his poetic talent and 'lively intelligence' he may have felt apart from his immediate social environment,[7] but the extent to which this was true can be exaggerated; it remains the case that Burns was a product of that environment, and throughout retained strong links with rural and small-town Ayrshire and the South-west. This essay explores this relationship through three aspects of the period which have recently attracted the attention of historians, and may be of some relevance to Burns studies.

First, the world of work, which is included not least because Burns's poetry is littered with references to the occupations which were commonplace in the countryside and expanding villages of Lowland Scotland in the second half of the eighteenth century. These include weavers, waulkers, tailors, millers, brewers, coopers, shoemakers, tenant-farmers, cottars, ploughmen and servants, as well as the tinkers and itinerant fiddlers who appear in 'The Jolly Beggars', as they did throughout rural Lowland Scotland. Simply by referring to them, Burns establishes himself as the product of a particular historical era, that is of fundamental agrarian change, the intensification of agricultural processing and the extension of small-scale rural manufacture, or 'industry in the countryside', known otherwise by economic and social historians since the early 1970s as 'proto-industrialisation'.

Scotland in the decades after 1750 underwent what was a highly compressed process of economic modernisation, a phenomenon which was accompanied by one of the fastest rates of urban growth in western Europe.[8] Transformation was underpinned by a revolution in agriculture, the organisational and technological aspects of which in Ayrshire at the time of Burns have been admirably described in a recent study by Gavin Sprott.[9] Part and parcel of the linked processes of agrarian and industrial advance were changes in social relationships, between masters and men (and women and child workers), landowners and tenants, and tenant-farmers and their servants and sub-tenants. The impact of these is something about which much more is now known.

One thing which has emerged quite clearly is that while the second half of the eighteenth century saw a general rise in living standards, the period was also one of profound and sometimes painful dislocation and adaptation for many thousands of ordinary people. 'Order and economy', both on the land and in the workplace, were amongst the key words used by those Scots who took upon themselves the responsibility of transforming Scottish society and creating a modern, competitive capitalist economy. What this meant for the lower orders was that landowners and urban employers paid increasing attention to the ways in which they organised production, with the rational management of labour and resources being a critical component of the search to improve efficiency and reduce operating costs.[10]

Burns is largely silent on the processes of change. In this regard the work of his part-contemporaries, Robert Fergusson and John Galt, better reflects the momentous shifts taking place in the world around them. Nevertheless Burns could be interested in, and was certainly conscious of, the effects of change in Ayrshire's rural economy. One of the most striking results of 'Improvement' was a distancing of the classes, and the creation of an army of landless wage labourers in the countryside, as sub-tenants and cottars found themselves squeezed out in the move by landowners to maximise estate revenue by amalgamating and enlarging farms and letting them out to fewer tenants on strictly controlled leases.[11] Although smaller family farms survived longer in Ayrshire than some other regions, consolidation was practised by the major landowners, and new techniques were encouraged. It was a process of adaptation which Burns's father struggled with grittily, but only with the greatest difficulty and little material success. This, as John Weston has shown, affected Burns deeply, as is revealed in his letters and much of his most bitingly sarcastic poetry, in which, often, the rich and landed were his targets.[12]

One poem which is lashed by anger and a hatred clearly born of intimate personal experience of the difficulties of the smaller tenant-farmer is 'The Twa Dogs', in which Caesar declares:

> I've notic'd, on our Laird's court-day,
> An' mony a time my heart's been wae,
> Poor tenant bodies, scant o' cash,
> How they maun thole a factor's snash;
> He'll stamp an' threaten, curse an' swear,
> He'll apprehend them, poind their gear:
> While they maun stan', wi' aspect humble,
> An' hear it a', an' fear an' tremble!

The reference to the factor is important: increasingly it was he who conducted the affairs of his landed master. The paternalist regime of former times, where the personal involvement and authority of the landowner in the day-to-day operation of the estate appears to have maintained at least the appearance of co-operation on the part of the tenantry, was disappearing and being replaced by the cold formality of his 'man of business'.

Single lines and stanzas reveal the same familiarity and empathy with the labouring poor, like the cottar in 'The Twa Dogs', 'howkin in a sheugh', who has nothing but his 'han-daurk' (the labour of his own hands) to support his wife and children. Similarly, his address 'To the Rev. John M'Math' opens with the lines:

> While at the stook the shearers cow'r
> To shun the bitter blaudin' show'r,

a powerful evocation of the enduring harshness of rural working conditions.

Despite the suffering which resulted for many with the introduction of the new regime in the Scottish countryside, there is something of a consensus amongst historians that, in the Lowlands at least, there was little visible popular opposition to it. When rural protest occurred, it generally took the form of what E.P. Thompson, in the English context, has called the 'anonymous tradition', where, for example, fences and plantations would be cut down or gates removed from their hinges during the night.[13] Foot-dragging and surliness — rather than outright demonstrations of hostility — were the most prudent options in Scotland, where control was firmly in the hands of a powerful rural elite, allied to a uniquely repressive, tightly-knit and pervasive system of state and church discipline.[14] Even so, it is at least worth noting that a few scattered instances of overt hostility to enclosure did occur in the south-west of Scotland, although some years before Burns was born,[15] and it is conceivable that he heard tales of the earlier disturbances at Irvine during his spell there as a flax-dresser. It was the quiescence of the Lothians that struck contemporaries, and which has had to be explained by modern historians.[16]

Levellers could pull down the occasional wall and Burns might periodically rail against the iniquities of agrarian capitalism, but the satisfaction of seeing an enclosure breached or the relief felt by plain and open speaking had to be tempered by the inescapable fact that in eighteenth-century Scotland the route to personal security and social advancement depended to a large degree on patronage and hence the goodwill of one's social superiors.[17] In these circumstances, not only for Burns, whose entry into a career in the Excise is a prime example of the need for connections in high places, but for thousands of his countrymen of similar rank, opposition had necessarily for most of the time to remain suppressed. By articulating his venom in pen and print Burns chose a potentially perilous path, although even he appears to have been conscious that there were limits to how far he could prudently go,[18] even when partially concealed behind the mask of poetic personae and barely controllable wit. That deep-seated resentments were present there is no doubt how-

ever, despite the superficial appearance of social harmony:
during the anti-Militia disturbances of 1797, for example, when
the local yeomanry was called upon to put down the disorders,
one reluctant tenant-farmer yeoman in Midlothian expressed
without ambiguity what he thought was the reality of the
situation:

> You quell the riot at the hazard of your *Life, Family and Property*,
> because you are stationary in the place, amongst those men you
> compel, and who you cannot live without, which if enraged, will
> never hesitate to destroy you, and your effects.

If it was only rarely that open conflicts occurred, those
occupying the lower rungs of the ladder in Scottish rural
society did have a view of the social order which they quietly
but forcibly expressed. As these were usually unrecorded, in this
respect the poetry of Burns, with his ear close to the ground,
becomes an invaluable source. The attitudes referred to can be
heard in 'The Twa Dogs', where, after work and 'twalpenny-
worth o' nappy', Luath reports that the poor

> . . . lay aside their private cares,
> To mind the Kirk and State affairs;
> They'll talk o' patronage and priests,
> Wi' kindling fury i' their breasts;
> Or tell what new taxation's comin',
> And ferlie at the folk in Lon' on.

Other aspects of drink-induced abandon and popular protest will
be examined later.

Tensions in social relations and the re-organisation of
production were by no means restricted to agriculture. Indeed
the second half of the eighteenth century saw equally momentous developments in manufacturing. During Burns's lifetime,
however, little of this was carried on in mills and factories,
usually seen as the symbols of the new industrial age. Yet that
Burns paid an unsuccessful visit to Carron ironworks in August
1787, after which he wrote his 'Verses, Written on a Window of
the Inn at Carron', provides a hint that he was aware that a new
era was in the making. The recollection by his travelling

companion that Burns after a second visit had been struck by
'the resemblance between that place, and its inhabitants, to the
cave of the Cyclops' confirms it.[19] Whether he ever appreciated
that the unfortunate porter who refused him entry on his earlier
visit had been following instructions laid down in 1765, not
only to monitor visitors, but more importantly to note the
movements in and out and the state of sobriety of the Carron
workers, and to 'preserve order, [and] prevent embezzlement',[20]
can probably never be known. Yet, just as rural society was
being refashioned by the ideology and tools of rational management, inside the walls and gates which surrounded Carron
works a new, regimented army of industrial workers — many
of them recruits from the surrounding countryside — was
being forged.[21]

Most work, however — even in manufacturing — was still
carried on in the household and small workshops. Nowhere was
this more so than in the ubiquitous task of hand-spinning. Such
work was done mainly by females; perhaps as many as eight out
of ten Scotswomen spent at least some part of their time
spinning, but more as the century wore on and the demands
of the burgeoning linen industry for yarn intensified.[22] And
indeed several references to spinning appear in Burns's poems
and songs, although they generally lack the the conviction of his
treatment of agricultural work.

In 'Bessy and Her Spinning Wheel', the task and situation of
the spinner are highly idealised, in a manner which has much in
common with the work of those poets and artists of the period
(such as Thomas Gainsborough or, in Scotland, David Allan),
whose purpose appears to have been to portray the rural poor as
hard-working and satisfied with — or at least resigned to —
their lot.[23] It is an ideologically loaded pastoral image of
domestic contentment which is in many ways similar to that
of 'The Cotter's Saturday Night', and therefore strangely at odds
with the radical empathy with the labouring poor which Burns
displays elsewhere. Here he is simply a vernacular poet, practising his art but disengaged from the the spinner's experience and
perception of her world. Thus the last lines of the poem run:

Wi' sma' to sell, and less to buy,
Aboon distress, below envy,
O wha wad leave this humble state,
For a' the pride of a' the Great?
Amid their flairing, idle toys,
Amid their cumbrous, dinsome joys,
Can they the peace and pleasure feel,
Of Bessy at her spinnin wheel?

Although it may be argued that as in 'The Cotter's Saturday
Night' Burns here celebrates the dignity of labour, the image is
in many respects unconvincing, and bears a strong resemblance
to the prescriptive role laid out for women by Scottish moralists
from the 1760s, in which complacency and domesticity were
deemed essential virtues.[24] It is certainly at odds with the reality
of desperately poor pay for increasingly long hours of repetitive
work, in addition to a myriad of other domestic tasks which
females from the middle and lower ranks had to perform. Yet
spinning was something which thousands of females had to do in
order to earn the pittance which supplemented many household
economies precariously balanced on the edge of subsistence,
especially if young children had to be fed. To engage in hand-
spinning was necessary simply to survive where Scotland's large
army of single women was concerned.

Historical reality is turned on its head, however, in 'O Leave
Novels', where the poet, in playful and seductive mood, urges
'Mauchline belles' to put aside their books, with their power to
arouse, and so become 'baited hooks' for 'rakish rooks, like Rob
Mossgiel'. Instead, they are urged, 'Ye're safer at your spinning
wheel'. In fact, the spinning household, where an older woman
might supervise half-a-dozen younger single spinners, was
described by one observer as having been the 'Grand Theatre'
of courtship in Scotland prior to the era of the flax spinning mill,
the magnet for males anxious to find suitable marriage partners.
The best spinners, that is those who could draw the longest and
most even yarns, which sold at the highest prices, were evidently
considered the best prospects.[25] But it was a female-generated
culture of independence and conviviality — jokes and song —
and not the silent and submissive world of Burns's Bessy.

There are, however, poems and songs in which images are partly constructed from the actuality of part-time rural manufacturing. In 'There Was a Lass' Duncan Davidson marries Meg the spinner, who afterwards spends time spinning in the evening. It is clear from others, too, that Burns was well aware of the nature of the spinning routine. In 'The Twa Dogs', for example, Caesar refers to

> A country lassie at her wheel,
> Her *dizzens* done, she's unco' weel

— a comment which alludes to the quantity of work a spinner was expected to put out during a day.

However, where Burns most accurately reports the lot of the female spinner at the end of the eighteenth century, he does so humorously, but almost certainly unwittingly, in the song, 'The weary Pund o' Tow'. In this, which Burns adapted from a popular song, the husband complains that, although he has bought his wife a stone of lint 'as gude as e'er did grow',

> . . . a' that she has made o' that
> Is ae poor pund o' tow.

His nagging brings an unexpected but understandable response:

> She took the rock, and wi' a knock
> She brak it o'er my pow.

We can feel with the woman here, although the poem's purpose seems to have been to inspire sympathy for the male who finds himself married to a woman who is considered to be an unwilling spinner and therefore an unsatisfactory wife.

Nevertheless, the 'weary pund o' tow' theme is one which evidently struck a deep chord in eighteenth- and early nineteenth-century Scotland, for there were several tunes and songs based upon it, one of the best-known being 'The Rock and the Wee Pickle Tow'. A version of it was written in 1825, during a lengthy and violent dispute in one of Glasgow's East-End cotton mills. Here the striking workers adapted the traditional tune and its eighteenth-century thrust, 'The spinning, the spinning, it gars my heart sob/ When I think o' the beginnin o't', and turned it into what is one of the earliest surviving strike songs in Scotland. It may be crude but in its directness it contrasts sharply with songs written both by Burns and Alexander Ross (who wrote the best-known adaptation of 'The Rock and the Wee Pickle Tow'), who were outsiders and poets rather than workers struggling against the encroachment of 'blacklegs' to defend their livelihoods. It begins with the lines,

> We are the braw chiels that
>   belongs to the wheel
> That earns their bread by the
>   spinning o't
> Ne'er let your hearts tumble down
>   to your heels
> But stand on your feet for
>   the Spinning o't

and develops into a vicious verbal attack on the proprietors of the mill at the heart of the dispute.[26] Burns by contrast is detached. Beyond the sphere of farming labour he becomes an Enlightened observer, generalising in a tired classical allusion to Carron, and displaying much less compassion for the lot of the female spinner than the male cottar. There is irony in the fact that many cottar households were sustained in part by the earnings from spinning done by female members.

The second theme is that of Burns and the kirk. Burns's most forceful and expressive poetry is that which springs from personal experience — as has just been seen. Other immediate sources of inspiration were church matters and theological disputation, and in particular the practices and demeanour of the elders of the parish kirk session. An example of the former is 'The Holy Tulzie'; of the latter the epistle 'To The Rev. John M'Math', where the poet confesses that when confronted by the elders,

> . . . I gae mad at their grimaces,
> Their sighan, cantan, grace-prood faces,
> Their three-mile prayers, an' hauf-mile graces,
> Their raxan conscience,
> Whase greed, revenge, an' pride disgraces
> Waur nor their nonsense.

The manner in which the Scottish kirk exercised its authority, and the social consequences thereof, are subjects which have recently attracted considerable historical interest. Of many things which have become clearer, one is the pervasiveness — sometimes the brutality and ugliness — of godly discipline and its agents at the parish level. Several features stand out: first, the zealousness and single-mindedness of many elders in their pursuit of fornicators, adulterers, Sabbath-breakers, drinkers, swearers and other delinquents. Second is the severity of the questioning of those suspected of improper or anti-social acts, and even the cruelty with which some of the elders and their agents went about the business of enforcing repentance on offenders — for example by appointing midwives to inspect the breasts of women suspected of concealing pregnancy. This was the practice in the Ayrshire parish of Kirkoswald, for example.[27] Third, there was the punishment of the guilty. Adultery, for example, could result in as many as twenty-six consecutive appearances in front of the parish congregation on the high, backless stool of repentance, sitting upon which required absolute concentration if a fall was to be avoided. Heavy fines were also imposed, while ducking and the shaving of women's hair as well as standing in the jougs were other punishments used. Banishment from the parish — and thus loss of status and livelihood — was not unknown.[28] What is clear too is that the system had an impact, with the 'savage and exemplary' sentences handed out in St Andrews in the early 1590s, for example, leading to the virtual elimination (for a time) of cases of fornication and adultery, while counties with low ratios of illegitimacy in the later sevententh century and first half of the eighteenth, such as the Lothians and Fife, were generally those where church authority was most readily accepted.[29]

Also evident, however, are the fissures within the Established Church of Scotland, not only between the 'Auld Lichts' (the Evangelicals) and the 'New Lichts' (the Moderates), but also those which led to schisms in the form of secessions so numerous that by 1800 over 20 per cent of Lowland Scots adhered to dissenting congregations, a much higher figure than previously thought.[30] Many of those who remained were hostile to the heritors and kirk sessions; this was especially so amongst men and women of Burns's social status — small farmers, artisans and tradesmen and the lower middle class. Rather than being a watertight means of reinforcing social control, as was thought by generations of historians, the kirk, it has been persuasively argued, was commandeered by the discontented, and used as a vehicle for popular protest. This showed itself in frequent and sometimes violent disputes about pews (the availability and price of), and precentors (the removal of), but mainly about patronage (and the imposition by heritors of unpopular ministers). It was over these issues that the rural poor in Scotland channelled their anger at landowners (who were also heritors), the distancing of the social classes, and agrarian improvement.[31] Dissenting congregations can be seen in the same light, although their social composition tended to be relatively high, comprising not peasants and the rural poor but 'the upper echelons of the agricultural workforce'.[32]

Burns does not fit neatly into this pattern of religious fractures: the Moderate wing of the Church of Scotland, to which he was inclined, was also the party of the landed interest, and the object of much of the popular opposition which occurred after 1750. Yet he was the product of a society and class in which religious questions loomed large and resentment at the pious intrusion of the kirk in so many areas of everyday life burned deep. This, rather than theological disputation, was the principal spur. Burns's weapon was language and he vented his wrath through verse; others recorded their hostility in less permanent ways (unless they were recorded in the kirk session minutes): by refusing to stand before the congregation, or continuing to work on the Sabbath or to use profane language, in dancing, drunkenness or by frequent acts of fornication.[33]

This leads to another factor which serves to bed Burns even more firmly not only within Lowland rural society but in his native Ayrshire. There is no reason to believe that the kirk sessions of that county were not as strongly committed to the control of public and private morality as anywhere else in Lowland Scotland. In Ayrshire and the south-west, however, unlike the rest of the country, the level of illegitimate births rose

markedly from the mid-eighteenth century. The local weaken-
ing of godly discipline which this points to has been accounted
for by the two historians of sexual behaviour in early modern
Scotland by reference to a long-standing tradition of resistance to
authority (seen in the strength and character of the Covenanting
movement) and 'an unusual level of resistance' by males to
church discipline, which manifested itself in the refusal on the
part of a high proportion of men to admit responsibility in
paternity cases which were brought before the session.[34] In
short, Burns was born and brought up in a region of religious
rebelliousness, which is reflected in the outrageous suggestion he
makes in the 'Poetical Epistle To A Tailor', where he is
confronted by a kirk elder:

> A furnicator-loun he call'd me,
> An' said my fau't frae bliss expell'd me;
> I own'd the tale was true he tell'd me,
> 'But what the matter?'
> Quo' I 'I fear unless ye geld me,
> I'll ne'er be better'.

Burns here ridicules and challenges the kirk session, whose
members are unlikely to engage in the grotesque form of
surgery which alone will remove the root cause of the sin.

Grievances about a particular elder and popular opposition to
the entering of a new minister were necessarily parish-based. The
final part of this essay examines another aspect of the local
community and Burns's relation to it. For a long time historians
have searched for solidarity in later eighteenth-century Scotland
in terms of class and a growing attachment to radical political
ideology. But to analyse divisions in Scottish society simply in
terms of class and radicalism is too restrictive and fails to recognise
that there were several solidarities in later eighteenth-century
Scotland.[35] Occupation, gender and religious sympathy are
another three, which could each unite or divide different groups
of people, or, depending on the circumstances, overlap. Sometimes identities adopted seem to modern eyes to be contradictory. If class mattered, it was not selfconscious. Where it can
be detected at all, it is within the local community.

The community itself could be a particularly potent source of group cohesion. Of this Burns was made acutely aware during the seven years he spent as an Excise officer, his experience of which caused him to ask, despairingly, in 'Lines Written on a Window at the King's Arms Tavern, Dumfries':

> Ye men of wit and wealth, why all this sneering
> 'Gainst poor Excisemen? give the cause a hearing:

Burns's identification here is with his fellow officers, for whom there was little popular sympathy in the 1790s — it had been only within living memory that even those nearer the top of the social scale (and then not uniformly) had given them the support they required in order to carry out their duties effectively. From the end of the seventeenth century, as in France and elsewhere in early modern Europe, communities in Scotland had closed ranks to oppose what were seen to be, and treated as, unwelcome agents of the centralising state and a restriction on the rights of merchants to trade as they saw fit, while the taxes they collected were regarded as unwarranted impositions on the standard of living of the poor.[36] During the first half of the century, riots following attacks on officers of the Customs and Excise were the most common form of crowd-based disorder in Scotland. Nowhere were these more frequent or outrageous than in the south-west. The anti-authoritarianism of the region is thus further emphasised. One frustrated officer in Dumfries reported to his superiors in Edinburgh in 1724 that it was impossible to stop the cross-border traffic in illicit brandy, 'for there will be two or three hundred men & women', with no respect for the law, to assist 'at ye unloading of a small boat'.[37] Frequently, troops had to be called in to protect the officers from being mobbed, beaten and even taken prisoner, as they went about their business.

Although by Burns's time comparatively little of the mob violence which had formerly been directed at Customs and Excise officers was to be seen, smuggling along the Ayrshire and Galloway coastline was still rife and much pride was taken in tax evasion and an ability to hoodwink the 'gaugers'.[38] It was this attitude which Burns detected, understood, but necessarily — if reluctantly — had to counter.[39]

Yet the collective anger of the community could still be registered violently in the second half of the eighteenth century. Indeed the power of the Scottish mob, noted much earlier in the century by Daniel Defoe, who described the Scots as a 'hardened, refractory and terrible people', could be considerable. Recent research has uncovered evidence of greater social tension and much more rioting in Scotland than has hitherto been recognised. As has already been suggested, older notions, which have their genesis in nineteenth-century efforts to portray Scotland as a tame, quiescent, kirk-controlled society, are currently being revised.[40]

One event which demonstrates the turbulence of the period is the parliamentary election, on the character and results of which, despite the small numbers of registered electors (4000 at most, who sent forty-five MPs to Westminster), and the power of patronage to achieve the desired outcome, the great mass of the unenfranchised in Scotland could still have an impact. How this happened can be seen in the following extract from an early nineteenth-century description of an election in the Angus town of Forfar, where the popular favourite was the local candidate, Donald Ogilvie. Not all the electors were inclined to support him, however. Consequently, according to one visitor, although the populace (or non-electors)

> [had] no vote . . . by their violent conduct [they] seem to force the reluctant part of the Magistracy to vote as they choose — they are threatening Provost Yeaman personally to break all his windows if he does not vote for Ogilvie — Meantime Ogilvie is encouraging this spirit by every Means in his power — Showering money among the crowd — giving them . . . Porter . . . keeping a Band [of] Music & processions constantly in action, in short the Town is in a complete uproar . . .

and so it goes on.[41] Readers of Burns have come across this before, in his election poems, the 'Epistle to Robert Graham of Fintry' and 'The Heron Ballads'. These, with their rollicking rhythms, vibrant, colourful and sometimes earthy language and imagery, capture almost exactly the characteristics of elections in Scotland's far-from-douce burghs, including their parochialism:

> Yon beardless boy comes o'er the hills
> Wi's uncle's gowd, and a' that:
> But we'll hae ane frae 'mang oursels
> A man we ken, an' a' that.

The community too was involved *en masse* in other boisterous events, such as Hallowe'en and Hogmanay, both of which feature in 'The Twa Dogs'. Hallowe'en, for example, was a time when

> . . . *rural life*, of every station,
> Unite in common recreation;
> Love blinks, Wit slaps, an' social Mirth
> Forgets there's *Care* upo' the earth.

Another uproarious festive occasion in eighteenth-century Scotland was the King's birthday, an event which has until very recently escaped the notice of virtually every Scottish historian, but to which references are to be found scattered throughout eighteenth- and early nineteenth-century literature, as in Robert Fergusson's energetic 'The King's Birth-Day in Edinburgh', and John Galt's penetratingly accurate account in *The Provost*. Burns, too, acknowledges the day in his poem 'The Dream', a satirical address to King George III. Further examination of the poem and its context may contribute something to our understanding of the nature of Burns's egalitarianism and his uncompromising attacks on authority.

The King's birthday celebrations were the most notable of a series of orchestrated festivities the initial purpose of which was to celebrate the Restoration of Charles II, but which were later associated with support for the Protestant Hanoverian succession and the expanding British Empire. Flags were hoisted, bells rung and toasts drunk on the birthdays of various members of the royal family as well as on the news of military and naval victories.[42] Burns himself wrote 'A Toast' to commemorate the anniversary of Admiral Rodney's naval victory over the French in 1782. Given his Jacobite sentiments and later sympathy for revolutionary France, Burns's loyalism might at first seem surprising:

The next in succession, I'll give you the King,
Whoe'er would betray him, on high may he swing;
And here's the grand fabric, our free Constitution,
As built on the base of the great Revolution.

Patriotic outpourings and the sentiments these represent were
much more widespread in post-Union than might at first be
assumed, particularly after the failure of the final rising, in
support of Charles Edward Stuart, in 1745. Loyal North
Britons were anxious to dispel fears that beneath every
Scotsman's kilt there lurked a Jacobite rebel. Nor was there
necessarily any contradiction between patriotic pride and
political radicalism.[43] Sentimental Jacobitism, a tide of feeling
and current of thought which was recreating Scotland's recent
history, was both drawn on and sustained by Burns, and could
and did flourish — in the person of James Boswell, for
example — alongside affection for and appreciation of the
benefits of Hanoverian rule.[44] Eighteenth-century Scots were
confused about their identity within the framework of Great
Britain, but increasingly, as they became more confident
within the Union and began to enjoy the rewards it produced, and aware too of their part in making it successful, they
had no difficulty about identifying themselves as Britons:[45]
indeed many gloried in it, as well as in being Scots, and, in
Burns's case, in being an Ayrshireman too.

During King George III's long reign the birthday celebrations
were held each year on the 'glorious' fourth of June. Although
the nature of the festivities varied from place to place, and
depended on what funds were available (and upon the prevailing
public mood), at their grandest they featured formal processions,
loyal toasts, small-arms and cannon fire, and bonfires in the
streets. Normally the costs were met and the displays sponsored
and publicly supported by the burgh councils and their guests,
drawn from the ranks of the local elite — senior customs and
excise officers, lawyers, ministers, merchants, employers and
other leading citizens, who were surrounded by great watch-
ing, cheering crowds. Although it was mainly a feature of urban
society, the inhabitants of villages and even workers in the

countryside could find themselves recipients of food, drink, fire and music provided by local landowners or employers.

In the towns, however, the day commonly culminated in varying degrees of outrage, as sections of the crowd, the usual restraints on their behaviour weakened by the voluminous quantities of liquor they had consumed, turned on the authorites and pelted them with mud, stones, fireworks and, not infrequently, dead cats and dogs. Order was often restored only when troops were called for (although this could exacerbate an already tense situation), or after the rioters had exhausted themselves after several hours' rampaging.

It is important to establish that this behaviour was the norm *and* that it was tolerated (albeit with growing unease) by the authorities, regardless of the discomfort it caused them. Demands that the more disgraceful aspects of the crowd's activities should be discouraged did not meet with as much favour amongst the middle and upper classes as might be anticipated. This, it seems, was largely because, as some more perceptive contemporaries recognised, the King's birthday provided a necessary safety valve, an opportunity for those in lowly positions to express their frustrations and resentments — to ritually attack and humiliate those who usually stood above them, but without threatening the social order itself. In England and elsewhere in continental Europe where there were obvious inequalities in wealth and status similar temporary purges were to be found.[46] Only in Scotland, however, did this happen so regularly on the King's birthday.

Almost without fail, after a period of time during which the world was temporarily turned upside down, order and normality returned. In their poetry which the occasion inspired, Fergusson and Burns were likewise engaged in a process of inversion, their raw material being the bland, reverential birthday 'Odes' which were written each year, such as that which appeared in the *Scots Magazine* in October 1739, which portrayed a benign Caesar-like figure, Protestant and anti-Rome, a defender of Liberty and lover of peace, hailed by a 'joyous throng' of Britons. The familiarity of the opening line of 'A Dream', 'Guid-Morning to your Majesty', reveals immediately that something different is about to take place.

The suggestion, made many years ago that 'A Dream', which is highly critical of William Pitt, corruption, taxes and even members of the royal family, was a somewhat daring venture for Burns to have engaged in can be quickly dismissed.[47] The King's birthday was a rare quasi-institutionalised occasion in the Scottish calendar when it was considered legitimate (for those in power there was little choice) for the lower orders to castigate and even engage in ritual assaults on their superiors. By general agreement, particularly unpopular individuals or institutions might be set upon by the mob. In Edinburgh those unfortunate individuals who were singled out by the crowd were

> seized and carried to the . . . Square, and there burghered as it was called — that is had their bottoms brought hard down upon the ridge of the box three times, with severity proportioned to the caprice of the inflictors . . .

(Burns, too, engages in personal attacks, but alone and without the sustaining power and shelter of the mob, which he had grown above, and to which he could no longer belong.) Effigies of out-of-favour politicians were also burnt, while there were also separate instances where a prison and a brothel were attacked. The King's birthday mobs could be both radical and conservative, democrats and opponents of John Wilkes and Thomas Paine. Usually concerned to right a locally-perceived wrong, a King's birthday riot was a form of community politics, where the plebs (or the 'labouring poor') acted while the discomfited patricians looked on. It was the most explosive act in the theatre of provincial politics which in other guises had its counterparts throughout Britain.[48] What is perhaps unusual about 'A Dream' is that it deals with national politics (but so too did the King's birthday mob in Edinburgh in 1792, which paraded with an effigy of Henry Dundas), and is critical, albeit in a mildly satirical way, of the monarch himself. Yet this was not unknown, although the evidence so far uncovered suggests that the typical King's birthday rioter was a staunch Hanoverian rather than a supporter of the exiled Stuart dynasty, or indeed a republican.

The levelling or reductive aspect of the King's birthday disorders is also worthy of note. The rioters' targets invariably included those who set themselves apart from the 'people', who turned on the magistrates and their official parties, whose public toasting and feasting was after all a provocative and shameless display of local power and privilege, increasingly resented as the gulf between the social classes grew, in terms of wealth, residence, and culture. Analysis of crowd behaviour and particularly attempts to define popular attitudes in the early-modern period are methodological minefields. Yet on one level the actions of the King's birthday crowds can safely be interpreted as representing an enduring dislike on the part of the ruled of pomposity and pretension; in literature this is most vividly portrayed by Galt in *The Provost* where the smug and superior Provost Pawkie is felled by a dead cat. The symbolism of the cat is inadequately understood, but it was certainly used as a means of humiliation in both France and Germany.[49] Levelling of another kind can be seen in the propensity of the Edinburgh and Glasgow mobs on the King's birthday to threaten middle- and upper-class passers-by with demands for money, or that they take off their hats. Often these were forcibly removed and then kicked up and down the street. In Burns the beliefs which produced this type of behaviour find expression in many of his poems, but are perhaps best expressed in 'For A' That and A' That':

> Ye see yon birkie, ca'd a lord,
> Wha struts, and stares, and a' that;
> Tho' hundreds worship at his word,
> He's but a coof for a' that.

The prose has been traced to Paine's *Rights of Man*;[50] the poetry, however, taps a deeper chord, which is self-evidently Scottish, but is recognisable in popular attitudes throughout Europe.

To conclude: it can reasonably be argued that the vituperativeness of Burns's attacks on the rich and those in authority owed much to his own personal circumstances and character, the 'Passions' of which he wrote, 'when once they were lighted up, raged like so many devils, till they got vent in rhyme'. Rightly, it has been suggested, the carnivalesque in Burns's poetry, as well as his use of 'flyting', were features which were rooted in a Scottish literary tradition which in the latter case stretches back into the streets of the medieval burgh. He could be ironic and self-ironic, adopting poses for the sake of his art, and given his poetic aspirations, and connections, could hardly fail to be influenced by the cultural values and social outlook of Scotland's intellectual elite. Yet we should not underestimate the extent to which Burns's attitudes and sentiments and indeed the tone and rhythms of much of his most powerful poetry echo contemporary life and perceptions of the world at the lower levels of society in Lowland Scotland in the later eighteenth century.

The apparatus of social control in Scotland was immensely strong, but there were ways in which it could be pricked. Despite its best efforts, the kirk had not managed to suppress amongst the Scottish people either a desire for release, or an enjoyment of the carnal, especially in the last case in Ayrshire. Burns's biting anti-authoritarian poetry thus sits no more uncomfortably in the context of Scottish society in the 1780s and 1790s than a newly–called minister who was unable to enter his church because of the presence of a chanting, stone-carrying crowd, or a violently thrown, distended, and mud-covered cat, wrapped around a magistrate's neck. Too often our images of Scotland in the period have been drawn from what we know of Edinburgh's drawing-rooms and coffee-houses; the obsession of present-day intellectuals with civic humanism and Scotch philosophy; and the couthy cap-touching portraits of social harmony painted by Dean Ramsay, Henry Gray Graham and their followers. In all this Burns has a place. But there was another less restrained, less deferential, more rumbustious, Scotland — of which Burns was also part and upon which his poetic imagination fed. Of this, much of his most compelling poetry is a potent record.

Notes

1. Good examples are, D. Daiches, *Robert Burns* (London, 1950), and T. Crawford, *Burns: A Study of the Poems and Songs* (Edinburgh, 1960).
2. See, for example, two recent essay collections: T.M. Devine & R.

Mitchison (eds.), *People and Society in Scotland, Vol* 1. 1760–1830 (Edinburgh, 1988), and R.A. Houston and I.D. Whyte (eds.), *Scottish Society,* 1500–1800 (Cambridge, 1989).

3. See the Editors' 'Introduction', in I.L. Donnachie & C.A. Whatley (eds.), *The Manufacture of Scottish History* (Edinburgh, 1992).

4. T.C. Smout, *A History of the Scottish People,* 1560–1830 (London, 1969, 1971 edn.), 417.

5. K.G. Simpson, 'Burns and Scottish Society', in J. Dwyer & R.B. Sher (eds.), *Sociability and Society in Eighteenth Century Scotland* (Edinburgh, 1993, 213; for a fuller treatment of this theme, see K.G. Simpson, *The Protean Scot: The Crisis of Identity in Eighteenth Century Scottish Literature* (Aberdeen, 1988).

6. C. McGuirk, 'Scottish Hero, Scottish Victim: Myths of Robert Burns', in A. Hook (ed.), *The History of Scottish Literature, Vol* 2, 1660–1800 (Aberdeen, 1987), 221.

7. Simpson, 'Burns and Scottish Society', 210.

8. T.M. Devine, 'Urbanisation', in Devine & Mitchison, *People and Society,* 27–52.

9. G. Sprott, *Robert Burns, Farmer* (Edinburgh, 1990); the principal authority on Burns's Ayrhshire background, however, is still Dr John Strawhorn.

10. C.A. Whatley, 'The Experience of Work', in Devine and Mitchison, *People and Society,* 227–51.

11. M. Gray, 'Scottish Emigration: The Social Impact of Agrarian Change on the Rural Lowlands, 1775–1875', in *Perspectives in American History, VIII* (1973), 112–44.

12. J.C. Weston, 'Robert Burns's Satire', in R.D.S. Jack & A. Noble (eds.), *The Art of Robert Burns* (London & New Jersey, 1982), 36–58.

13. E.P. Thompson, 'Patrician society, plebeian culture', *Journal of Social History,* 7 (1974), 388.

14. For a brief introduction, see C. Larner, *Enemies of God: The Witch-hunt in Scotland* (London, 1981), 53–9.

15. J. Leopold, 'The Levellers' Revolt in Galloway in 1724', *Scottish Labour History Society Journal,* 14 (1980), 4–29; J. Strawhorn, *The History of Irvine* (Edinburgh, 1985), 71, 84.

16. Larner, *Enemies of God,* 49–53; and especially T.M. Devine, 'Social stability in the eastern Lowlands of Scotland during the

agricultural revolution, 1780–1840', in T.M. Devine (ed.), *Lairds and Improvement in the Scotland of the Enlightenment* (Dundee, 1979), 59–70.

17. For recent studies of the operation of patronage, see A. Murdoch, '*The People Above*': *Politics and Administration in Mid-Eighteenth Century Scotland* (Edinburgh, 1980); J.S. Shaw, *The Management of Scottish Society, 1707–1764* (Edinburgh, 1983); R.M. Sunter, *Patronage and Politics in Scotland, 1707–1832* (Edinburgh, 1986); M. Fry, *The Dundas Despotism* (Edinburgh, 1992).

18. T. Crawford, *Boswell, Burns and the French Revolution* (Edinburgh, 1990), 51–7.

19. J. Kinsley (ed.), *The Poems and Songs of Robert Burns* (Oxford, 1968), 1242.

20. Scottish Record Office, Carron MSS, GD 58/2/1/1, Minute Book, General Meetings, 171.

21. Whatley, 'Experience of Work', 231–9.

22. A.J. Durie, *The Scottish Linen Industry in the Eighteenth Century* (Edinburgh, 1979), 38, 159.

23. J. Barrell, *The dark side of the landscape: the rural poor in English painting, 1730–1840* (Cambridge, 1983 edn.), 65–88; on links between Burns and Scottish painters, see D. MacMillan, *Scottish Art, 1460–1990* (Edinburgh, 1990), 126–32, 165–78.

24. J. Dwyer, *Virtuous Discourse: Sensibility and Community in Late Eighteenth-Century Scotland* (Edinburgh, 1987), 117–40.

25. University of Dundee Archives, MS 11/5/14, C. Mackie, 'History of the Flax Spinning from 1806 to 1866', 16–19.

26. For a fuller discussion, see C.A. Whatley, 'Women, girls and vitriolic song: a "Note" on the Glasgow cotton strike of 1825', *Scottish Labour History Society Journal* (1993).

27. R. Mitchison & L. Leneman, *Sexuality and Social Control: Scotland, 1660–1780* (Oxford, 1989), 202.

28. See C.G. Brown, *The Social History of Religion in Scotland Since 1730* (London, 1987); L. Leneman, 'The Kirk Session and Social Control in Early-Modern Scottish Cities: A Preliminary Inquiry', in *Popular Religion and Society* (Association of Scottish Historical Studies, St Andrews, 1991), 78–89.

29. G. Parker, 'The "Kirk By Law Established" and the Origins of "The Taming of Scotland": St Andrews 1559–1600', in L. Leneman (ed.), *Perspectives in Scottish Social History* (Aberdeen,

1988), 17; Mitchison and Leneman, *Sexuality and Social Control*, 147.

30. C. G. Brown, *The People in the Pews: Religion and Society in Scotland since* 1780 (Economic & Social History Society of Scotland, 1993), 13.

31. C.G. Brown, 'Protest in the Pews: Interpreting Presbyterianism and Society in Fracture During the Scottish Economic Revolution', in T. M. Devine (ed.), *Conflict and Stability in Scottish Society*, 1700–1850 (Edinburgh, 1990), 83–105.

32. Brown, *The People in the Pews*, 29.

33. There are countless examples, but for an introduction, see Mitchison and Leneman, *Sexuality and Social Control*, 200–30.

34. *Ibid.*, 145–6.

35. C.A. Whatley, 'An Uninflammable People?', in Donnachie & Whatley, *The Manufacture of Scottish History*, discusses this briefly in relation to the 'Radical War' of 1820, 69–71.

36. C.A. Whatley, 'How tame were the Scottish Lowlanders during the Eighteenth Century?', in Devine, *Conflict and Stability*, 6–12.

37. Scottish Record Office, Customs and Excise Minute Books, CE 51/1/2, Collector (Dumfries) to the Board, 1 June 1724.

38. L.M. Cullen, 'Smuggling in the North Channel in the Eighteenth Century', *Scottish Economic & Social History*, 7 (1987), 20–1; R. Goring, 'Eighteenth-Century Scottish Smugglers: The Evidence from Dumfries and Montrose', *Review of Scottish Culture* 3, 1987, 53–65.

39. For a little-known but instructive account of Burns's career in the service of the Excise, see G. Smith, *Robert Burns the Exciseman* (Ayr, 1989).

40. For a brief statement of the older view, see B. Lenman, *Enlightenment, Integration and Industrialisation: Scotland 1746–1832* (London, 1981), 11; for a recent survey, see I.D. Whyte, 'A Relatively Orderly, Authoritarian Society?', *Scottish Economic & Social History*, 12 (1992), 86–9

41. University of Dundee Archives, MS 15/114/2, Diary of Thomas Handyside Baxter, 1829–30; several entries for June and July 1830 refer to the conduct of the Forfar election. I am grateful to Mrs Joan Auld, Archivist, for drawing my attention to this source.

42. For a full account, see C.A. Whatley, 'Royal Day, People's Day: The Monarch's Birthday in Scotland, c.1660–1860', in R.A.

Mason & N. Macdougall (eds.), *People and Power in Scotland: Essays in Honour of T.C. Smout* (Edinburgh, 1992), 170–88.

43. See T.C. Smout, 'Problems of Nationalism, Identity and Improvement in later Eighteenth-Century Scotland', in T.M. Devine (ed.), *Improvement and Enlightenment* (Edinburgh, 1989), 1–21; H. Cunningham, 'The Language of Patriotism, 1750–1914', *History Workshop Journal*, 12 (1981), 8–33; L. Colley, 'The Apotheosis of George III: Loyalty, Royalty and the British Nation 1760–1820', *Past and Present*, 102 (1984), 94–129.
44. W. Donaldson, *The Jacobite Song: Political Myth and National Identity* (Aberdeen, 1988), 72–89.
45. L. Colley, *Britons: Forging the Nation*, 1707–1837 (New Haven & London, 1992), 123–32.
46. B. Bushaway, *By Rite: Custom, Ceremony and Community in England*, 1700–1880 (London, 1982), 168; for a Europe-wide survey, see P. Burke's seminal *Popular Culture in Early Modern Europe* (London, 1978).
47. J.L. Robertson, *Burns; Poetical Works* (London, 1904, 1966 edn.), 570.
48. See E.P. Thompson, 'The Patricans and the Plebs', in E.P. Thompson, *Customs in Common* (1991, 1993 edn.), 16–96.
49. R. Darnton, *The Great Cat Massacre And Other Episodes in French Cultural History* (New York, 1984), 89–96.
50. Crawford, *Boswell, Burns and the French Revolution*, 62.

6
'My Tocher's the Jewel':
Love and Money in the Songs of Burns

Donald A. Low

In writing far more songs about love than about any other subject, Robert Burns shows a preference and habit which belong to most prolific song-writers. Just how marked is the bias in his case is illustrated by J.C. Dick's decision in 1903 to arrange Burns's songs under subject headings.[1] Dick's edition has 354 songs, grouped according to theme into nine categories: Love — Personal, Love — General, Love — Humorous, Connubial, Bacchanalian and Social, The Jolly Beggars, Patriotic and Political, Jacobite, and Miscellaneous. The first three categories account for 209 songs, considerably more than half the total number.

In the course of preparing my own chronologically arranged edition, I came to notice one recurrent thematic concern relating to love which is very characteristic of Burns: the relationship between love and money.[2] It would be possible to arrange songs which refer to this subject into three groups — personal, general, and humorous. What follows here is a brief survey of a representative selection of these songs.

One song which has a direct bearing on the topic of love and money is 5, 'O Tibbie, I hae seen the day':

CHORUS
O Tibbie, I hae seen the day,
Ye wadna been sae shy;
For laik o' gear ye lightly me,
    But, trowth, I care na by.

Yestreen I met you on the moor,
Ye spak na but gaed by like stoure:

Ye geck at me because I'm poor,
　　But fient a hair care I.
　　Tibbie, I hae &c.

I doubt na, lass, but ye may think,
Because ye hae the name o' clink,
That ye can please me at a wink,
　　Whene'er ye like to try.
　　Tibbie, I hae &c.

But sorrow tak him that's sae mean,
Altho' his pouch o' coin were clean,
Wha follows ony saucy quean
　　That looks sae proud and high.
　　Tibbie, I hae &c.

Altho' a lad were e'er sae smart,
If that he want the yellow dirt,
Ye'll cast your head anither airt,
　　And answer him fu' dry.
　　Tibbie, I hae &c.

But if he hae the name o' gear,
Ye'll fasten to him like a brier,
Tho' hardly he for sense or lear
　　Be better than the kye.
　　Tibbie, I hae &c.

But, Tibbie, lass, tak my advice,
Your daddie's gear maks you sae nice,
The deil a ane wad spier your price,
　　Were you as poor as I.
　　Tibbie, I hae &c.

Scots Musical Museum, no. 196, 1788, signed X. Hastie MS, f. 50.

laik o' gear	lack of money	*fient*	the devil a
lightly	slight, disparage	*clink*	cash
trowth	truly	*quean*	lass
by	about it	*airt*	direction
yestreen	yesterday evening	*lear*	learning
gaed	went	*kye*	cattle
stoure	dust	*diel a ane*	not a single one
geck	toss your head, scorn	*spier*	ask

Written when the poet was in his late teens, and arguably Burns's first masterpiece, this song conveys throughout a strong feeling of contempt for Tibbie. The essential reason is that she has recently presumed to look down her nose at Burns because he lacks gear, whereas she has the 'name o' clink', being assured of 'your thousand mark'. A version of 'O Tibbie, I hae seen the day' is included in Burns's first Commonplace Book, under the date September 1784, with two additional stanzas:

> When comin' hame on Sunday last
> Upon the road as I cam' past
> Ye snufft an' gae your head a cast
>   But trouth I caretna by. —
>
> There lives a lass beside yon park
> I'd rather have her in her sark
> Than you wi' a' your thousand mark
>   That gars you look sae high.

'Tibbie' was probably Isabella Steven of Littlehill, close to Lochlie, which Burns's father farmed from Whitsun 1777, when Burns was eighteen. In *Burns: A Biography of Robert Burns* (1992), James Mackay notes that according to tradition Isabella Steven came into a legacy of £75, on the strength of which she rejected Burns for another suitor.[3] Were the Stevens possibly also prejudiced against Burns's youth?

What stands out about the song is its decisive tone. The song-writer's contempt for Tibbie's preoccupation with money is very characteristic. The song shows that when still very young Burns was capable of writing derisive words and matching them to music with considerable skill and feeling for the spirit of a tune. (The air, *Invercauld's Reel*, had been printed in Stewart's *Reels*, 1762, and McGlashan's *Strathspey Reels*, 1780, and was clearly already very popular. In his Commonplace Book, Burns describes it as 'Invercald's reel — Strathspey'.) Whether or not Burns had entertained hopes of marrying Tibbie, he is determined to make plain, presumably to mutual friends and acquaintances, that by placing money — 'the yellow dirt' — above love, Tibbie has got her values fundamentally wrong.

This remains a consistent position in serious (as distinct from

comic) songs concerning love throughout Burns's songwriting
career. Moreover, he is impartial with regard to gender.
Whether the one who suffers because of the intrusion of
mercenary thinking is male or female, Burns objects on
principle. We observe his utterly uncompromising spirit in
174 (*Scots Musical Museum*, no. 312, 1792, signed B) written
from the point of view of a girl who knows that her lover's true
concern is limited to her *tocher* or dowry:

> O meikle thinks my luve o' my beauty,
>   And meikle thinks my luve o' my kin;
> But little thinks my luve I ken brawlie
>   My tocher's the jewel has charms for him.
> It's a' for the apple he'll nourish the tree;
>   It's a' for the hiney he'll cherish the bee;
> My laddie's sae meikle in love wi' the siller,
>   He canna hae luve to spare for me!
>
> Your proffer o' luve's an airle-penny,
>   My tocher's the bargain ye wad buy;
> But an ye be crafty, I am cunnin,
>   Sae ye wi' anither your fortune maun try.
> Ye're like to the timmer o' yon rotten wood,
>   Ye're like to the bark o' yon rotten tree,
> Ye'll slip frae me like a knotless thread,
>   And ye'll crack your credit wi' mae nor me.

'O meikle thinks my luve o' my beauty' is one of Burns's
finest — and also one of his most aggressive — songs, partly
based on traditional material, including probably lines 5–6, and
the final four lines, which he had sent to Tytler of Woodhou-
selee in August 1787, as 'a sample of the old pieces that are still to
be found among our Peasantry in the West. I once had a great
many of these fragments and some of these here entire; but as I
had no idea then that any body cared for them, I have forgot
them'.[4] Noting that Nathaniel Gow claimed to have written the
tune, Burns commented, 'It is notoriously taken from *The
muckin o' Geordie's byre*. It is also to be found, long prior to
Nath[1] Gow's aera, in Aird's *Selection of Airs and Marches* . . . under
the name of *The highway to Edin*.'[5] The strong tune and Burns's

skill in matching to it the bitter words of an insulted girl together ensure that the song has unity.

'There's auld Rob Morris that wons in yon glen' offers further proof that, even when he was not personally involved, Burns responded with sympathy to the plight of a lover adversely affected by inequality in financial status:

> There's auld Rob Morris that wons in yon glen,
> He's the king o' gude fellows and wale of auld men;
> He has gowd in his coffers, he has owsen and kine,
> And ae bonie lassie, his dawtie and mine.
>
> She's fresh as the morning, the fairest in May;
> She's sweet as the e'enin amang the new hay;
> As blythe and as artless as the lambs on the lea,
> And dear to my heart as the light to my e'e.
>
> But oh, she's an Heiress, auld Robin's a laird;
> And my daddie has nocht but a cot-house and yard:
> A wooer like me maunna hope to come speed;
> The wounds I must hide that will soon be my dead.
>
> The day comes to me, but delight brings me nane;
> The night comes to me, but my rest it is gane:
> I wander my lane like a night-troubled ghaist,
> And I sigh as my heart it wad burst in my breast.
>
> O had she but been of a laigher degree,
> I then might have hop'd she wad smil'd upon me!
> O, how past descriving had then been my bliss,
> As now my distraction no words can express!

Select Collection, no. 17, 1793

Burns's point of departure in writing this song about the opposition between love and wealth was a song in the *Tea-Table Miscellany* about youth versus wealthy age:

brawlie	very well	*an*	if
tocher	dowry	*timmer*	wood
hiney	honey	*crack*	boast of
siller	silver, money	*mae nor*	more than
airle-penny	earnest money		

MITHER

Auld Rob Morris that wins in yon glen,
He's the king of good fellows, and wale of auld men,
He's fourscore of black sheep, and fourscore too,
Auld Rob Morris is the man ye maun loo.

DOUGHTER

Had your tongue, mither, and let that abee,
For his eild and my eild can never agree:
They'll never agree, and that will be seen;
For he is fourscore, and I'm but fifteen.

George Thomson evidently suggested a song on the basis of the traditional one, because Burns wrote to him in November 1792,

> I have partly taken your idea of 'Auld Rob Morris'. — I have adopted the two first verses, and am going on with the Song on a new plan, which promises pretty well. — I take up one or another just as the Bee of the moment buzzes in my bonnet-lug.[6]

Later, he demurred at Thomson's attempt to modify his diction in the song:

> There is a naiveté, a pastoral simplicity, in a slight intermixture of Scots words and phraseology, which is more in unison (at least to my taste, and I will add, to every genuine Caledonian taste,) with the simple pathos, or rustic sprightliness, of our native music, than any English verse whatever. — For instance, in my Auld Rob Morris, you propose instead of the word, 'descriving', to substitute the phrase 'all telling', which would spoil the rusticity, the pastoral, of the stanza.[7]

The seventeenth-century air is in Craig's *Scots Tunes*, 1730, p. 45; *Orpheus Caledonius*, 1733, no. 30, and other collections.

A debate between an old woman who candidly urges caution and realism about the significance of worldly possessions in the choice of a husband, and a young woman who is determined to marry for love alone is the subject of 198, 'In simmer when the hay was mawn' (*Scots Musical Museum*, no. 366, 1792). Partly no doubt because of inherited song convention with regard to such a debate, Burns seeks to do justice to both speakers, and certainly the older woman cites proverbial sayings which give point to the viewpoint of long experience. In this song, too, however, the balance of sympathy is on the side of romantic love, rather than of mere prudential reasoning. From a memorable argument we are unlikely to forget the young woman's response to Robie, in contrast to the unromantic Johnie o' the Buskie-glen, or her heartfelt final answer:

> In simmer, when the hay was mawn
>   And corn wav'd green in ilka field,
> While claver blooms white o'er the lea,
>   And roses blaw in ilka bield,
> Blythe Bessie in the milking shiel,
>   Says, I'll be wed come o't what will;
> Out spak a dame in wrinkled eild: —
>   O gude advisement comes nae ill.
>
> Its ye hae wooers mony ane,
>   And lassie ye're but young ye ken;
> Then wait a wee, and canie wale,
>   A routhie butt, a routhie ben:
>
> There's Johnie o' the Buskie-glen,
>   Fu' is his barn, fu' is his byre
> Tak this frae me, my bonie hen,
>   It's plenty beets the luver's fire.
>
> For Johnie o' the Buskie-glen,
>   I dinna care a single flie;
> He loes sae weel his craps and kye,
>   He has nae loove to spare for me:
> But blythe's the blink o' Robie's e'e,
>   And weel I wat he loes me dear;
> Ae blink o' him I wad na gie

wons	lives	*laird*	landowner
gude	good	*cot-house*	cottage
wale	pick	*yard*	garden
gowd	gold	*maunna*	must not
owsen	oxen	*dead*	death
kine	cattle	*my lane*	alone
dawtie	pet	*ghaist*	ghost
e'enin	evening	*laigher*	lower
lea	pasture	*descriving*	describing

For Buskie-glen and a' his gear.

O thoughtless lassie, life's a faught,
    The canniest gate, the strife is sair;
But ay fu'-han't is fechtin best,
    A hungry care's an unco care:
But some will spend, and some will spare,
    An' wilfu' folk maun hae their will;
Syne as ye brew, my maiden fair,
    Keep mind that ye maun drink the yill.

O gear will buy me rigs o' land,
    And gear will buy me sheep and kye;
But the tender heart o' leesome loove,
    The gowd and siller canna buy:
We may be poor, Robie and I,
    Light is the burden Loove lays on;
Content and Love brings peace and joy,
    What mair hae Queens upon a throne.

Scots Musical Museum, 366, 1792, signed R. 'Written for this Work by
Robert Burns'. Hastie MS, f. 90.

Burns acknowledged 'In simmer when the hay was mawn' in a
letter to George Thomson of October 1794.[8] Allan Cunningham comments that the song

> has the air and tone of the ancient lyrics of Caledonia. It hovers
> between the dramatic and the sentimental, and partakes of the
> character of both. Our old songs abound with conversations, and
> questions, and replies.[9]

The air *The country lass* is in *Orpheus Caledonius*, 1733, ii., no. 38.

Burns does not take romantic love so solemnly, though, that he
misses opportunities in song to share jokes about wooers interested
in young women with attractive dowries. Often, no doubt, song
tradition suggested the point of view which he develops. An
example of this type of song is 140:

> There's a youth in this city, it were a great pity
>   That he from our lasses should wander awa;
> For he's bonie and braw, weel-favor'd with-a'.

An' his hair has a natural buckle and a'.
His coat is the hue of his bonnet sae blue;
His fecket is white as the new-driven snaw;
His hose they are blae, and his shoon like the slae,
And his clear siller buckles, they dazzle us a'.

For beauty and fortune the laddie's been courtin;
Weel-featur'd, weel-tocher'd, weel-mounted and braw;
But chiefly the siller, that gars him gang till her;
The Pennie's the jewel that beautifies a'.
There's Meg wi' the mailin that fain wad a haen him;
And Susie whase daddy was laird o' the Ha':
There's lang-tocher'd Nancy maist fetters his fancy —
But th' laddie's dear sel he lo'es dearest of a'.

Scots Musical Museum, 257, 1790, signed Z. Hastie MS, f. 51v.

This is an original song in which Burns cleverly develops a hint about a good-looking but mercenary-minded Scots wooer. 'The air', he writes, 'is claimed by Niel Gow who calls it his lament for his brother. The first half-stanza of the song is old; the rest is mine' (*Notes On Scottish Song*, 48). *Neil Gow's Lament* is in his second collection of *Reels*, 1788.

Another successful song on the same theme is 300:

mawn	mown	*loove*	love
claver	clover	*blink*	glance
lea	pasture	*wat*	know
blaw	blow	*wad na*	would not
bield	shelter	*gear*	possessions
-shiel	hut	*faught*	struggle
eild	age	*gate*	way
advisement	advice	*sair*	hard
canie wale	choose with care	*ay*	always
routhie	plentiful	*fu'-hant*	full-handed
butt	outer room	*fechtin*	fighting
ben	inner room	*unco*	formidable
fu'	full	*syne*	then
byre	cowshed	*maun*	must
beets	'adds fuel to fire' (B)	*yill*	ale
dinna	do not	*rigs*	ridges
flie	fly	*leesome*	lightsome
craps and kye	crops and cattle	*gowd and siller*	gold and silver

Awa' wi' your witchcraft o' Beauty's alarms,
The slender bit beauty you grasp in your arms,
O, gie me the lass that has acres o' charms!
O, gie me the lass wi' the weel-stockit farms!

    Chorus
Then hey, for a lass wi' a tocher,
    Then hey, for a lass wi' a tocher,
Then hey, for a lass wi' a tocher;
    The nice yellow guineas for me!

Your beauty's a flower, in the morning that blows,
And withers the faster the faster it grows;
But the rapturous charm o' the bonie green knowes,
Ilk Spring they're new deckit wi' bonie white yowes.
    Then hey &c.

And e'en when this Beauty your bosom has blest,
The brightest o' beauty may cloy, when possest;
But the sweet yellow darlings wi' Geordie imprest,
The langer ye hae them, — the mair they're carest!
    Then hey &c.

Select Collection no. 100, 1799.

Though its deft phrasing carries Burns's distinctive stamp, 'Awa wi' your witchcraft o' Beauty's alarms' was possibly suggested by a song in *The Tea-Table Miscellany* entitled 'Lass with a Lump of Land':

Gi'e me a lass with a lump of land,
    And we for life shall gang the gither,
Though daft or wise, I'll never demand,
    Or black or fair, it maks na whether.

fecket	sleeved waistcoat, vest	*till*	to
snaw	snow	*mailin*	small-holding,
blae	blue		land held on lease
shoon	shoes	*fain*	glad
slae	sloe	*wad a haen*	would have had
siller	silver	*laird*	squire
-tocher'd	furnished with a dowry	*lang*	long
gars	makes	*sel*	self

I'm aff with wit, and beauty will fade,
  And bloom alane is na worth a shilling:
But she that's rich, her market's made,
  For ilka charm about her is killing . . .

Love tips his arrows with woods and parks,
  And castles, and riggs, and muirs, and meadows,
And naithing can catch our modern sparks,
  But well-tocher'd lasses, or jointur'd widows.

Burns sent his song to Thomson in February 1796. Thomson had proposed gathering Irish airs in one volume, and Burns commented enthusiastically:

The twenty-five Irish Songs, in one number, is a business that you will find your account in more than anything. — I shall chearfully undertake the task of finding verses for them. I have already, you know, equipt three Irish airs with words, and the other day I strung up a kind of rhapsody to another Hibernian melody which I admire much.[10]

Thomson liked the song, commenting, 'With you the subject is something new indeed. It is the first time I have seen you debasing the god of soft desire, into an amateur of acres and guineas'.[11]

'Awa wi' your witchcraft o' Beauty's alarms' shows how readily Burns can enter into the spirit of traditional song, even when this entails setting aside his personal convictions in order to create a convincingly shameless admirer of 'the sweet yellow darlings wi' Geordie imprest'. In song, as in the rest of his creative work, he does nothing by halves.[12] His superbly inclusive sense of humour continues to challenge the merely correct.

weel-stockit	well-stocked
tocher	dowry
knowes	mounds
yowes	ewes
e'en	even

Notes

1. *The Songs of Robert Burns Now First Printed With The Melodies For Which They Were Written: A Study In Tone-Poetry*, By James C. Dick. Henry Frowde, 1903.
2. *The Songs of Robert Burns*, (London, 1993). All references are to this edition, by song numbers.
3. *Burns*, 80.
4. *The Letters of Robert Burns*, ed. G. Ross Roy, (Oxford, 1985), Letter 126; I, 147.
5. *Notes on Scottish Song by Robert Burns*, ed. J.C. Dick (London, 1908) 54
6. Letter 518; *Letters*, II, 160.
7. Letter 535; *Letters* II, 181.
8. Letter 644; *Letters*, II, 317.
9. *Works of Robert Burns*, 1834, iv, 239.
10. Letter 689; *Letters*, II, 376.
11. *The Works of Robert Burns*, ed. James Currie, 1800. iv. 256.
12. Other songs which allude to the theme of love and money are

> 104 'My heart is a-breaking, dear Tittie'
> 125 'O, wilt thou go wi' me, sweet Tibbie Dunbar?'
> 206 'Ithers seek they kenna what'
> 234 'O ken ye what Meg o' the mill has gotten' (second version)
> 321 'Tibbie Fowler o' the glen'.

7
Editing Robert Burns
in the Nineteenth Century

G. Ross Roy

Most people think of editing as collecting together a series of essays by other people to form a more or less unified whole, or of a single person collecting or selecting the output of a single author, arranged in a particular order (chronological, subject matter, and so on), to which the editor may or may not add notes. But there is a good deal more to being an editor than that. In almost every edition the editor has had to make choices, sometimes the author himself acts in this capacity; having produced variant readings of a text, he at some later date opts for the one or the other. John Masefield, for example, could never quite decide how he wanted the opening line of his best-known poem 'Sea Fever' to read. In the first edition it is, 'I must down to the sea again, to the lonely sea and the sky', but this was later amended to, 'I must go down to the sea again, to the lonely sea and the sky'. Some later printings, however, return to the earlier readings, while some retain the amendment.

So one could argue that the earliest form of editing is that which the author applies to his own creations. Robert Burns made such a choice in 'The Holy Fair' when at the suggestion of Hugh Blair he changed the original reading in the 1786 edition:

> For Moodie speels the holy door,
> Wi' tidings o' salvation

to read 'tidings o' damnation' in the edition of 1787. Using major editions of 1800, two in 1834, 1856, 1877, two in 1896, and the two major twentieth-century editions of 1968 and 1986, I find that they all give the reading 'damnation' but that three of these editions do not indicate the earlier 'salvation'.[1] At the end of the poem the word 'houghmagandie' is glossed as 'fornication' in the 1800 edition, but the word is not glossed in one of the 1834 editions and is called 'loose behaviour' in the other. Thereafter it is again glossed as 'fornication'.

We can assume that Burns preferred 'damnation' as more descriptive of the 'fire and brimstone' type of preaching which was done at these holy fairs, because the reading was retained in Burns's day in both the 1793 and 1794 editions of his poetry, and we know that he used a set of sheets of the earlier of these editions in setting up the 1794 one.

In the two lines which I quoted above there is another form of editing exercised by the poet: the name 'Moodie' is indicated ★★★★★★. Half concealing a proper name in this way was, of course, commonplace in the eighteenth century, but it certainly was also a form of self-censorship or silent editing on the part of the author. Of the seven nineteenth-century editions I noted earlier, only James Currie in 1800 followed Burns with the use of asterisks – from caution, no doubt.

There was another form of editing, the intervention of others than the author to make alterations in a text. One of the best-known of these concerns 'Tam o'Shanter' where in the MS which Burns sent to Francis Grose for inclusion in *The Antiquities of Scotland* (Vol. II, 1791), Burns added after:

> Wi' mair o' horrible and awefu',
> Which even to name wad be unlawfu'

these four lines:

> Three Lawyers' tongues, turn'd inside out,
> Wi' lies seam'd like a beggar's clout;
> Three Priests' hearts, rotten, black as muck,
> Lay stinking, vile, in every neuk.

These lines were removed from the poem when it was reprinted in Burns's edition of 1793 upon the advice of Alexander Fraser Tytler, himself a lawyer. Perhaps where the lines appear in the poem they do contradict what the poet has said in the preceding line, because Burns claims that the mere naming of them 'wad be unlawfu', so that the poem may in fact benefit from omitting them, although Tytler's suggestion that the passage be removed was probably a question of giving offence rather than improving 'Tam o'Shanter' as a work of art.

I have mentioned censorship, and it must be admitted censorship and editing overlap, and continue to overlap in almost all of the editions of Burns's work which I shall consider in this essay. The nineteenth- and early twentieth-century editor saw no impropriety in thus 'cleansing' the mouth of Scotia's Bard. Keeping back from the public poems which he had written was, in Burns's case, just being prudent — thus 'Holy Willie's Prayer' was published only once (in 1789) during the poet's lifetime, and that was surely a piracy of which he knew nothing. The serious question of editing Burns's work arose only after his death.

Soon after Burns's funeral friends realised that his family would be destitute unless assistance was forthcoming. An edition of his works was agreed upon, the profits from which were to be made over to Mrs Burns. We need not here go into the difficulty there was in finding someone, preferably someone who had known Burns quite well, to take up the task of editing the poet's works — it suffices to say that finally the job fell to Dr James Currie (1756–1805), a native of Dumfriesshire who had spent most of his working life in Liverpool. Certainly Currie knew Scotland and the literature of the country, although he had met the poet only once.[2] Currie set about collecting material for his edition, which was to be a major biography (Robert Heron had published a *Memoir of the Life of the Late Robert Burns* in 1797 but it ran to only a few pages and is today of interest only to the literary historian) and was to include all of Burns's poems and songs as well as his correspondence. In the event Currie turned up very few new poems, relying on the two-volume set of *Poems, Chiefly in the Scottish Dialect* of 1793 and James Johnson's *Scots Musical Museum*, five of the six volumes of which had appeared by the year of Burns's death. In order to write a biography Currie needed, in addition to direct contact with friends, to have available letters from and to the poet. Like most people of the period, Burns had kept most of his, but it was not uncommon for correspondents to request the return of their letters when the addressee died, and it is not improbable that some were returned in this way. Apparently Maria Riddell exchanged the poet's letters to her for hers to him, and she appears to have destroyed them. The most notorious collection of Burns letters to be withheld, and quite understandably, were those to Mrs Agnes M'Lehose (the famous 'Clarinda') from her 'Sylvander'. These love letters to a woman whose husband was still living, although not with her, were published in part in an unauthorised edition in 1802, but it was not until 1843 that the lady's grandson published a complete edition of the Clarinda-Sylvander correspondence.

What Currie came up with was a goodly number of letters both from Burns and to him. Once he had used the letters he does not appear in several instances to have kept them together, because individual letters and manuscripts of poems have emerged from a number of places and are now to be found in various collections throughout the English-speaking world. Perhaps the most unexpected place to find a Burns manuscript is in France at the Bibliothèque Municipale in Nantes.

One major collection of letters, which occupies the entire fourth volume of Currie's edition, is the correspondence between Burns and George Thomson, editor of *A Select Collection of Original Scotish [sic] Airs*, which appeared in eight parts between 1787 and 1818, to which Burns devoted an enormous amount of energy, writing, re-writing and collecting songs and selecting others for Thomson to use from anywhere he could lay hands on them. Thomson apparently got back his letters to Burns and probably destroyed them while sending Currie altered copies of them. At the same time he very heavily scored through certain passages in Burns's letters which Thomson did not want the public to see. Here we have, then, the earliest example of tampering with a text which is to go before a reading audience. The work starts without delay in Burns's first letter to Thomson. In September 1792 the latter had written to Burns in Dumfries asking if he would collaborate in the undertaking, and offering to pay 'any reasonable price you shall please to demand'. Note the word 'reasonable', for Thomson was a prudent man; we find him bickering over money with Beethoven at a later date when the musician supplied some arrangements for the edition. To this letter Burns replied on 16 September happily accepting the invitation, and adding (for Burns was not prudent in the way in which Thomson was), 'As to remuneration, you may think my Songs either *above* or *below* price; for they shall absolutely be the one or the other. — In the honest enthusiasm with which I embark in your undertaking, to talk of money, wages, fee, hire, &c. would be downright Sodomy of the Soul!'[3] To this expression Thomson appended a note: 'I presume Dr C. will think it right to substitute some other word for *Sodomy*', so the equally prudent Dr Currie printed '*prostitution of the soul!*' (IV, 5).

One of the most interesting disagreements which Burns and Thomson had concerned the wording of 'Scots Wha Hae', to use the song's popular title. Burns sent the song to Thomson probably on 1 or 2 September 1793, telling him that it was to be sung to the tune 'Hey tutti taitie', claiming that it was the air to which Bruce's warriors marched to Bannockburn. The words he sent began:

> Scots, wha hae wi' Wallace bled,
> Scots, wham Bruce has aften led,
> Welcome to your gory bed, —
> Or to victorie. —

In his answer Thomson downplayed the air, saying, 'I never heard any one speak of it as worthy of notice' (Currie, IV, 115). In place of it Thomson asked Burns if they could not substitute 'Lewie Gordon' which had a longer final line, and would allow the first stanza to read 'Or to *glorious* victorie' and he went on to propose changes for each of the six stanzas, including such wooden lines as, 'Let him, *let him* turn and flie', 'But they shall, *they shall* be free' and 'Let us, *let us* do, or die!' (IV, 115–16). A few days later Burns sent another version of the song to Thomson who was still not satisfied, although it would appear that the text of his answer to Burns which Thomson sent to Currie was deliberately incomplete. Finally Burns answered, quoting Pope, 'Who shall decide, when Doctors disagree?'[4] and rejecting Thomson's proposed alterations. Currie, when he edited this exchange, obviously sided with Thomson and appended a footnote to the first version of the song, 'A more finished copy will be found afterwards' (IV, 110). Posterity, of course, has decided otherwise.

It must be admitted that Currie was preparing an edition which would appeal to a broad general public, in the event 2000 copies were sold, so that it was no doubt permissible for him to omit some of Burns's brief comments on songs he was considering for inclusion in Thomson's work. In fact, Currie alerts the reader to this in a footnote when he says of these lists, 'All his [Burns's] remarks of any importance are presented to the reader' (IV, 117). But Thomson and Currie obviously conspired to maintain a picture of a pure, if one is not to say emasculated, poet. A letter of September 1793 includes a reworking of Tom Brown's 'Caelia's Rundlet of Brandy' from D'Urfrey's *Pills to Purge Melancholy* which opens with these lines:

> The other night, with all her charms,
>   My ardent passion crowning,
> Fair Celia sank within my arms
>   An equal transport owning. —

Burns then goes on to mention several other songs, including one of which he says, 'take the following old Bacchanal', whereupon he sets down a sixteen-line song beginning 'Deluded swain, the pleasure/ The fickle Fair can give thee', all but four lines of which are his own. Thomson, however, notes to Currie, '*Nothing* in this letter for the general eye, nor are any of the Songs Mr Burns's own, except the first which is too warmly coloured. G. T.'[5] Currie heeded the admonition, and in his edition we find all mention of the 'too warmly coloured' song deleted without, as Currie sometimes did, any indication that material had been omitted. Ironically, though, Currie did include all of 'Deluded swain' even though Thomson had believed Burns's statement about its being traditional (IV, 135–6).

One of the most interesting pieces of editing which I have come across is a letter to Burns's friend John Ballantine of 18 April 1787 concerning a shipment of copies of the Edinburgh edition of his poems. The letter was not reproduced in early editions, but a facsimile of it was published in the 'Stothard' reissue of the 1820 Currie. One usually accepts a facsimile as a genuine representation of what was written, but the entire second sentence has been removed. It reads, 'I have no acquaintance with Forsyth; and besides I believe Booksellers take no less than the unconscionable, Jewish tax of 25 pr Cent. by way of agency' (*Letters*, I, 105), so it is not surprising that the editor did not want it to appear. True there were unobtrusive asterisks where the deletion has been made, but these are so small that on the original facsimile they might be taken for periods made by the author himself. When I first compared a photocopy of the original manuscript, which is in the Bodleian Library, with the facsimile I learned a lesson about so-called foolproof evidence.

My last example of Currie's editing consists of adding rather than deleting a sentence to a text. Today it is well known that Burns wrote a collection of bawdy poems known as *The Merry Muses of Caledonia*, but to the potential audience for his 1800 edition Currie went to great pains to hide from his readers the facts about the poet's involvement with such material, just as certain letters in which Burns openly avowed having had sexual affairs were kept from the public. Burns had written and collected bawdy poetry for some time, as a letter to a friend makes clear. The recipient was John M'Murdo, chamberlain to the Duke of Queensberry at Drumlanrig, and a trustee of funds raised for Jean and her children after the poet's death. In his letter to M'Murdo, tentatively dated February 1792, Burns repaid six guineas which he had owed for some time. The text, as published by Currie, continued:

> I think I once mentioned something of a collection of Scots songs I have for some years been making: I send you a parcel of what I have got together. I could not conveniently spare them above five or six days, and five or six glances of them will probably more than suffice you. A very few of them are my own. When you are tired of them, please leave them with Mr Clint, of the King's Arms. There is not another copy of the collection in the world; and I should be sorry that any unfortunate negligence should deprive me of what has cost me a good deal of pains. (II, 438)

Sir,

I have taken the liberty to send a hundred copies of my book to your care. — I have no acquaintance with Forsyth; and besides I believe Booksellers take no less than the unconscionable, Jewish tax of 25 p[er] cent. by way of agency. — I trouble you then, Sir, to find a proper person, of the mercantile folks I suppose will be best, that for a moderate consideration will retail the books to subscribers as they are called for. — Several of the Subscription bills have been mislaid, so all who say they have subscribed must be served at subscription price; otherwise those who have not subscribed must pay six shillings. — Should more copies be needed, an order by post will be immediately answered. —

My

My respectful Compliments to Mr Aiken. I wrote him by David Shaw which I hope he received. —

I have the honor to be,
with the most grateful sincerity,
Sir,
your obliged & very humble serv.t

Robert Burns

Edin.r 18th April
1787

Original manuscript published with permission of the Bodleian Library.
MS. Montague d.2, fol. 69r.

Sir.

I have taken the liberty to send a hundred copies of my book to your care. . . . . . I trouble you then, Sir. to find a proper person, of the mercantile folks I suppose will be best, that for a moderate consideration will retail the books to subscribers as they are called for. — Several of the Subscription bills have been mislaid, so all who say they have subscribed must be served at subscription price; otherwise those who have not subscribed must pay six shillings. — Should more copies be needed, an order by post will be immediately answered. — My respectful Compliments to Mr Aiken — I wrote him by David Shaw which I hope he received. —

I have the honor to be, with the most grateful sincerity, Sir. your obliged & very humble servt

Robert Burns

Edin. 18th April 1787

Facsimile manuscript, with the second sentence removed.

A glance at the manuscript shows that Currie made some trivial alterations to the text and added one sentence: 'A very few of them are my own.'

I had puzzled for years about this. We know that Currie withheld letters altogether, and that he deleted passages when he did not deem the material in them to be appropriate for the general public. Why then, I wondered, had he not just ignored the letter altogether, working the passage about the money (which had acutely embarrassed the poet) into the biography? The reason became apparent some years ago. The first edition of *The Merry Muses* had been known in only one copy, that of the Earl of Rosebery, but the volume was imperfect, wanting the date on the title-page, which is torn. In those days paper was watermarked with the date of manufacture, and the Rosebery copy has leaves watermarked 1799 and 1800, leading scholars to assume a date of 1800. When I was able to purchase another copy of the book I was surprised to find that the date on the title-page was 1799, although the leaves were watermarked both 1799 and 1800. Accepting the 1799 date for the title-page is not a great problem, because papermakers might start using the new year's date late in the previous year. Now it became clear to me why Currie had tampered with Burns's text. Through his Scottish connections he must have heard of the publication of *The Merry Muses*, perhaps even owned a copy, and realised that the best way to protect Burns from accusations of being a pornographer would be to publish the offending letter, but to try to whitewash Burns with the inserted sentence.

The story does not end there. Under-the-counter editions of *The Merry Muses* proliferated, particularly one falsely dated 1827, but in fact probably first published in 1872, which went through a number of editions through 1930. These editions contained Burns's material, but also included material which was not by Burns, and two letters from Burns. One of these, to the poet's Edinburgh friend Robert Ainslie, described in graphic detail Burns's love-making with Jean. To put rumours to rest about Burns and *The Merry Muses* the Editor of the *Burns Chronicle*, Duncan M'Naught, prepared an edition of *The Merry Muses* which had the sanction of the Burns Federation, although

M'Naught was not foolhardy enough to use his own name, preferring the pseudonym Vindex. The title itself sets the tone of the volume: *The Merry Muses of Caledonia; (Original Edition) A Collection of Favourite Scots Songs Ancient and Modern; Selected for use of the Crochallan Fencibles . . . a Vindication of Robert Burns in Connection with the Above Publication and the Spurious Editions which Succeeded it* (Kilmarnock, 1911). M'Naught and the Burns Federation appeared further to distance themselves from *The Merry Muses* by adding to the title-page: 'Printed and Published under the Auspices of the Burns Federation. For Subscribers only. Not for Sale'; interestingly these last words are exactly those used on the title-pages of the so-called 1827 editions. The text begins with an 'Introductory and Corrective' of twenty-five pages in which Vindex speaks of the 1799 edition as a 'mean-looking volume' (p. xvii). With this volume Currie would appear to have carried the day. There was one problem for M'Naught. Instead of using the known copy of the first edition of *The Merry Muses* and incorporating Currie's manufactured disclaimer, the editor copied the poems from the so-called 1827 edition. This text, however, included Burns's letter to Ainslie, and whereas Vindex could deny that Burns had written many (and by inference any) bawdy songs, there was no way that he could find another author for Burns's letter. When the sheets were printed, prudence took hold, and the leaf (pp. 137–8) containing the letter was cancelled and the volume bound up without it.

With this we can leave James Currie and his edition of Robert Burns. Misguided as an editor by today's standards, he was not different from others in his time.

Although Robert Hartley Cromek published an entire book containing material which had been overlooked by Currie, his *Reliques of Robert Burns* (1808) will not be discussed in detail because most of the material which appeared in his book did so for the first time, although he did complete a letter from Burns to William Chalmers of 27 December 1786 which had first appeared in Currie. Oddly enough there seems to have been no reason for Currie to delete the passage, which is a somewhat wordy comment on St John the Divine, other than to save space.

Included also in the *Reliques* are eleven letters to Margaret Chalmers (not related to William) whose father had a farm near Mauchline. According to Cromek, 'The following fragments are all that now exist of twelve or fourteen of the finest letters that Burns ever wrote.'[6] Cromek goes on to say that the letters had been destroyed without saying how he managed to obtain the fragments which he printed. It is possible that he had access to the manuscripts before they disappeared – if so, then he was responsible for our having only a portion of the letters as they were written.

The next major edition of Burns was the work of Allan Cunningham, himself a poet. It appeared in eight volumes as *The Works of Robert Burns; With his Life*, and was published in London to where Cunningham had moved as a young man. Like Currie's, Cunningham's first volume contains the life, a biography which has aroused a great deal of adverse comment during this century; perhaps the best-known is that in Franklyn Bliss Snyder's *Life of Robert Burns*:

> This biography certainly pictures Burns more or less as he actually was, but is absolutely unreliable as regards specific facts. Anything that Cunningham says may be true; nothing that he says should be believed without corroborating testimony.[7]

Since the volume of biography is ancillary to the seven of work by Burns, we need not spend our time hunting out his omissions and fabrications.

Although Cunningham claimed in the Preface to the first volume that he had arranged Burns's works, 'as much as might be in the order of their composition'[8] he did not, in fact, keep very rigorously to this claim. Poems from the editions of 1786, 1787, and other sources are printed in no apparent order and there is a section in the third volume under the heading 'Epitaphs, Epigrams, &c., &c.' Cunningham says further in his Preface: 'Of verse, one hundred and odd pieces will be found in this edition, which are not in Currie's octavos' (I, v), and this is true, but that is not to say that he was printing them for the first time. In fact only eight poems in Cunningham are published for the first time, and none of these is a major work.

According to the editor, 6000 copies of the first volume were sold when a second edition of it was called for. Early in 1835 the first volume only was reissued and in a new Preface Cunningham wrote that there were many Burns MSS which had 'remained till now in manuscript–nay, such was their abundance, that the hitherto unknown and unacknowledged poems, songs, and letters, contained in this edition alone, would make a separate volume of great and abiding interest' (I, viii). Note the repeated implication that he has added genuinely new poems and songs.

The strength of Cunningham's edition lies in the forty-two previously unpublished letters which he added to the canon. I have already mentioned the most important new letter — it is the one to Robert Ainslie, here published incomplete, to be completed in *The Merry Muses* of 1872 (VI, 241–2). It seems probable that Ainslie still had Burns's letters and allowed Cunningham to have access to them. Another absent letter of about 1 June 1788 to Ainslie concerns May Cameron who was pregnant by Burns, but whether Cunningham declined it, or Ainslie withheld it, is not certain. In his later years Ainslie became conservative and quite pious, dissociating himself from the young poet with whom he had caroused in earlier times.

There was an expanded version of the Border Tour of May 1787 which had first been published in Currie, although even Cunningham left the work incomplete. Burns's Tour in the Highlands of August and September 1787 was also published, although this manuscript seems to have disappeared. Finally, and this is an important addition, Cunningham included notes to the poems and songs, and occasionally to the letters. To the poem 'Hallowe'en' the editor added 129 lines of notes as well as quoting John Mayne's poem of the same name which was published in 1780, and which Cunningham suggests may have influenced Burns. Given that Jean died in the year of the edition, and that Agnes M'Lehose, about whom Cunningham wrote in the biography but without publishing her letters, lived until 1841, there is a good possibility that the editor obtained some of his information from people who had known Burns. The remainder he got from his own imagination.

The same year, 1834, saw the first two of five volumes which made up *The Works of Robert Burns*, edited by James Hogg and William Motherwell. These contain poems and songs, as does the third volume; Burns's correspondence forms the continuation of Volume III and Volume IV. The final volume came out in 1836, consisting mainly of the posthumous 'Memoir of Burns' written by Hogg, who had died the previous year. Unfortunately the 'Memoir' is poorly regarded by modern Burns scholars. As it happens I own one volume of Currie's 1820 edition which has been very extensively annotated in Hogg's and other hands for use in the Hogg and Motherwell edition, but as this is to be incorporated into the Stirling/South Carolina edition of the Works of James Hogg I shall not delve further into what editorial alterations were made by the editors of the edition which appeared between 1834 and 1836.

Robert Chambers (1802–71) was the next editor who produced an important edition of Burns's works. With his brother William he was first bookseller and then publisher in Edinburgh. In 1838–9 he brought out *The Life of Robert Burns*, *The Poetical Works* and *The Prose Works of Burns* in a popular and inexpensive edition called 'The People's Edition'. These were expanded and combined into a four-volume set in 1851–2 and in its final form in 1856–7. As is the case with earlier collected editions, most of the new material which appears in Chambers consists of letters, although he did add a few new poems. The most important poetic material is the additional stanzas of 'The Vision', a poem which had been first published in the Kilmarnock edition in 1786. According to Chambers the additional stanzas were retrieved from a manuscript recently discovered. To the text as originally printed he added no fewer than fourteen stanzas, only one of which was admitted to the canon by James Kinsley in 1968. The almost forty new letters include an important group to Robert Graham of Fintry, who as a Commissioner of the Scottish Board of Excise was influential in Burns being appointed to that body. Probably the most important letter from Burns to Graham was written on 31 December 1792, when Burns's loyalty had been called into question, and the poet wrote to his benefactor to save his job, but that letter had been first published by Cromek in 1808. A letter from Burns to George Thomson also appears in the fourth volume of 1852. Thomson must have supplied the text of it to Chambers shortly before he died in 1851, and he apparently withheld a sentence of Burns's. The poet mentioned that he was returning material to Thomson with 'alterations & remarks on the margin of each song' (IV, 202). The omitted sentence follows: 'You may perhaps think me hard as to 'Cauld kail in Aberdeen,' but I cannot help it' (Letters, II, 384–5). The new letter adds little to our understanding of the relationship between the two men, but it underscores the vanity of Thomson in wishing to be seen in the best possible light by readers of his correspondence with Scotland's greatest poet.

Chambers' edition was a popular one which remained in print in various forms until it was completely revised by William Wallace in 1896. Chambers was the last major editor who had the opportunity to be in touch with people who had known the poet. His method of weaving poems, letters and his own narration into one long biography of Burns makes accurate the title *Life and Works*. It also makes it a rather dated text for the scholar of today.

The publication in 1843 of *The Correspondence between Burns and Clarinda*, edited by Agnes M'Lehose's grandson, made available almost all of those torrid epistles, and so for the first time readers could judge the affair from all the known evidence.

William Scott Douglas was the editor of an edition of the poetry and prose which appeared in six volumes between 1877 and 1879. It is an important edition, with three volumes of poetry and the remaining three devoted to the correspondence, both poetry and prose set out in chronological order. According to the Preface the editor's plan is to publish 'the author's text with critical exactness, unabridged and untampered with, and recording the numerous and interesting variations in his manuscripts and several authorised editions' (I, vii). He goes on to say that he and his publisher (the firm of William Paterson) have made every effort to locate Burns manuscripts and to collate them with printed texts. Returning to 'The Holy Fair', we find some contradiction with this claim: names of people are filled in without indication that they replaced the asterisks in the first edition; the substitution, however, of 'damnation' is noted in a footnote with 'Altered from "salvation" by suggestion of Dr Hugh Blair' (I, 272), but the editor does not say that the word 'salvation' did in fact appear in 1786. True to his declared policy, a manuscript of the poem in the British Museum was consulted and variants noted.

In trying to give the world a completely accurate version of Burns's poems Scott Douglas faced the problem which every editor eventually faces: what to do when there are two or more texts which do not agree. Take, for example, the poem which the editor entitles 'A Poet's Welcome to his Love-Begotten Daughter', first published in 1799 by Stewart & Meikle of Glasgow (where it carried the title 'Burns's Address to his Illegitimate Child'). It differs considerably from the version to be found in the Glenriddell MS. Unfortunately the latter does not contain the stanza

> Lord grant that thou may ay inherit
> Thy mither's person, grace, an' merit,
> An' thy poor, worthless daddy's spirit,
>   Without his failins,
> 'Twill please me mair to see thee heir it,
>   Than stocket mailens (I, 73)

which Scott Douglas includes. Technically a manuscript source should outweigh a printed one as copy-text, but Scott Douglas wisely included the stanza, adding a note which said, 'By some inadvertency, as we suppose, Burns, in transcribing the poem, had omitted Stewart's closing verse . . . which is so fine that it cannot be dispensed with' (I, 73–4). Later Scott Douglas was vindicated when another manuscript in Burns's hand was forthcoming, and it contained the lines missing in the Glenriddell text.

Thus, although not adding significantly to the poetic canon, Scott Douglas did give readers a much more reliable text. Where the edition really stands out is in the new letters by Burns which are added in Volumes IV - VI. There are no fewer than ninety-eight new ones, the most notable collection being eighteen hitherto unpublished letters from Burns to George Thomson, and in addition Scott Douglas completed twenty-two others – letters which had originally appeared in Currie. We are not surprised to find one letter which Thomson had withheld from Currie in which Thomson had returned 'Scots Wha Hae' altered as he saw fit. In reply the poet told his editor that to alter the line 'Welcome to your gory bed' as Thomson wished would not do. 'Your idea "honor's bed" is, though a beautiful, a hackney'd idea; so, if you please, we will let the line stand as it is' (VI, 284). It is interesting to note that either Thomson withheld or Currie chose not to publish (probably the latter) some letters or portions of letters which are neither indiscreet nor do they show Thomson in a bad light *vis-à-vis* Burns. For example, the letter which Burns wrote in January 1795 appears in Currie (IV, 216–9) and contains the entire text of 'For a' That, and a' That', but omits a paragraph saying how busy he (Burns) had been because of the illness of the Supervisor of Excise, and writing admiringly of a copy of Pindar which Thomson had sent him. In supposedly completing the letter, Scott Douglas omitted the poem which Burns had sent, his 'Ode to Spring' (VI, 333), although he does refer the reader elsewhere in the edition. When we look this up, however, we find that Scott Douglas's version shows only one of three stanzas (III, 17), and that one emasculated. In a lengthy footnote Scott Douglas quotes the first line of the poem (with a crucial word omitted) with the following comment, 'Reader, we can follow the bard no farther in this very original "Ode"' (III, 18). Neither Currie nor Scott Douglas included the first sentence Burns wrote to Thomson after the ode, 'Now for decency' (*Letters*, II, 336).

With the centenary of the poet's death approaching, plans were set afoot to capitalise on the event: there was a huge exhibition in Glasgow, speeches aplenty and several editions of Burns's works. The long popularity of Robert Chambers's *Life and Works of Robert Burns* naturally suggested a revised edition of that work. The set came out in 1896 retaining the name of Chambers, and crediting the revision to William Wallace. The poetry remained much as it had been presented in earlier editions and over forty new letters were collected and woven into the narrative as had been the case in earlier editions. As we have come to expect, Wallace was discreet in quoting Burns. A letter to Robert Ainslie after they had parted when Burns was on his Border tour, dated from Newcastle on 29 May 1787, has a passage which reads, 'In the words of the Highlandman when he saw the Deil on shanter-hill in the shape of five swine — "My hair stood and my p— stood, and I swat & trembled" (*Letters*, I, 119), which becomes the tamer 'My hair stood . . . and I swat and trembled' (Wallace, II, 118), although the editor was honest enough to indicate his deletion with an elipsis. As I mentioned with respect to Chambers, the inclusion of both poetry and letters in the narration may be an annoyance to today's reader, but for several years it was rated the most important of all editions of the complete works.

Wallace followed this feat with another important edition whose title speaks for itself: *Robert Burns and Mrs Dunlop Correspondence now Published in Full for the first Time* (London, 1898). Having access to the collection of manuscripts formerly at Lochryan, but by 1898 in the Adam Collection in Buffalo, New York, Wallace was able to add to the substantial number of letters to Mrs Dunlop which were published by Currie an additional thirty-three letters, and to give the full text of several more. It seems likely, though, that one letter was either not available or that part of it was deliberately ignored by Wallace. That is the extended letter which Burns wrote between 20 December 1794 and 12 January of the following year. A small part of the letter had appeared in Currie, but not the part in which Burns wrote to Mrs Dunlop about Dr John Moore's letter to him concerning the execution of Louis XVI and Marie-Antoinette: 'I cannot approve of the honest Doctor's whining over the deserved fate of a certain pair of Personages. – What is there in the delivering over a perjured Blockhead & an unprincipled Prostitute into the hands of the hangman . . .' (*Letters*, II, 334).

When I mentioned Wallace's edition as the most important edition of the complete works, I was not including the final nineteenth-century collection I shall mention. This was William Ernest Henley and William F. Henderson's *The Poetry of Robert Burns*, another centennial offering which appeared in four volumes during 1896 and 1897. The edition added eleven formerly uncollected poems, but the great strength of this work was in the annotation. Henley had good Edinburgh connections, and it was no doubt a coup for the publishers (T. C. & E. C. Jack, of Edinburgh) to get him to collaborate. As far as we can tell though, the editing was done by Henderson, and from a certain point of view it remains the best edition there is yet. (I am not forgetting James Kinsley's 1968 edition.) Where Henderson excels is in tracing the roots of Burns's poems, and almost half of each volume is given over to notes. For example, Henderson takes the sixteen lines of 'A Red, Red Rose' and shows that almost every phrase in the song had been published before Burns did so. A short quotation will make the point:

> Now fare thee well my Dearest Dear,
>   And fare thee well awhile,
> Altho' I go I'll come again
>   If I go ten thousand mile,
>   Dear Love,
>   If I go ten thousand mile.
>   (III, 403)

This is from a black-letter ballad which long predates Burns. Henderson, like everyone else, can only marvel at how Burns took undistinguished verse and wove it into truly great poetry.

Henley, for his part, wrote his famous essay entitled simply 'Life, Genius, Achievement' in which he set out the poet's claim to fame, and while so doing tried to debunk a good deal of the falsity which had grown up around him. Once the essay appeared in 1897 there was an outcry from all over Scotland and elsewhere claiming that Henley had treated Scotia's Bard unfairly, but that is another story. In their Preface the editors had written that they wanted to produce a text which was 'as nearly complete as existing canons of taste will permit' (I, v) and that this text should be 'as nearly classic as a systematic and, in so far as might be, an exhaustive collation of authorities — books, proof-sheets, tracts, broadsides, periodicals, and MSS — could secure' (I, v-vi). In a phrase which would have made Hugh MacDiarmid happy, the editors say that their annotations go to show that Burns was 'not the founder of a dynasty, but the heir to a flourishing tradition and the last of an ancient line . . .' (I, vii).

To sum up, then, we find that the editing of Burns over a century was much like the editing of other poets, with the important difference that he wrote in a dialect unknown outside Scotland, and not well known within — the proof of this last statement lies in the fact that he felt it necessary to append a glossary to his Kilmarnock edition, when its sale was not expected to reach much beyond Ayrshire. Early in the nineteenth century censorship applied to passages which might give offence, either for political or social reasons. As these reasons for eliminating such passages became less important, cleansing literature of passages which were obscene or sexually descriptive, even suggestively so, became a greater editorial concern. I have said nothing about editors who were so willing to add poems to the Burns canon that they accepted obviously spurious work of third-rate quality — these were acts of over-zealousness. Burns's editors operated as Henley and Henderson stated, within the 'existing canons of taste'. They served as well as they were able to.

Notes

1. *The Works of Robert Burns; With an Account of his Life* . . . by James Currie, 8th edn. 4 vols. (London, 1820), III, 33; *The Works of Robert Burns; With his Life,* by Allan Cunningham, 8 vols. (London, 1834), II, 107; *The Works of Robert Burns,* ed. the Ettrick Shepherd [James Hogg] and William Motherwell, 5 vols. (Glasgow, 1834–6), I, 30; *The Life and Works of Robert Burns,* ed. Robert Chambers, 4 vols. (Edinburgh, 1856–7), I, 266; *The Works of Robert Burns,* ed. William Scott Douglas, 6 vols. (Edinburgh, 1877–9), I, 272; *The Life and Works of Robert Burns,* ed. Robert Chambers, rev. William Wallace, 4 vols. (Edinburgh & London, 1896), I, 361; *The Poetry of Robert Burns,* ed. William Ernest Henley and Thomas F. Henderson, 4 vols. (Edinburgh, 1896–7), I, 40; *The Poems and Songs of Robert Burns,* ed. James Kinsley, 3 vols. (Oxford, 1968), I, 132; *The Complete Works of Robert Burns,* ed. James A. Mackay (Alloway, 1986), p. 136.

Further references to these editions will appear in the text. The editions of 1968 and 1986 were noted to show continuity into this century, but will not be cited further.

2. See R. D. Thornton, *James Currie the Entire Stranger and Robert Burns* (Edinburgh & London, 1963).

3. *The Letters of Robert Burns*, 2nd edn., ed. G. Ross Roy. 2 vols. (Oxford, 1985), II, 149. Further references to this work will be given in the text.

4. Alexander Pope, *Moral Essays. Epistle III*, line 1. *Letters*, II, 248.

5. See *Letters*, II, 249, where full details of Burns's sources are set out.

6. *Reliques of Robert Burns*, ed. R. H. Cromek (London, 1808), p. 37.

7. Franklyn B. Snyder, *Life of Robert Burns* (New York, 1932), p. 489.

8. *The Works of Robert Burns; With his Life*, ed. Allan Cunningham. 8 vols. (London, 1834), I, v.

8
Burns As Sassenach Poet

R.D.S. Jack

The adjective in my title is important. In current usage, it means 'English' with disparaging tonal force. One of the sad side-effects of the recent expansion of Scottish literary courses at University has been the increase in the number of students who look at nationality first and literary quality second or never. In this essay, therefore, I am replying to those who have welcomed additional Scottish courses in the negative spirit of 'Thank God, I don't need to do Shakespeare now'. The title, then, does not suggest the (self-evidently ludicrous) proposition that Burns is an 'English' poet. It is the counter-rhetoric of exaggeration designed to awaken such blind adulators to the error of their critical ways.

Of course, objective views of Burns were not exactly thick on the ground even before the respectable canon had expanded beyond the Ayrshire poet and Walter Scott. Early editions of the *Letters* simply expurgated those epistles, which showed the hero in a less than perfect light, on the circular sophistry that a perfect individual could not have written in that manner. The holograph letter suggesting that Jean Armour was lucky to have been cruelly treated by such a great poet was therefore disowned as a forgery because early eulogisers shared Burns's opinion of his own magnificence.[1]

The development of Scottish literature as a distinct discipline has re-defined the terms for such purification of image rather than replacing it with critical objectivity. Historically, this is understandable. Until the late 1950s, most Scots were taught to condescend to their own literature. In resuscitating pride, we found it necessary to use 'English' literature and the 'English' literary tradition as a counter-paradigm against which to measure 'Scottishness'. I have always seen that as a necessary intermediary stage in rehabilitation. It ought now to be over; the full canon having been rescued, we can admit that English and Scottish are not discrete terms culturally or linguistically.

Briefly, as a paradigm works synchronically and absolutely, the non-literary grounds for acceptance are drawn in contrast to what Scots value *now* as defining their sense of identity. I have argued this case more fully elsewhere, but essentially the line of divine judgement uses the predominant counter-culture as the type of Hell.[2] On the side of the good come writers who write in Scots, are concerned with Scottish history strained through the left-wing radicalism of today and who can, preferably, be associated with the lower classes. Burns, of course, fits each of these predetermined, non-literary values. Poor Drummond of Hawthornden — every bit as much of a nationalist; every bit as much a product of his own literary/cultural imperatives — is furiously dismissed. If we continue to place obstacles in the way of honest historical research and the different definitions of 'Scottish' in successive centuries; if we continue to question those writers who choose English as a medium, prefer the metaphysical and conceptual to the political and empirical and who, perhaps, have had the misfortune to be born into the middle classes, then we simply reply to the false critical measure of the English tradition with an equally distorted eclectic measure of our own. What follows is a practical proof of how mythologising, even in the case of Burns, not only distorts but may diminish the quality of the writer in order to narrow him in accommodation to the limitation of a critical version of 'political correctness'.

My method is simple. Using first Pope and then Wordsworth, I shall isolate in each case the perversions and diminutions perpetuated by those who see the English poets as '*sassenach*' threats to Burns's Scottishness. It is unnecessary, I am sure, to cite the frequent occasions on which Burns praised the former and the latter praised Burns. Much of this will, anyway, arise from the argument naturally.

All my major concerns in the neoclassical context may be regarded as rhetorical. First of all, there is the issue of Scots or English language. Correctly, modern scholars and writers are concerned with the distance Scots has fallen from the days of the late-medieval makars. When Dunbar wrote, Middle Scots was a full, literary language although already narrowing and firmly associated with writing and poetic convention. Our current linguistic defensiveness is superimposed upon Burns because it is correctly seen that, in his day, Scots had become an essentially lyrical dialect needing outside conceptual boosting from English. The paradigmatic answer is to stress that Burns writes well only in Scots and that he was reviving that dialect in outraged opposition to the treacherous, manneristic anglicisation of the Castalians and Drummond. There is descriptive truth in much of this but rhetorical persuasiveness in hardly any.

The architect of the Scottish vernacular revival, Allan Ramsay, did not see himself as linguistically limited, as he thought in rhetorical rather than nationalist terms primarily. When the Easy Club flourished, Ramsay first took an English neoclassical pseudonym in Isaac Bickerstaff, only later preferring Gavin Douglas.[3] We are, I am sure, correct in believing that Burns wrote most easily and forcefully in Scots (or at least a heavily Scotticised English); we would also be correct in fearing that he never fully mastered the English neoclassical couplet; we would be wrong if we turned from these conclusions to suppose that he viewed language politically or defensively.

Like Ramsay and the Scottish late-medieval makars, he thought of language in terms of hierarchically arranged and linguistically distinguished styles. Thick Scots was linguistically most suited to colloquialism and rhetorical denigration, issuing from the flyting traditions. Hence, poor Willie Wastle's wife becomes the subject of a latter-day flyting:

> Auld baudrans by the ingle sits,
>   An wi' her loof her face a washin;
> But Willie's wife is nae sae trig,
>   She dights her grunzie wi' a hushian:
> Her waly nieves like midden-creels,
>   Her feet wad fyle the Logan-water;
> Sic a wife as Willie's wife,
>   I wad na gie a button for her.

This is the equivalent of the medieval low style.

Burns's other styles may be briefly noted. The middle style is Anglo-Scots and is the norm for his writing. Middle high is a purer English, which can be used seriously to note a higher theme or comically, as in 'Holy Willie's Prayer', to suggest hypocrisy. The highest style is Latinate English and out of this variety Burns turns what might have been, viewed nationalistically, linguistic disadvantage into poetic strength. In 'Tam o' Shanter', for example, the reader who misses the Scots vowels in the middle style of the descriptive passages:

> She prophesied that late or soon,
> Thou would be found deep drown'd in Doon;[4]

loses the rhetorical force intended by the poet, but so does the reader who Scotticises the linguistically marked change from middle to middle high in:

> But pleasures are like poppies spread,
> You seize the flower, its bloom is shed;
> Or like the snow falls in the river,
> A moment white — then melts for ever.[5]

To deny this is to deny Burns' debt to Dunbar as well as Pope.

Burns admitted his essentially neoclassical, rhetorical training in his letter to Moore, where he proclaimed himself a product of Murdoch's interest in figures of style and thought.[6] Poetically, the verse headings he employs most regularly return to the classics or to Pope and his followers, while eulogy frequently is associatively focused in a manner which makes Burns's high evaluation of English and neoclassicism quite clear:

> I've scarce heard ought describ'd sae weel,
> What gen'rous, manly bosoms feel;
> Thought I, 'Can this be Pope or Steele,
>   Or Beattie's wark;'
> They told me 'twas an odd kind chiel
>   About Muirkirk.[7]

It is only one step beyond limiting the symptoms of linguistic variety on pseudo-patriotic grounds to misunderstanding the whole literary motivation. Suppose you are thinking in modern,

nationalist terms and are faced with the following description of
Dame Scotia's garments in 'The Vision':

> Her *Mantle* large, of greenish hue,
> My gazing wonder chiefly drew;
> Deep *lights* and *shades*, bold-mingling, threw
>   A lustre grand;
> And seem'd, to my astonish'd view,
>   A *well-known* Land.

The infrequency with which this allegoric vision of Scotland's
grandeur is invoked at Burns suppers is directly, I fancy, related
to the archaicised, anglicised nature of its medium. Only if we
move from linguistic variety to the medieval/classical concept of
decorum — the relating of stylistic levels appropriately to
subject — can one account for the highest vision of Scotland
being presented in a middle high style (English) with elements of
high style (compound adjectives à la Spenser/Drummond)
embedded in it.

Take another example from a very different and apparently
less promising source: 'The Jolly Beggars'. This anarchist cantata
has quite properly been linked with contemporary radical visions
and frustrations in Scotland. It ends with two songs by the bard-
persona. In the first of these he seems to denigrate the arch-priest
of Scottish literary mannerism, James VI, and his 'maister poete',
Alexander Montgomerie, by specifically scorning the 'Castalian
band' founded by the former and the 'Heliconian' stanza
practised by the latter:

> I never drank the Muses' Stank,
>   Castalia's burn an' a' that,
> But there it streams an' richly reams,
>   My Helicon I ca' that.

Closer reading corrects the favoured impression. He denies
drinking of Castalia but he re-invents Helicon. He then
proceeds to a recitativo whose fourteen-line bob and wheel
stanza is rhetorically highly complex and formally returns in the
artifice of a circle to that which opened the cantata. But there is
more. The fourteen-liner with its aabccbdede rhyme followed

by a 'wheel' with internal rhyme is the Heliconian stanza used by
Montgomerie in his long verse-song 'The Cherrie and the Slae'.
I set out the first stanza of that poem preceded by the opening
stanza of 'The Jolly Beggars':

> When lyart leaves bestrow the yird,
> Or wavering like the Bauckie-bird,
>   Bedim cauld Boreas' blast;
> When hailstanes drive wi' bitter skyte,
> And infant Frosts begin to bite;
>   In hoary cranreuch drest;
> Ae night at e'en a merry core
>   O' randie, gangrel bodies,
> In Poosie-Nansie's held the splore,
>   To drink their orra dudies:
> Wi' quaffing, and laughing,
>   They ranted an' they sang;
> Wi' jumping, an' thumping,
>   The vera girdle rang.
>
> 'The Jolly Beggars'

> About a bank with balmie bewes,
> Where nightingals their nots renews
> With gallant goldspinks gay,
> The mavise, mirle and rogne proud,
> The lintwhite, lark and laverock loud,
> Saluted mirthful May:
> When Philomel had sweetly sung,
> To Progne she deplored
> How Tereus cut out her tongue
> And falsely her deflorde;
> Which storie, so sorie,
> To shew ashamd she seemde,
> To heare her, so neare her,
> I doubted if I dream'd.
>
> 'The Cherrie and the Slae'[8]

Which, then, is the more appreciative view of Burns? That he
was simply negating the rhetorical skills of the Castalians or that
he was redefining wittily the purposes of that skill? In denying
Castalia, he is using one of the most common rhetorical

topoi — disclaiming the very complexity he is practising. Without doubt, he had learned of the modesty topos[9] from Murdoch as a common means of opening or concluding your verse and seen it practised by Dunbar and Henryson. Here he not only re-invents one aspect of the stanza; heuristically, he gives his down-to-earth theme new rhetorical dignity by expressing it in the highest artistry. Moreover, unlike Montgomerie, his art is not to flaunt the makar's virtuosity but to conceal it. Only once the proper rhetorical context has been defined and similarities as well as differences noted can full tribute be paid to Burns the poet.

This provides a convenient transition from the past and Pope to the future and Wordsworth. Honest comparative criticism involves assessing similarities as well as differences against the changing modes and conventions of literary history. To assess Burns's intrinsic literary strengths and (dare I note it) limitations or to evaluate his place in literary history as a non-English poet influenced by English neoclassicism and anticipating English Romanticism, one must first of all be freed from the prejudice that linking his name with Wordsworth's is, somehow, bound to discredit Ramsay or Dunbar. (And in case any reader should find such pleading unnecessary, the present writer, after giving an Immortal Memory linking Burns to Fergusson, was condemned in the vote of thanks for linking an Ayrshire poet with one from Edinburgh!) I propose, therefore, to change the bias of the study in this section. I am still concerned with what we may miss, in terms of underestimation or false conclusions, by drawing too rigid a division between English and Scottish authors. But, whereas Pope could be employed to pinpoint primarily misjudgements concerning Burns, Wordsworth serves to highlight ways in which the Scottish poet influenced later English practice as well. Open study of why Wordsworth admired Burns, where he followed his example and where he did not, should cast further light on the apparent paradox that a Scot whose strengths were the very rhetorical ones disclaimed in the *Preface to Lyrical Ballads* should so impress the author of that critical credo that he embarked on a sort of Burnsean pilgrimage. It may also help to answer the seldom posed question of what 'glories of English literature' would not have existed or would have existed in a different form had there not been an Alloway peasant farmer influenced by Pope and Scottish folk tales in roughly equal measure.

The classical topos on which comparison of literary texts was based had the form *'varius sis sed tamen idem'*, emphasising both sameness and variation, Imitation and Invention. This would be the formula used by rhetorical teachers such as Murdoch. Following its guidelines, I shall organise my study of Burns and Wordsworth round five major areas of shared concern. Of these, the first two will emphasise contrast, the second two similarity and the last a near counterpoise between acceptance and rejection.

The order of study, placing the areas of disagreement first, has been dictated by the neoclassical portion of the essay. In one sense, the more one believes Burns to be a product of neoclassical practice, the less convinced can one be that he has the right to be claimed as a Romantic, incipient or otherwise. And of all the Romantics in England, Wordsworth should be the most antipathetic because his theoretical position as set out in the *Preface to Lyrical Ballads* is nothing if not a gauntlet thrown down to Pope, rhetorical artifice and poetic diction. Personification, a device regularly used by Burns, becomes the type for all these figures and is duly sacrificed in favour of 'a selection of language really used by men':

> The Reader will find that personifications of abstract ideas rarely occur in these volumes; and are utterly rejected as an ordinary device to elevate the style, and raise it above prose. My purpose was to imitate, and, as far as is possible, to adopt the very language of men; and assuredly such personifications do not make any natural or regular part of that language. They are, indeed, a figure of speech occasionally prompted by passion, and I have made use of them as such; but have endeavoured utterly to reject them as a mechanical device of style, or as a family language which writers in metre seem to lay claim to by prescription.[10]

Students today with their lack of a continuous reading in literature of the past fail to see what a massive challenge

Wordsworth has set himself — nothing less than rejection of the classical vision of aesthetics which had dominated Western Literature from Aristophanes and Quintilian to Pope. Nor has he done this to substitute an easier poetic method — the disclaiming of all those clear 'signs' of poesie are somewhat analogous to a cripple deciding to seek a cure by burning his crutches. If you deprive yourself of all the most obvious means of 'signing' your topic's importance and verse's distinctive use of language, then you have to convey your sense of 'the glory and the dream' without warning your audience linguistically that it should have importance for them. I am not surprised therefore that Wordsworth lends himself to parody:

> I put my hat upon my head
> And walk'd into the Strand,
> And there I met another man
> Whose hat was in his hand.

The truly wondrous thing, in my opinion, is how much of his verse, written in strict accordance with the stylistic masochism of the *Preface, cannot* be so caricatured. If the significance of, say, Simon Lee's ankles is not directly conveyed by the moral and spiritual context of the direct message, there is nothing stylistically to romanticise them, nothing verbally to suggest to the reader that he ought to reconsider his reaction to them.

Burns, by way of contrast, is an unrepentant rhetorician. Imagistically he is unadventurous. Striking conceits occur most often in his bawdy verse and even there are part of an established convention of indirection. Elsewhere, love being like a red, red rose or Clarinda like the sun scarcely suggests any ambition to outdo Donne and the metaphysicals. True, his rhetoric is seldom of the overtly virtuosic sort anticipated by the Castalians. His is the classical aim of using art to conceal art (*ars est celare artem*). But the rules of rhetoric were hierarchical with as many guides for low and middle style as for high. In using 'rhetorical' now to mean only the sort of speech delivered by Shakespeare's Antony at Caesar's funeral, we lose sight of the comprehensiveness of the original concept. 'Tam o' Shanter', for example, seems couthy and colloquial; it is drawn from a folk-tale but it is a valuable

exercise to look at the variety of effects Burns gains within it by
the single device of repeating a word or words at the beginning
of a line. Early on that device is employed to convey increased
conviviality in the pub but elsewhere it is used to stress dignity,
to convey a flyting, to underline comic incongruity, to parody
posturising and so on:

> The night drave on wi' sangs and clatter;
> And aye the ale was growing better:
> The landlady and *Tam* grew gracious,
> Wi' favours, secret, sweet, and precious:
> The Souter tauld his queerest stories;
> The landlord's laugh was ready chorus:
> The storm without might rair and rustle,
> *Tam* did na mind the storm a whistle.

The very next verse paragraph begins with a personification of
'Care' precisely as defined and renounced in the *Preface* by
Wordsworth. The Burns of decorum, levels of style, figures
of speech and thought is not the Burns who inspired Words-
worth nor the romanticised mythical figure created later by the
Burns cult.

Also implicit in the *Preface* is a new view of originality, moving
attention away from authorities and placing it firmly within what
Coleridge would define as the Secondary Imagination.[11] This is
another reaction against classical and neoclassical views of
Imitation and Invention. In relegating Invention from its prime
position to the subsidiary non-creative, kaleidoscopic function
of Fancy, they at once withdrew the need to work from earlier
writers and originated the modern, perjorative concept of
plagiarism. Burns is so far from this position that one critic
has called him 'Of all the great poets the least original; almost,
one might say, the most anxious not to be original'.[12] And if that
is doubted, the reader might turn to Thomas Crawford's *Robert
Burns* and the sections in the notes headed 'English Literary
Tradition' and 'Sources and Parallels'.[13] Crawford's approach is
neither overly ingenious nor relentlessly comparative. The work
has rightly been awarded a high critical evaluation for the clarity
of its exposition and its explication of Burns's ideas in their

sociological and philosophical context. Yet, in a work such as this, the list of Burns's literary authorities and sources includes 123 entries, most with multiple sub-references. There are many Scots names and poems, of course, but forty-seven of the authors alone are English. Wordsworth may be a poet of the synthesising imagination, creating anew; Burns in these terms would remain a bard of the classical invention or the romantic fancy, drawing his inspiration widely from earlier authorities.

Why, then, did Wordsworth revere Burns, convey that reverence to Dorothy, ally himself with Gilbert Burns and embark on his literary pilgrimage as Russell Noyes and others have established?[14] It is, perhaps, a simplification to say that it was the 'Scottish' Burns who thrilled Wordsworth and the 'English' Burns whom he preferred to forget but, with modifications, that generalisation is a fair starting point. Unlike Coleridge, Wordworth was not much concerned with the internal logic of criticism; his was essentially a heuristic approach. Views which helped him to understand his own creative strengths (such as the child being father of the man and our life a process of forgetting) appeared as general tenets when, in fact, they were primarily aids to a particular genius's own creative processes. I do not believe, therefore, that had I presented Wordworth with this essay's neoclassical arguments, he would have been much concerned. For him Burns exemplified two *other* crucial literary beliefs and these were the focus of the lakeside poet's interest.

In 'The Prelude', Wordsworth mapped out the best possible training for the poetic imagination — delayed schooling, maximal access in the early years to folk-tales and that literature of fantasy whose powers he praised in Book V against the limitations of restrictive reasoning:

> Forgers of lawless tales! we bless you then,
> Impostors, drivellers, dotards, as the ape
> Philosophy will call you: then we feel
> With what, and how great might ye are in league,
> Who make our wish our power, our thought a deed;
> An empire, a possession: Ye whom Time
> And Seasons serve; all Faculties; to whom

> Earth crouches, th' elements are potter's clay,
> Space like a Heaven fill'd up with Northern lights;
> Here, nowhere, there, and everywhere at once.

This was not Wordsworth's own experience. He had endured the prison house of schooling at the set time and progressed to University. Burns, on the other hand, had gone to school late after having imbibed from his mother and Betty Davidson (the old maid, full of 'ignorance and credulity' noted in the letter to Moore) folklore inhabited by 'devils, ghosts, fairies, brownies, witches, warlocks, spunkies, kelpies, elf-candles, dead-lights, wraiths, apparitions, cantraips, giants, inchanted towers, dragons and other trumpery'.[15] That irrational belief in the power of faerie which Burns sometimes boasted of, sometimes found exasperating; that ability at once to accept emotionally but reject rationally, most clearly enacted in 'The Address to the Deil', was for Wordsworth a consistently envied ideal or Idea.

The other ideal realised by Burns and worshipped by Wordsworth was that of the rustic. Wordsworth was perfectly honest. In shunning imitation of literary authorities he moved, of necessity, to imitating rural language for he was not of that group whose linguistic directness he idealised. One needs only to think of the effect of Wordworth entering a lakeside pub on the assembled rustics and compare it with the easy spirit of shared conviviality expressed by Burns in the first 'Epistle to John Lapraik' to share the English poet's concern:

> On Fasteneen we had a rockin,
> To ca' the crack and weave our stockin;
> And there was muckle fun and jokin,
>   Ye need na doubt;
> At length we had a hearty yokin,
>   At *sang about.*

Again it is easy to mock the English poet; few cronies of the Duck and Feathers would have been likely to refer to gypsies in the Wordsworthian terminology as 'vagrant dwellers in the houseless woods'. Again, however, I am much more impressed by the English poet's success in using simple language shared with prose than I am alienated by his lapses. And he *does* see that his own version of rustic speech must be a 'selection', 'purified' by his own sensibilities.

Related to this concept of the rustic is Wordsworth's desire to champion their cause and invert the usual intellectual, spiritual hierarchy. Here, also, Burns provides the type. Wordsworth over and over again in the *Preface* elevates the emotions and the heart above the reason. Now, if there is one prevalent theme in Burns's philosophy it is summed up (and repeated in an almost infinite variety of forms) by the phrase 'The heart's aye the part aye'. Even the moral connotation which follows that line — making us right or wrong — was accepted by Wordsworth. And if there is a dialectical technique favoured by Burns, it is assuming initially that the mind and status define hierarchical superiority, followed by an overturning which exalts the poor in the name of the heart and charity. (See 'A Man's a Man'; 'Address to the Unco Guid'; 'The Jolly Beggars'; 'MacPherson's Farewell'; 'The Lament of Mary Queen of Scots', etc etc.)

There are, of course, other reasons for Wordsworth's enthusiasm for Burns but my intention is, economically, to present the proper techniques of comparative analysis, its value and its limitations. In placing the ideas of education and the rustic firmly on the positive side, I am urging that even distinctions here should be positively construed. Wordsworth and Burns were not educated in the same manner, nor were they champions of the emotions or rural living in the same manner or from the same perspective. But that is the point, in this instance. It was as an ideal that Wordsworth worshipped Burns, and from that view the phrase 'poetic *pilgrimage*' is an accurate one.

Most comparisons dwell in a less clear land, however. It is not misleading, for example, to link Wordsworth and Burns as poets of Nature and the outdoors. Only because Wordsworth shared this view did he find Burns's failure to rhapsodise on the beauties of Arran surprising. Had Wordsworth been able to look out over the Firth of Clyde practically every day, that lovely island would certainly have become a source of his musings on the powers of Nature to encourage or correct the rudimentary conscience:

> One impulse from a vernal wood
> May teach you more of man,
> Of moral evil and of good,
> Than all the sages can.

What a reading of Wordsworth and Burns provides at the most basic level is a removal of the reader's focus from town or study to unspoiled nature. But while Nature in Wordsworth is, predominantly, either an aesthetic end in itself or a means of explaining the mysteries of man, morals and metaphysics, for Burns it is more simply the most 'naturally' available repository for imagery. Very occasionally, in his attempts at high serious-ness, as in 'The Vision', Burns may touch on Nature's power to offer correction or benediction:

> I saw thee★ seek the sounding shore,
> Delighted with the dashing roar;
> Or when the *North* his fleecy store
>   Drove thro' the sky,
> I saw grim Nature's visage hoar,
>   Struck thy young eye.
>
> Or when the deep-green-mantled Earth,
> Warm-cherish'd ev'ry floweret's birth,
> And joy and music pouring forth,
>   In ev'ry grove,
> I saw thee eye the gen'ral mirth
>   With boundless love.

Actually, this is rather close to the later Wordsworthian view of Nature's capacity for benevolence and malevolence, and there is a temptation to draw 'The Vision' and 'The Prelude' together. But *varius sis* would remind the more careful comparative critic that the idea of Nature *mère* and *marâtre* pre-dates both writers; that 'The Vision' is neither a typical Burnsean poem nor one which Wordsworth, given his views on allegorisation, artifice and the high-style, would have read with any pleasure. Burns never praises Arran's beauty because his use of Nature is, poetically, more pragmatic and personal than Wordsworth's.

★ Coila — Ayrshire, as allegoric character.

Had he made love on Arran, he would have sung its beauties enthusiastically; not having had any experiences on the island, he was neither the man nor the poet to gaze at it carefully in an effort to transform it into a touchstone for the spirit, the heart or the mysteries of moral philosophy.

To sum up, there does seem to me an analytic, critical value in comparing Wordsworth and Burns. The base for this is the later poet's known acquaintance with and enthusiasm for the earlier writer's work. But just as rejection of any discussion on grounds of national antagonism (Scots/Sassenach) seems to me sophistically based, so imprecise yoking of the two is equally irresponsible. Broadly, I have argued that in the five areas I have chosen, those focused on rhetoric and imitation *predominantly* draw the two apart; those based on the imagination and rustic experience draw them together *once the distinction between ideal and actuality has been clearly identified*; that centred on Nature works *outwards* from a central truth whose importance is similarly accepted but differently interpreted.

The reader, then, who reads only Scottish poets and so ignores Pope and Wordsworth will, I fear, achieve an inadequate view both of Burns and of his contribution to literature within Britain. More generally, I believe that such an approach works against the freedoms permitted by a discipline of the imagination. As a former student of law and one who began with 'parliamentary longings', I have nothing but admiration for the codes which determine the vision I am lamenting in its literary application. Necessary practical considerations accustom one to myths of exclusion and opposition. These correctly condition one's perspective on literature and one's evaluation of it. I simply maintain that if one thinks in terms of Scots and Sassenachs in the realms of the imagination, one is going, unnecessarily, to misjudge and, simply, to miss out. If Burns had not inspired Wordsworth's journey, the world would have lost '*The Solitary Reaper*'. For the student and the scholar who deprives himself of it on the proudly expressed nationalist grounds of 'Thank God I don't need to *do* Wordsworth!' I have genuine pity and (as these are actual quotations) some sense of 'professorial' guilt:

Behold her, single in the field,
Yon solitary Highland Lass!
Reaping and singing by herself;
Stop here, or gently pass!
Alone she cuts and binds the grain,
And sings a melancholy strain;
O listen! for the Vale profound
Is overflowing with the sound.

No Nightingale did ever chaunt
More welcome notes to weary bands
Of travellers in some shady haunt,
Among Arabian Sands:
A voice so thrilling ne'er was heard
In spring-time from the Cuckoo-bird,
Breaking the silence of the seas
Among the farthest Hebrides.

Will no one tell me what she sings?-
Perhaps the plaintive numbers flow
For old, unhappy, far off things,
And battles long ago:
Or is it some more humble lay,
Familiar matter of to-day?
Some natural sorrow, loss, or pain,
That has been, and may be again?

Whate'er the theme, the Maiden sang
As if her song could have no ending;
I saw her singing at her work,
And o'er the sickle bending:-
I listened, motionless and still;
And, as I mounted up the hill,
The music in my heart I bore,
Long after it was heard no more.

Notes

1. *The Letters of Robert Burns*, ed. G. Ross Roy, 2nd edn. (Oxford, 1985), 2 vols., I, 250-1 (No. 215: To Robert Ainslie.)
2. See 'Scottish Literature: The English and European Dimensions',

in *Renaissance Culture in Context*, ed. Jean R. Brink & William F. Gentrup (Cambridge, 1993), 9–17.

3. *The Works of Allan Ramsay*, 6 vols., Scottish Text Society (Edinburgh & London, 1944–74), V, 28.

4. 'Would', 'found/drowned', and 'Doon', while having different vowel sounds in English, could all be given the same [u] sound in Ayrshire Scots.

5. The stylistic transition would be the same whether the intention were seriously decorous or to satirise the posturising of a pompous narrator-persona.

6. *Letters*, I, 135. (No. 125: To Dr John Moore.)

7. Here, the verse of a Scots vernacular poet is boosted by association with neoclassical moral poetry written in English.

8. *A Choice of Scottish Verse* 1560–1660, ed. R.D.S. Jack (London, 1978), 46.

9. See E.R. Curtius, *European Literature and the Latin Middle Ages* (New York, 1953), 83–91.

10. Wordsworth citations follow the Oxford edition of his *Works*, ed. by Ernest de Selincourt & Helen Darbishire.

11. Samuel Taylor Coleridge, *Biographia Literaria*, ed. J. Shawcross, 2 vols. (Oxford, 10th edn. rev., 1973), 202 (Ch. 13).

12. Alexander Gray, *A Timorous Civility* (Glasgow, 1966), 142.

13. Thomas Crawford, *Burns: A Study of the Poems and Songs* (Edinburgh & London, 1960), 394–6.

14. Russell Noyes, 'Wordsworth and Burns', *Publications of the Modern Language Association*, 59 (1944), 813–32.

15. *Letters*, I, 135 (Note 125: To Dr John Moore).

9
Burns and Scottish Nationalism

Andrew Noble

On the face of it one could hardly imagine a less fruitful field of inquiry than the one suggested by this title. Can any nation ever have so enthusiastically and constantly granted so singular a role to a poet as its exemplary representative? He is omnipresent in our commercial iconography. Like Banquo's descendants, an endless stream of Burns Suppers passes before us. In a life replete with thwarted desires, his nationalist aspiration seems one granted to him in life and death:

> As I have but slender pretensions to philosophy, I cannot rise to the exalted ideas of a Citizen of the world at large; but have all those national prejudices, which, I believe, glow peculiarly strong in the breast of a Scotchman. — There is scarcely any thing to which I am so feelingly alive as the honour and welfare of old Scotia; and, as a Poet, I have no higher enjoyment than singing her Sons and Daughters.[1]

This, like so many successfully self-promoting protestations made in the early stages of Burns's career, stressing his rural, provincial and ethnic limitations, is not to be taken at face value. Would, in any case, a true *naif* be even aware of that central tension among eighteenth-century men of letters between local and cosmopolitan attachments? In Burns modesty and foxiness often go together. If national prejudices did glow in the heart of this 'peasant' poet and his prosperous Scottish audience, the causes of the inflammation were not only diverse but, in reality, divisive.

For Burns's contemporary middle- and upper- class audience fervour for Scotland combined with the innate conviction that membership of the British state provided the sole means of social, political stability and economic improvement. T.C. Smout has lucidly defined this phenomenon of 'concentric' national identity, whereby Scottish *and* British allegiances are not only compatible but desirable.[2] Sir Walter Scott and his works represent the zenith of this concept. Burns, not only influenced by quite other experiences and forces of social deprivation and, ironically, by English dissent in both eighteenth-century political theory and poetry, came to quite different conclusions about the Hanoverian British State. It was a conclusion, as we shall see, further strengthened by his interpretation of the revolutionary events in America and France which were so important to the development of his political thought.

This divergence between Burns's radical politics and those of his conservative social superiors is essential to an understanding of the 'meteoric' flight-path of his poetic career which began in a blaze of celebrity in Edinburgh and ended in near-isolated death in Dumfries where his dying wish not to have the soldiers of the British militia shoot over his grave was disobeyed. He, who had briefly been the applauded epicentre of Edinburgh society, had, in the dark shadows of the French Revolution and the consequent treason trials, become a hunted, haunted, marginal figure:

> The shrinking Bard adown an alley sculks,
> And dreads a meeting worse than Woolwich hulks —
> Tho' there his heresies in Church and State
> Might well award him Muir and Palmer's fate . . .[3]

Why, almost two hundred years after his death, should the degree of Burns's political dissent still be a matter of relative ignorance in Scotland? In part, it is due to the fact that the young poet, as we shall see, ambitiously colluded with the 'patriotic' expectations of his audience. In part, it is due to the fact that as he increasingly hardened in his opposition to that audience and as the political situation became darker and, finally, dangerous he felt curbed in what he could say. He wrote in 1788 about his pro-Jacobite comments on a Stirling Castle window:

> Why will great people not only deafen us with the din of their equipage, and dazzle us with their fastidious pomp, but they must also be so very dictatorially wise? I have been question'd like a child about my matters, and blam'd and schooled for my

Inscription on Stirling window. Come Clarinda — 'Come, curse me Jacob; come, defy me Israel!'[4]

At his most depressed, Burns felt that the censorious external pressure was so great that he had no recourse but to submissive silence:

> In politics if thou would'st mix,
>   And mean thy fortunes be;
> Bear this in mind, be deaf and blind,
>   Let great folks hear and see.
> ('Lines Written on windows of the Globe Tavern, Dumfries')

The combination of his craft with his explosive temperament, however, did not allow such final, submissive silence. What it did induce was a brilliant series of poetic strategies employing a Swiftian capacity for personae, political allegory and historical analogy, too wittily intelligent to allow him to be clearly marked out for suppression. If, however, establishment Scotland was to have as its representative man a poet from the people, it was utterly unacceptable that he should be not only radically discontented but profoundly more intelligent than his audience. Thus in his life Burns had to bend to his audience's condescending specifications. His posthumous reputation was to fare even worse. Francis Jeffrey, his first major Scottish critic, employed the then-vast prestige of *The Edinburgh Review* to consolidate the policy adopted by polite Edinburgh to deal with Burns. In his 1808 review of Cromek's *Reliques of Robert Burns*, Jeffrey drew a fundamental aesthetic distinction, which is also a moral and political distinction, between the compliant, pastoral sentimentalist and the rough, licentious man of the people. Revolutionary politics, as always, were tinged with disruptively erotic menace. Thus Jeffrey largely dismissed Burns's love poetry as being in bad taste and socially presumptuous 'since it is seldom accommodated to the timidity and "sweet austere composure" of women of refinement'. His political satires are similarly discounted: 'They seem to have been written, not out of playful malice, but out of a fierce and ungovernable anger'.

In the long shadow cast by the French Revolution Burns and his vengeful anger haunted establishment Scotland as a microcosm of the terrifying macrocosm of the anarchic mob. This is why Jeffrey, loathing the poetry and politics of the young Wordsworth, was so intent on isolating Burns's poetry from the contagion of English Romantic republicanism. Thus Wordsworth's world of 'hysterical schoolmasters and sententious leechgatherers' had nothing to do with 'the authentic rustics' of Burns's 'The Cotter's Saturday Night'. This was essentially a critical judgement based on political loyalty. Jeffrey believed that Wordsworth's prosody was 'infantine'. That is to say, it had a regressive power to undermine not only traditional literature but the hierarchical stability of the state. Burns's poetic language, on the other hand, was, according to Jeffrey, a traditional endorsement of language and thereby politics.[5]

If a Scottish Whig could achieve such a degree of personal, poetic and political distortion, what might be expected of a Scottish Tory? Our answer can be found in this report of 1844:

> 'The Burns Festival' — a meeting at which the people of Scotland of all ranks assembled in large numbers to do honour to their great national poet — was celebrated in the vicinity of Ayr on the 6th of August 1844. Not fewer than 80,000 persons were present on the occasion; and when they marched in procession with playing bands and streaming banners past the platform on which the *Dii Majores* of the jubilee were stationed, the spectacle was in the highest degree exhilarating. It was a demonstration worthy of the nation, and of the genius which the nation delighted to honour. In the afternoon about 2000 of the assembly dined together in an elegant pavilion extemporised for that purpose. The Earl of Eglinton was in the chair: Professor Wilson acted as croupier; and it was then that he delivered the following oration, in proposing a toast 'The Sons of Burns,' who were present as guests at the entertainment.[6]

Professor John Wilson (Christopher North), not so much a gambler with as destroyer of greater men's reputations, was, inevitably, the day's chief orator. Wilson here is preaching to the converted, a crowd completely in his power and behaving precisely in reverse fashion to that of a revolutionary mob. With his characteristic, loquacious rhetoric Wilson attempts to square the circle of how Burns, representative of the earthiness, irreverence and, more evasively, the eroticism of the Scottish common people, could end up as a totem of pietistic social harmony and, indeed, defender of the British realm:

> But they who know Burns as we know him, know that by this sometimes unregulated and unguarded sympathy with all appertaining to his kind, and especially to his own order, he was enabled to receive into himself all modes of their simple, but not undiversified life, so that his poetry murmurs their loves and joys from a thousand fountains. And suppose — which was the case — that this unguarded sympathy, this quick sensibility, and this vivid capacity of happiness which the moment brings, and the frankness of impulse, and the strength of desire, and the warmth of blood, which have made him what he greatly is, which have been fire and music in his song, and manhood, and courage and endurance, and independence in his life, have at times betrayed or overmastered him — to turn against him — to turn against him all this self-painting and self-revealing, is it not ungrateful, barbarous, inhuman? Can he be indeed a true lover of his kind, who would record in judgement against such a man words that have escaped him in the fervour of the pleading designed to uphold great causes dear to humanity? — who would ignobly strike the self-disarmed? — scornfully insult him who, kneeling at the Muses' confessional, whispers secrets that take wings and fly abroad to the uttermost parts of the earth? Can they be lovers of the people who do so? who find it in their hearts thus to think, and speak, and write of Robert Burns? — He who has reconciled poverty to its lot, toil to its taskwork, care to its burden — nay, I would say even grief to its grave? And by one Immortal Song has sanctified for ever the poor man's Cot — by such a picture as only genius, in the inspiring power of piety, could have painted; has given enduring life to the image — how tender and how true! — of the Happy Night passing by sweet transition from this worky world into the Hallowed Day, by God's appointment breathing a heavenly calm over all Christian regions in their rest — nowhere else so profoundly — and may it never be broken! — as over the hills and valleys of our beloved, and yet religious land.

It cannot be said that the best biographers of Burns, and his best critics, have not done, or desired to do justice to his character as

well as to his genius; and, accordingly as the truth has been more
entirely and fearlessly spoken, has he appeared the nobler man. All
our best poets, too, have exultingly sung the worth, while they
mourned the fate of him, the brightest of the brotherhood. But
above, and below, and round about all that they have been
uttering, has all along been heard a voice, which they who know
how to listen for it can hear, and which has pronounced a decision
in his favour not to be reversed; for on earth it cannot be carried to
a higher tribunal. A voice heard of old on great national
emergencies, when it struck terror into the hearts of tyrants,
who quaked, and qualified, and quitted for aye our land before 'the
unconquered Caledonian spear' — nor, since our union with
noblest England, ever slack to join with hers and fervid Erin's sons,
the thrice repeated cry, by which battle-fields are cleared; but
happier, far happier to hear in its low deep tone of peace. For then
it is like the sound of distant waterfalls, the murmur of summer
woods, or the rolling sea in its rest. I mean the Voice of the People
of Scotland — the Voice of her Peasantry and her Trades — of all
who earn their bread by the sweat of their brow — her Working
Men.[7]

The prose of this Scottish Salieri is aesthetically wholly
deplorable but socially deeply revealing. Wilson's sprawling
writings on Burns are arguably the *ur*-texts of millions of
subsequent garrulous 'Immortal Memories'. They are also key
documents in revealing the anxiety-ridden consciousness of
establishment Scotland in relation to the problems of class and
ethnicity wherein Burns's posthumous reputation has such a
central role. The tortuous illogic of Wilson's prose (he was
Professor of Philosophy at Edinburgh University) should not
disguise the corrupt clarity of his political manipulation. After
the French Revolution nineteenth-century British society
lived in fear of a subterranean explosion of the common
people. Wilson, not alone, deeply feared that Burns's legacy
might, in a Scottish context, be a trigger for such an explosion.
While this political paranoia might now be considered un-
realistic, it is the only adequate explanation of his writings on
Burns.

The nature of Wilson's argument is, obliquely if not terribly subtly, not so much to subvert as invert Burns's attitude to both class and nation. Although Wilson initially implicates him in deliberately ill-defined sexual and political irregularities of his own class, Burns is, then, absurdly defended by Wilson against those critics who, less than friends of the people, would attack him on these very grounds. Subsequently Burns is defined as the reconciler of the poor to their lot by that apparent hymn of burgeoning evangelical Toryism, 'The Cotter's Saturday Night'. This quite ignores all the contrary poetic evidence of rancorous Scottish discontent:

> Arouse my boys! exert your mettle,
> To get auld Scotland back her *kettle*!
> Or faith! I'll wad my new pleugh-pettle,
>   Ye'll see't or lang,
> She'll teach you, wi' a reekan whittle,
>   Anither sang.

> This while she's been in crankous mood,
> Her *lost Militia* fir'd her bluid;
> (Deil na they never mair do guid,
>   Play'd her that pliskie!)
> An' now she's like to rin red-wud
>   About her *Whisky*.

> An' L-d! if ance they pit her till't
> Her tartan petticoat she'll kilt
> An' durk an' pistol at her belt,
>   She'll tak the streets,
> An' rin her whittle to the hilt,
>   I' th' first she meets!

('The Author's Earnest Cry and Prayer, to the Right Honorable,
    the Scotch Representatives in the House of Commons')

It is a typical Burns evasive strategy to insert a darker, menacing section into what is mainly a light, comic satire on English taxation of Scottish whisky exports. This somewhat histrionic celebration of atavistic Scottish violence, a threat Walter Scott took with complete seriousness, is, however, quite outdone by the poem's biting 'Postscript' where, as chillingly as Blake's blood running down palace walls, Burns sees Celtic Scotland as victim of British Imperialism:

> But bring a SCOTCHMAN frae his hill,
> Clap in his cheek a *highlan gill,*
> Say, such is royal GEORGE's will,
>   An' there's the foe,
> He has nae thought but how to kill
>   Twa at a blow.

> Nae cauld, faint-hearted doubtings tease him;
> Death comes, with fearless eye he sees him;
> Wi' bluidy hand a welcome gies him;
>   An' where he fa's,
> His latest draught o' breathin lea'es him
>   In faint huzzas.

The conversion of the Jacobite enemy of the British state into its bleeding, dispensable cutting edge — Pitt the elder's boasted achievement — was not the least of the multiple ironies which Burns saw as a consequence of the loss of Scottish nationhood. Such a poetry of radical, ethnic discontent became, however, increasingly submerged by the floodtide of Victorian prosperity in Scotland. The suppers became increasingly gargantuan and bibulous; Burns's poetic voice drowned out by the vacuous rhetoric and the kitsch music. A culture which could accept Wilson's vision of England, Scotland and *Ireland* in a tripartite defensive, imperial alliance was quite incapable of detecting a contradiction between its vaunted Scottishness and its devotion to the Union. What Burns had actually written was censored for subversive content so that subsequent 'Burnsian' nineteenth-century Scottish poetry became merely the stuff of narrow, couthy, politically quiescent sentimentality.

In his own lifetime Burns had realised — in poetics, if not politics, he was essentially aristocratic — that his example had provoked a generation of wholly inadequate imitators: 'Besides, my success has encouraged such a shoal of ill-spawned monsters to crawl into public notice under the title of Scots Poets, that the very term, Scots Poetry, borders on the burlesque'. This, however, was not a border resistant to the celebratory effusions of the nineteenth century. Here, for example, is that fine twentieth-century cultural critic, William Power's, account of the zenith of Victorian junketings:

> The record among Burns celebrations is still held by the Centenary Banquet in the City Hall, Glasgow, on January 25, 1859. Over and above 'The Immortal Memory', which was replied to by Burns's son, Colonel William Nicol Burns, there were twenty-two toasts and fifteen replies, with appropriate musical items between. The chairman was Sheriff Sir Archibald Alison, and among other speakers were Henry Glassford Bell, Dr Norman MacLeod, Professor Nichol, Sir David Brewster, Colin Rae Brown, Monkton Milnes and Samuel Lover. The band and organ were in full blast; the vocalists were Messrs. Fulcher (of 'Hurrah for the Highlands!'), John Muir, Stembridge Ray and Robson. The average middle-class audience in Scotland today is rather diffident about the Scottish National Anthem, perhaps regarding it as savouring of Sinn Feinism, or, worse still of 'commonness.' The 'fifty-niners, on whom the light of Kipling had not dawned, had no such qualms. Their memorable jamboree began with 'Solo, "Scots Wha Hae", by Mr Fulcher, Chorus to be sung by Company, standing'. And the final item of the Gargantuan programme reads — 'Solos, "Auld Lang Syne" — the Vocalists — Chorus by the Company, standing, accompanied by Band and Organ'. At which of the not so very wee short 'oors ayont the twal' this item was reached, and what company responded to the call to Attention, tradition sayeth not. But one may be certain that on January 16, 1859, Blanket Bay was the favourite resort, and the druggists' shops were busier than the Exchanges.[8]

Nor was Burns to be rescued by major Victorian Scottish writers from this self-congratulatory, middlebrow tidal wave. Politically sympathetic, Hugh Miller could see nothing but confusion in Burns's apparently absurd conflation of Jacobite and Jacobin politics.[9] Carlyle, the high priest of the British Empire, was antipathetic to Burns's democratic politics but, to a degree, refashioned the poet in his own 'heroic' image to make him a creature of politically thwarted will and 'savage' integrity. Partly reacting against Carlyle, R.L. Stevenson created a Burns self-undermined by ambitious social and, more dangerously, erotic role-playing. Ironically, Carlyle and Stevenson see Burns, respectively, within the Calvinist categories of election and damnation. Neither of these Anglo-Scots, while aware of his revolutionary politics, connects these with his national aspirations.

While Scottish writers either could or would not defend Burns's creative reputation from the excesses of popular nineteenth-century culture, a radical change took place in the early twentieth century. The First World War saw the breaking of the great continental empires and the beginning of the irretrievable erosion of the British one. The Scottish economy, especially the heavy industrial base, was fundamentally damaged. It was a time of political and economic turmoil and the new writers of the Scottish Renaissance, analogous to Burns in his time, were influenced both by the domestic economic distresses and the examples of foreign, national and radical, revolution. A conflict, at the least polemically vicious, broke out between these new writers and the mainly middle-class controllers of the media, university and church. At root was the question of whether the Union should be maintained. Thus all the bitterly personalised aesthetic wranglings as the avant-garde attempted to destroy the literary stereotypes of pseudo-Celticism, the Kailyard and, not least, the character and works of Burns, were symptoms of the fundamental issue of Scotland's true political nature and economic problems and, hence, future. William Power recalled thus the distribution of forces drawn up in the late nineteenth century which were to do battle after 1919:

> When I was quite a young boy I became aware that my compatriots were divided into two opposite camps. On one side were those who accepted Robert Burns as the representative Scot, quoted from him on all possible occasions, and thought him the greatest poetic genius that the world had produced. On the other side were those who ignored or disparaged Burns, read and re-read the Waverley Novels with something like ostentation, and spoke with affectionate reverence of 'Sir Walter'. The Burnsites, as a rule, were militant dissenters or mild free-thinkers; their national heroes, apart from Burns, were Willie Wallace and John Knox; they admired the Covenanters and execrated Claverhouse. The

Scottites were Episcopalians, or staunch adherents of the Established Church; they respected Robert the Bruce, not as the victor of Bannockburn, but as the restorer of the British dynasty; idolised Mary Stewart, made a hero of Montrose, covertly admired Claverhouse, and crooned Jacobite songs. Most of the Burnsites were Radicals. All the Scottites were ardent Tories. Both camps were represented in my own little circle, but the Scottites predominated. I do not remember seeing a portrait or bust of Burns in any of the houses I visited, but the physiognomies of Scott and Disraeli were familiar to me, and in the dining-room of one of my relatives a place of honour was given to portraits of Montrose and Dundee.

This partisan way of looking at Burns was, of course, fatal to a true appreciation of his writings. By one section of his fellow-countrymen he was regarded as a miracle of genius, a pattern of manhood, and an apostle of freedom; by another, as a lewd fellow of the baser sort, with a knack of rhyming and an itch for notoriety. The Burnsites have gained in strength recently. They now include members of all classes and political parties. The high priest of the Burns cult for many years was the Earl of Rosebery. Professor W.P. Ker, whose sympathies were strongly Conservative, wrote a pamphlet to prove that Burns, had he lived to-day, would have been an ardent Imperialist and Unionist, resolutely opposed to Scottish Home Rule, and rejoicing in the concentration of all political and social and literary interests in London. The average Burns Club is solidly middle-class in composition and sentiment, and a proposer of 'The Immortal Memory' would be reasonably safe in combining his laudation of Burns with a denunciation of Socialist doctrines.[10]

Such testimony as this demonstrates why, in their own time, the Scottish Renaissance writers were almost wholly unsuccessful in assigning Burns his true national or international place. The key work of the period, Catherine Carswell's biography with its realistic presentation of the man, its fine sense of the poetry, and its political and intellectual grasp of the late eighteenth century, was savaged in the pages of the *Burns Chronicle*. The Revd Lachlan MacLean Watt and his ilk ruled. Somebody actually sent Mrs Carswell a bullet. The support of D.H. Lawrence and, at home, critics of the power and penetration of Edwin Muir and Hugh MacDiarmid did the book's reputation little, if any, good. Muir despaired of Scotland not least because it seemed to have mythified its actual history into an escapist sequence of 'legendary' personalities. Chief among these was Burns whose image Muir saw as a compensatory fantasy for both Scottish class and sexual neuroses. Less well known than he should be for his satiric wit, Muir wrote in 1936, in the depths of the Depression, this account of a Burns celebration inspired by the rhetoric of Ramsay MacDonald:

Mr Ramsay MacDonald recently unveiled some new statuary in the Burns Mausoleum at Dumfries and made it the occasion for a speech. This event was not of any intrinsic importance, but it has considerable symbolic interest. The setting itself was involuntarily symbolic. The unveiling of the statuary took place in a churchyard; between one and two hundred people were gathered within the gates; outside were several thousands, some unemployed among them. When Mr MacDonald started by addressing his audience as 'friends', there were some jeers from the crowd outside, and shouts of 'What about the means test?' But these interruptions soon subsided, and Mr MacDonald succeeded in making a very long and very involved speech, after having released the Scottish Standard which draped the figure of Burns at the plough.

The symbolism implicit in this scene is quite casual and involuntary. The churchyard could hold only a certain number of people; the 'platform party' (in Scotland one is always hitting against platform parties) was naturally chosen from the more well-to-do admirers of the poet: landlords, baronets, and officers in the British Army. Objectively one can see that, Scotland being what it is, a ceremony in honour of its greatest poet should take just this form and no other. But at the same time one is driven to ask what can have happened to Burns since his death to make him now the implicit property of the middle and upper classes, when he was the property of the poor man at the beginning. This change may be briefly described by saying that Holy Willie, after being the poet's butt, has now become the keeper of his memory.

I think I have said enough to show that Burns has been unostentatiously but securely swallowed and digested by Holy

Willie during the century and a bit since his death. Burns was not
the revolutionist whom Mr MacDonald makes him out to be, but
he was an honest writer. And though he was a revolutionist, he
showed his sympathy with the French Revolution in a quite
practical way, without stopping to consider whether it was a mere
revolution in the circumstance or a revolution in soul. We cannot
imagine the Burns whose statue Mr MacDonald unveiled sending
arms even to the constitutional government of Spain against the
expressed wishes of the established order, as the living Burns did to
the leaders of the French revolution against a similar prohibition.
Something has happened to him since his death, and it is what
happens to all writers after their death, no matter what they have
written. It may not be true that all writers reflect the economic
ideology of the society in which they live — I do not think it is
— but it does seem to be true that their writings are finally and in
the long run made to reflect that ideology, by a process of
elimination and transformation, until the most influential classes in
society can finally put their seal on the result.[11]

Given the modern poet's genius and pugnacity, the most bitter
battles over Burns and his self-elected cult inevitably involved
Hugh MacDiarmid. Manic, where Muir tended to depression,
MacDiarmid went headfirst for every Scottish sacred cow.
MacDiarmid saw the World Federation of Burns Clubs as the
inversion of the internationalisation of Scottish consciousness
which he, as Modernist, desired. He saw a planet colonised by
ersatz Scottish groups and demanded:

Are the young Scots of today — the Free Scots — going to
tolerate any longer the infernal insult to Burns, this base betrayal of
the historical function of the Scottish spirit? Scotland will signalize
that it has come to itself again and resumed its proper attitude to
world affairs when it makes a bonfire of all the worthless, mouldy,
pitiable relics that antiquarian Burnsians have accumulated at
Mauchline, Dumfries and elsewhere and reconcentrates on the
living message of Burns's poetry the world wide attention devoted
today (at least once a year) to the mere man and his uninteresting
love affairs and the ramifications of the genealogies of his
acquaintances and the poor bric-a-brac of his *lares* and *penates*
and the witless lucubrations of the hordes of bourgeois 'orators'

who annually befoul his memory by the expression of sentiments utterly antipathetic to that stupendous element in him which ensures his immortality.

. . . Burns knew what he was doing when he repudiated all the canting Anglicisers and reverted to the Scots tongue and the Scots spirit — and the need to follow his lead at long last is today a thousand times greater than when he gave it.

We can if we will. We can still rescue Scotland from the crash of England's collapse and the ruins of an Empire vitiated by England's infernal Ascendancy policy. We can still affirm the fearless radical spirit of the true Scotland. We can even throw off the yoke of all the canting humbug in our midst. We can rise and quit ourselves like men and make Scotland worthy to have had a Burns — and conscious of it; and we can communicate that consciousness powerfully to the ends of the earth.

We can if we will — if we won't, we won't, the Burns cult will remain a monstrous monument to Scotland's refusal to follow Burns's lead — a monument to the triumph of his enemies.[12]

To this polemic should be added a strange, chilling English-language sonnet written in 1923, eleven years before, called 'They know not what they do':

> Burns in Elysium once every year
> Ceases from intercourse and turns aside,
> Shorn for a day of all his rightful pride,
> Wounded by those whom yet he holds most dear.
> Chaucer he leaves, and Marlowe, and Shakespeare,
> Milton and Wordsworth — and he turns to hide
> His privy shame that will not be denied
> And pay his annual penalty of fear.
>
> But Christ comes to him there and takes his arm.
> 'My followers, too,' He says, 'are false as thine,
> True to themselves, and ignorant of Me.
> Grieve not thy fame seems so compact of harm,
> Star of the Sot, Staff of the Philistine,
> Truth goes from Calvary to Calvary.'

Much of the power of MacDiarmid's early Scottish-language lyric poetry emanates from a Christ-besotted atheism. While

Burns himself did feel that his grief and tears for the world agonisingly exceeded his faith, Christ did not figure among the many historical and literary models with whom he chose to identify. Tristram Shandy was often a comic alternative self.[13] Othello also preoccupied him; perhaps not so much as a menacing, dark erotic outsider but as a man who, unrewarded, had done the state some service.[14] An actual poet who had done the Scottish state enormous, largely unrecognised, service was his personally and poetically adored predecessor, Robert Fergusson. In Fergusson Burns saw prefigured (as MacDiarmid partly saw his own fate in that of Burns) his own fiscal, psychological and, most important, creative divorce from his fellow-countrymen:

> (O Ferguson! thy glorious parts
> Ill-suited law's dry musty arts!
> My curse upon your whunstane hearts,
>   Ye Enbrugh Gentry!
> The tythe o' what ye waste at cartes
>   Wad stow'd his pantry!)
>
>   ('To William Simpson, Ochiltree')

In Fergusson Burns saw a particular Scottish symptom of what he conceived of as a general poetic fate. While he would not have placed himself in the supreme pantheon of English poets celebrated in MacDiarmid's sonnet, he imaginatively fraternised with the near-contemporary English eighteenth-century poets whom he considered his peers. Like Goldsmith, Gray, Cowper and Churchill, he saw himself as a displaced, disorientated victim of the anti-poetic social, economic and political forces let loose in that century: 'There is not among all the Martyrologies that were ever penned, so rueful a narrative as Johnson's Lives of the Poets.'[15] He also felt that the quality and integrity of Scottish poetry and, hence, perhaps of Scotland itself was not diminished by seeing it in proper relation to its neighbour's extraordinary creative achievement:

> Yet all beneath th' unrivall'd Rose,
> The lowly Daisy sweetly blows;
> Tho' large the forest's Monarch throws

His army shade,
Yet green the juicy Hawthorn grows,
'Adown the glade.

('The Vision')

To MacDiarmid such endorsement of English creativity was anathema. Politically, culturally, aesthetically, psychologically, in the very rhythm of its blood, Scotland was for him essentially antipathetic to England. He conceived of himself and his creative generation as retrieving first in language and literature (politics would surely follow) the pre-Union essence of the Scottish spirit. This was a main cause of his ambivalence towards Burns expressed in his battlecry of going back to Dunbar and not Burns. In Dunbar he saw a pan-European consciousness, a non-provincialism not discernible to him in Burns. Even as early as 1930 in 'To Circumjack Cencrastus' we find this harsh assessment:

> I blink at Yeats as micht a man whom some
> Foul sorcery has changed into a pig,
> At Yeats, my kingly cousin, and mind hoo
> He prophesied that Eire 'ud hae nae Burns
> (Tho it has tried to mair than aince) but haud
> Its genius heich and lanely — and think o' Burns,
> That Langfellow in a' but leid and hoo
> Scots since has tint his maikles vir but hains
> His cheap emotions, puir ideas, and
> Imperfect sense o' beauty, till my race
> Lack ev'n the foetus luck o' Smith or Broon
> (A Hobson's choice to burse nae pigskin owre)
>   Bein' a' Jock Tamson's bairns.

As MacDiarmid aged, grew ever more disappointed in the savage torpor of his nation, ambivalence towards Burns darkened into condemnation. By the time MacDiarmid published the execrably written *Burns Today and Tomorrow* in 1957, Burns himself had become the initiator of the cult following that MacDiarmid had always loathed. In him by that point we can clearly discern the belated, creative rage postulated by Harold Bloom. He also felt crushed by the cultural juggernaut of the cult. At this point Burns and his late-eighteenth-century Scotland became totally obscured. On the one hand, the cult had evolved a series of sentimental, compensatory fantasies. On the other, MacDiarmid's anglophobic, polemical assault on the cult was based on a series of nationalistic premises which, at best, were gross simplifications and, at worst, inversions of the actual political and literary conditions prevailing in Burns's life and times.

We now need to turn, first, to what Burns conceived of as nationalism and, second, to the question of how his vision of nationalism evolved from, and was related to, the intellectual, economic, political and aesthetic forces prevailing in not only Europe but England itself. From the evidence of the letters, the key year is 1787. Here the young poet has just burst upon the Scottish scene and is in a state of high excitement from the creative energy within and the stimulating applause from without. In this letter we catch the bounce of the man at that time:

> On our return, at a Highland gentleman's hospitable mansion, we fell in with a merry party, and danced 'till the ladies left us at three in the morning. Our dancing was none of the French or English insipid formal movements; the ladies sung Scotch songs like angels, at intervals; then we flew at *Bab at the Bowster, Tullochgorum, Loch Erroch side,* &c. like midges sporting in the mottie sun, or craws prognosticating a storm in a hairst day. — When the dear lasses left us, we ranged round the bowl till the good-fellow hour of six; except a few minutes that we went out to pay our devotions to the glorious lamp of day peering over the towering top of Benlomond. We all kneeled; our worthy landlord's son held the bowl; each man a full glass in his hand; and I, as priest, repeated some rhyming nonsense, like Thomas a Rhymer's prophecies I suppose.[16]

There is much of the young Burns here with his dash-cutting, animal high spirits. He may have wanted to be the only rooster in the barnyard; he certainly wanted to be the most gorgeous one. Physically, instinctively, too, he is responding to a sense of national essence expressed in folk music and dance which Herder was simultaneously conceptualising in Germany. Undercut with comedy and irony though it is, there is also a sense of himself as national bard. Other reports of such bardic piety occur at this time:

> This morning I kneel'd at the tomb of Sir John the Graham, the gallant friend of the immortal Wallace; and two hours ago, I said a fervent prayer for old Caledonia over the hole in a blue whinstone where Robert de Bruce fixed his royal Standard on the banks of Bannockburn . . .[17]

If there is a youthful sense of self-dramatisation about this, it was a performance partly in tune with the growing, fervidly histrionic nationalism among the Scottish upper and middle classes of the late eighteenth century. We are still some years from the costumery, the Walter Scott-inspired borrowed tartan plumage of George IV's Edinburgh state visit, but the tide of national feeling is firmly set in that direction. This posturing nationalism was particularly fertile for the initial stage of Burns's career and seems to have come from post-Union Scotland's compulsion to believe itself productive of poetic peers of world and, more pertinently, English masters. James Macpherson, the Scottish Homer, and John Home, Shakespeare's rival, were lucrative stations to what was quickly to prove for Burns a bitter, impoverished cross. Perhaps subconsciously, resentment and guilt in the national psyche about the Union tended to generate, at the aesthetic level, compensatory 'heroic' Scottish figures.

Burns's early collusion in this attitude is certainly discernible in the same year, 1787, with his dedication of the much-demanded second edition of his poems 'To the *Noblemen and Gentleman* of the Caledonian Hunt'. In the dedication of his first edition, the Edinburgh literati had been soothed and manipulated by a poetic genius who entered centre-stage in the garb of spontaneous, artless country boy. A year later the tone was equally designed to arouse and satisfy more particular patriotic expectations:

> A Scottish Bard, proud of the name, and whose ambition is to sing in his Country's service, where shall he so properly look for patronage as to the illustrious names of his native Land; those who bear the honours and inherit the virtues of their Ancestors? — The

Poetic Genius of my Country found me as the prophetic bard
Elijah did Elisha — at the *plough*; and threw her *mantle* over me.
She bade me sing the loves, the joys, the rural scenes and rural
pleasures of my natal Soil, in my native tones: I tuned my wild
artless notes, as she inspired. — She whispered me to come to this
ancient metropolis, and lay my Songs under your honoured
protection: I now obey her dictates.

. . . Nor do I present this Address with the venal soul of a servile
Author, looking for a continuation of these favours: I was bred to
the Plough, and am independent. I come to claim the common
Scottish name with you, my illustrious Countrymen; and to tell the
world that I glory in the title. — I come to congratulate my
Country, that the blood of her ancient heroes still runs
uncontaminated; and that from your courage, knowledge and
public spirit, she may expect protection, wealth, and liberty.[18]

It is not known what these members of the eighteenth-century
'Ale and Quail Club' made of the compatibility of a poetry of
'wild artless notes' with such prose as is addressed to them here.
Certainly no less an authority than Coleridge was to attest to its
failure as a strategy for patronage. Burns attracted in his lifetime
only one patrician patron, the much-lamented, prematurely
dead James, Earl of Glencairn. Further, this particular economic
gulf between patrician sponsor and plebeian poet has to be seen
in the context of the general economic division prevailing in the
eighteenth century. Burns, as we shall see, is both representative
of and inspired witness to E.P. Thompson's thesis of a century
aggressively polarised between patricians and plebs.[19] In his
letters and in some of his most inspired political satire, Burns
analysed the aristocracy's burgeoning involvement in agrarian
capitalism with its harsh consequences for the common people.
Even less desirable was the licentious, anti-patriotic abuse of the
profits. Startlingly, this minor satirical miracle was composed
two years before the above dedication:

> Haith lad, ye little ken about it;
> For Britain's guid! guid faith! I doubt it.
> Say, rather, gaun as PREMIERS lead him,
> An' saying *aye* or *no*'s they bid him:
> At Operas an' Plays parading,

Mortgaging, gambling, masquerading:
Or maybe, in a frolic daft,
To HAGUE or CALAIS takes a waft,
To make a tour an' take a whirl,
To learn *bon ton* an' see the worl'.

There, at VIENNA or VERSAILLES
He rives his father's auld entails;
Or by MADRID he takes the rout,
To thrum *guittarres* an' fecht wi nowt;
Or down Italian vista startles
Whore-hunting amang groves o' myrtles:
Then bowses drumlie German-water,
To make himself look fair an' fatter,
An' clear the consequential sorrows,
Love-gifts of Carnival Signioras.

For Britain's guid! for her destruction!
Wi' dissipation, feud an' faction.

('The Twa Dogs. A Tale')

While Burns, for reasons both personal and national, may have
wished to perceive the contemporary Scottish aristocracy as a
conduit of an undivided, mythically democratic Scotland which
granted the common man prosperity and independence, almost
everything in his own life and the society he saw around him
testified to the opposite truth. His toil-wracked body, 'When
banes are craz'd and bluid is thin', the constant, soul-destroying
burden of debt which filled much of his life, the impoverished
living conditions and the stream of vagrant paupers were for him
overwhelming evidence of a Scotland more savage than benign.
As his nationalist thinking developed, his belief in the uncontaminated blood of Scotland's ancient heroes did not diminish.
Wallace and, less obviously, the House of Stewart were most
prominent in this legendary pantheon. These, often dismem-
bered, martyrs, had died in vain; their blood certainly did not
flow in the veins of their contemporary successors. If there was
to be a resurrected Scotland, it was not to come from its
establishment. In 1787, however, he was still prepared to
indulge that group; not least, perhaps, because they were at

that point indulging him. If there was an element of performance in Scottish political self-consciousness, there was no doubt who, in January 1787, was the star performer:

> The meeting was most numerous and elegant; all the different Lodges about the town were present, in all their pomp. The Grand Master who presided with great solemnity, and honor to himself as a Gentleman and a Mason, among other general toasts gave, 'Caledonia and Caledonia's Bard, Brother B-' which wrung through the whole Assembly with multiplied honours and repeated acclamations. As I had no idea such a thing would happen, I was downright thunder struck, and trembling in every nerve made the best return in my power. Just as I finished, some of the Grand Officers said so loud as I could hear, with a most comforting accent, 'Very well indeed!' which set me something to rights again.[20]

Burns is not alone among Scottish creative writers in acting out an archetypal Cinderella story with an unhappy ending. Peculiarly, too, he had an acute awareness that the pinnacle of his fortunes expressed in his first Edinburgh visit was to be extremely transient. He believed all true 'bardies' were, to a degree, second-sighted. Certainly he had a bleak prescience about his own subsequent career. His later life as marginal farmer, combined with that of Excise officer (a group defined by Dr Johnson in his Dictionary as 'wretches hired by those to whom the excise is paid') were harsh manifestations of economic pressures on him that, at best, restrained his poetic creativity and, at worst, eroded his integrity. Hence this little-known poem:

> Searching auld wives' barrels,
>   Ochon, the day!
> That clarty barm should stain my laurels;
>   But — what'll ye say!
> These muvin' things ca'd wives and weans
> Wad muve the very hearts o' stanes!
> ('An Extempore Effusion on being appointed to the Excise')

The degree to which Burns thought he had prostituted himself is allusively caught in the line 'But — what'll ye say' taken from

Ramsay's fine poem about the dying Edinburgh madam, Lucky Spence.

Burns's guilt, however, is as nothing compared to the subsequent transgressions of Scottish culture which from the early nineteenth century manipulated Burns into an icon of the very values he detested. Despite the acrimonious struggle of MacDiarmid and his generation, this bizarre figure still seems largely to have us in its thrall. Almost two hundred years from the poet's death, however, it is more than possible to argue that Burns's radical analysis of the Scottish situation was correct. First, many of the political, economic elements in which Burns diagnosed Scotland's ills at the end of the eighteenth century seem manifestly present at the end of the twentieth: the corrupting politics and psychology generated by the Union; the degeneration of parliament and of other British civic and fiscal institutions causing increasing disparity between rich and poor lie at the heart of Burns's political vision. Second, in the last three decades there has been a growing body of Scottish literary and historical scholarship which has gone a considerable way to revealing the poet and his age. A wider Scottish culture should be now receptive to these scholarly advances.

And what a truly great *poet* is revealed. He is the great synthesiser of the themes and forms of Scottish and English poetry in the late eighteenth century. With William Blake he is the lyrical and satirical Romantic precursor of the radical Romanticism of Shelley and Burns's fellow Scotsman, Byron. Like his fellow-dissenters he believed that British society was increasingly economically destructive of its common people by the savage labour practices of the new capitalism in agriculture and the early factories. Like them, too, he was a prophet against empire. Not anglophobic, he did, however, believe that England, especially in relation to America, had betrayed her own founding libertarian principles. Scotland he saw as not only a victim of British imperial ambitions but, especially in its degenerate ruling and professional classes, an active agent of them. For him a parcel of rogues had not only signed the Treaty of Union but continued in power. In political terms he thought

Scotland was ruled by Anglicised proconsuls, men notoriously more harsh to their own people. In literary terms sycophancy prevailed: 'Thou Eunuch of language — Thou Englishman who never was south the Tweed'.[21] Power and honour had abdicated as Scotland lived in the shadow of a dominant but degenerate England.

We should, however, leave the last word to the man himself. I choose 'Address of Beelzebub' to end partly because it is relatively unknown but mainly because in its formal skill and political power it brings together so much of what I have been trying to say. It was occasioned by events in the Highlands, prior to the Clearances, when the Highland chiefs were restraining their clansmen from seeking freedom and prosperity in North America. It is an ironic monologue of sustained brilliance in which Burns assumes the voice of an advisory devil to the Scottish aristocracy. It certainly deserves a wider audience:

> Long life, My Lord, an' health be yours,
> Unskaith'd by hunger'd Highlan Boors!
> Lord grant, nae duddie, desp'rate beggar,
> Wi' durk, claymore, or rusty trigger
> May twin auld Scotland o' a life,
> She likes — as lambkins like a knife!
>
> Faith! You and Applecross were right
> To keep the Highlan hounds in sight!
> I doubt na! they wad bid nae better
> Than let them ance out owre the water;
> Then up amang thae lakes an' seas
> They'll mak what rules an' laws they please:
> Some daring Hancock, or a Franklin,
> May set their Highland bluid a-ranklin;
> Some Washington again may head them,
> Or some Montgomery, fearless, lead them;
> Till (God knows what may be effecte,
> When by such heads an' hearts directed)
> Poor, dunghill sons of dirt an' mire,
> May to Patrician rights aspire;
> Nae sage North, now, nor sager Sackville,

To watch an' premier owre the pack vile!
An' whare will ye get Howes an' Clintons
To bring them to a right repentance,
To cowe the rebel generation,
An' save the honor o' the nation?
They! an' be damn'd! what right hae they
To meat, or sleep, or light o'day,
Far less to riches, pow'r, or freedom,
But what your lordships to gie them?

But hear, me lord! Glengary hear!
Your hand's owre light on them, I fear:
Your factors, grieves, trustees an' bailies,
I canna say but they do gailies;
They lay aside a' tender mercies
An' tirl the *Hullions* to the birses;
Yet, while they're only poin'd, and herriet,
They'll keep their stubborn Highlan spirit.
But smash them! crush them a' to *spails*!
An' rot the dyvors i' the jails!
The young dogs, swinge them to the labour,
Let wark an' hunger mak them sober!
The hizzies, if they're aughtlins fawsont,
Let them in Drury Lane be lesson'd!
An' if the wives, an' dirty brats,
Come thiggin at your doors an' yets,
Flaffin wi' duds, an' grey wi' beas'
Frighten awa your deuks an' geese;
Get out a horse-whip, or a jowler,
The langest thong, the fiercest growler,
An' gar the tatter'd gipseys pack
Wi' a' their bastarts on their back!

Go on, my lord! I lang to meet you
An' in my house at hame to greet you;
Wi' common lords ye shanna mingle,
The benmost neuk, beside the ingle
At my right hand, assign'd your seat
'Tween herod's hip, an' polycrate;
Or (if ye on your station tarrow),

Between almagro and pizarro;
A seat, I'm sure ye're weel deservin 't;
An' till ye come — your humble servant,
Beel Zebub *Hell*,
1st June, Anno Mundi 5790

Notes

1. The *Letters of Robert Burns*, ed. J. DeLancey Ferguson; 2nd edn., ed. G. Ross Roy, (Oxford, 1985), I, 97.
2. 'Problems of Nationalism, Identity and Improvement in later Eighteenth-Century Scotland', in *Improvement and Enlightenment: Proceedings of the Scottish Historical Studies Seminar, University of Strathclyde* 1987–88, ed. T.M. Devine, 1989. Smout argues for the inclusion of Burns in this dualistic category.
3. 'Fragment — Epistle from Esopus to Maria', in *Burns Poems and Songs*, ed. James Kinsley (Oxford, 1971), 608.
4. *Letters*, I, 220.
5. For a more detailed account of this, see my 'Versions of Scottish Pastoral: the Literati and the Tradition 1780–1830', in *Order in Space and Society*, ed. T. Markus (Edinburgh, 1982).
6. Introduction to 'Speech at the Burns Festival', *Essays Critical and Imaginative* by Professor Wilson, Vol. III (1867), 212.
7. *Ibid.*, 212–20.
8. William Power, 'The Song of Friendship', in *Robert Burns and Other Essays and Sketches* (London & Glasgow, 1926), 48.
9. Two recent fine studies of this apparent paradox are William Donaldson, *The Jacobite Song: Political Myth and National Identity* (Aberdeen, 1988) and Murray G.H. Pittock, *The Invention of Scotland: The Stuart Myth and the Scottish Identity, 1638 to the Present* (London, 1991).
10. William Power, 'Robert Burns', *op. cit.* 7–9.
11. 'Burns and Holy Willie', in *Edwin Muir: Uncollected Scottish Criticism*, ed. A. Noble (London & New York, 1982), 189–92.
12. 'The Burns Cult', *Hugh MacDiarmid: Selected Prose*, ed. A. Riach (Manchester, 1992), 103–5.
13. See for a full account of the Sterne connection K.G. Simpson's *The Protean Scot: The Crisis of Identity in Eighteenth-Century Scottish Literature* (Aberdeen, 1988).

14. Such references to *Othello* can be seen in *Letters*, I, 78, 105, 204, 216, 257.

15. *Letters*, II, 46.

16. *Letters*, I, 124–5.

17. *Letters*, I, 151.

18. *The Poems and Songs of Robert Burns*, ed. Kinsley, III, 977–8.

19. E.P. Thompson, 'Patricians and Plebs', *Customs in Common* (London, 1991).

20. *Letters*, I, 83.

21. *Letters*, II, 93.

10
Burns's Songs: A Singer's View

Jo Miller

In the original presentation of this essay the musical examples were sung. Although they are shown here on the page, I hope readers will try singing the songs for themselves. The main source for the examples is James Kinsley's edition, and in common with the most recent edition of Burns's songs I have tried to present versions in a form I have found to be singable.[1]

The intention here is to offer a personal choice of Burns's songs which I enjoy performing, and some comments on his activities as a songmaker. Although there has been growing consideration of the music of the songs, and its effect in combination with the texts,[2] there has been little exploration of how the songs (and indeed the poems) are performed: when, where and how do people sing them, and why? The views of musicians and their audiences provide invaluable information about why Burns's songs have the appeal they do. I look forward to further investigation in this area.[3]

The handful of Burns's songs heard at Burns Suppers is only the tip of an iceberg which broadens into a rich and rewarding repertoire of items by, or attributed to, Burns. As musicians get to know this repertoire they are led into an even greater storehouse of traditional songs and tunes, many current from Burns's time to the present day, kept alive in parallel musical activities like the fiddle and song traditions found throughout Scotland.

Alongside the song corpus itself, we should note the range of styles and contexts for performances of Burns's songs: from Burns Suppers to concert recitals and competitions; from arrangements with guitar and synthesiser to the domestic sing-song. Of course, something of this variety was also true in Burns's own lifetime: the musical melting-pot of eighteenth-century Scotland had room for him in the pubs of town and country amongst fiddle music and bawdry, but also in the drawing-rooms of the gentry.

Burns was intensely interested in discovering traditional songs and gathering information on their origin and authorship. His work for the *Scots Musical Museum* allowed him full rein here:

> I have been absolutely crazed about it [*SMM*], collecting old stanzas, and every information numbering respecting their origin, authors, &c. This last is but a very fragment business . . . a small account will be given of the Authors, particularly to preserve those of latter times . . .
>
> I have collected, begg'd, borrow'd and stolen all the songs I could meet with.[4]

Burns had access to all kinds of material, from chapbook songs and art songs to orally transmitted ballads and bawdry, and in order to learn new material he had to get right in among it. A twentieth-century concept in the disciplines of anthropology and ethnomusicology is that of 'participant observation': taking part in and becoming a student of a culture in order to learn about it, instead of remaining a more detached observer. This term well describes Burns: it is clear he was an active and conscious collector of traditional items, although we know little about his techniques apart from one or two glimpses in his letters. Mary Ellen Brown suggests much material was probably acquired informally and in company.[5] He is not the only source for much of the material he collected,[6] but he is an important one.

Singers who have tried a few Burns songs will quickly discover they can be technically challenging, with their wide ranges and large intervals.[7] As well as Burns's own experience of popular songs and tunes, he also knew contemporary composers and their work.[8] Many of the airs chosen for the *Scots Musical Museum* were derived from settings for instruments (mainly fiddle) rather than voice, and often have wider ranges and intervallic leaps easier to play than sing.

Many of the melodies are those of dance music — strathspeys, jigs and reels — which can be exhilarating to sing, although it may take a bit of practice to find the best version. I begin my own selection here with a well-known strathspey for which Burns made his own lyrics. **'Whistle o'er the lave o't'** [example 1] is known today as an instrumental tune, through Burns's texts (it also appears as 'Let me ryke up to dight that tear' in 'Love and Liberty — A Cantata'), and in traditional songs probably related to the original song Burns would have heard. Burns's text runs:

Example 1

First when Maggy was my care
Heaven, I thought, was in her air;
Now we're married — spier nae mair —
Whistle o'er the lave o't.

Meg was meek, and Meg was mild,
Sweet and harmless as a child —
Wiser men than me's beguil'd;
Whistle o'er the lave o't . . .

We know it was sung before this[9] — and more recently traditional versions have been recorded in Shetland, such as this one from John Irvine in 1959, which uses only the first part of the tune:

Minnie put me tae the well
Better she wad geen hersel
The bottom o the daffock fell
Hey tupsalteerie O.

Another verse is quoted as often following this:

My mother sent me tae the sea
For to gather mussels three
A sailor lad fell in with me
Whistle o'er the lave o't.[10]

One song in my own repertoire that's seldom heard is '**The rantin dog, the Daddie o't**', which uses a woman's voice. Two similar reel tunes are associated with this. It appears twice in the *Scots Musical Museum*, to both '**The East Neuk o Fife**' (no.277) [example 2a], and '**Whar'll bonny Annie lie**' (no.324) [example 2b]:

Example 2a

Example 2b

> O wha ma babie clouts will buy,
> Wha will tent me when I cry,
> Wha will kiss me where I lie?
> The rantin dog, the daddie o't.
>
> O wha will own he did the faut,
> Wha will buy the groanin maut,
> Wha will tell me how tae ca't?
> The rantin dog, the daddie o't.
>
> When I mount the creepie chair,
> Wha will sit beside me there?
> Gie me Rob, I'll seek nae mair
> The rantin dog, the daddie o't.

> O wha will crack tae me my lane,
> Wha will mak me fidgin fain,
> Wha will kiss me ower again?
> The rantin dog, the daddie o't.

There is a modern setting of this text by the much-neglected Scottish composer Francis George Scott (1880–1958),[11] who set the work of Burns, MacDiarmid, and other Scots poets, for voice and piano. I enjoy singing some of the composer's songs unaccompanied, as in this case. Scott's is a gentler melody [example 3] which brings out aspects of the text which are less evident when sung to the reel tunes. Donald Low says the song conveys 'passion . . . along with humorous acceptance'.[12] It is difficult to feel this about Scott's tune, which draws out and lingers on the last words of each line ('buy', 'cry', 'lie', etc.), and the feelings I have while singing '**O wha ma babie clouts will buy**?' to this melody are more complex than there is time for in the reel versions. They includes longing and loneliness as well as passion.

Example 3

One group of Burns's songs which have been increasingly heard in public recently are the bawdy songs (popular choices by women singers include '**Dainty Davie**' and '**John Anderson my Jo**'), only recently gathered together for consideration alongside the rest of Burns's songs in Donald Low's extremely usable edition.[13] One of my favourites is '**Greensleeves**' [example 4], to a popular tune of the day,[14] Elizabethan in origin, but still sung today:

Example 4

Green sleeves and tartan ties
Mark my truelove where she lies;
I'll be at her or she rise,
My fiddle and I thegither.

Be it by the chrystal burn,
Be it by the milk-white thorn,
I shall rouse her in the morn,
My fiddle and I thegither.

'**The Bob o Dumblane**' [example 5] I like for its tune — a jig — and the feel of the words rolling around on the tongue. It didn't appear in the *Scots Musical Museum*, although it was submitted:[15]

Example 5

Lassie, lend me your braw hemp-heckle,
And I'll lend you my thripplin kame:
My heckle is broken, it canna be gotten,
And we'll gae dance the Bob o' Dumblane.

Twa gaed to the wood, to the wood, to the wood,
Twa gaed to the wood, three cam hame:
An't be na weel bobbit, weel bobbit, weel bobbit,
An't be na weel bobbit, we'll bob it again.

Cedric Thorpe Davie, twentieth-century Scottish composer and writer on Scottish music generally, suggests three standpoints from which to study song: textual, musical, and the matching of the two elements.[16] He neglects, however, the dimensions of how singers feel and perform songs, and how they are received. In other words, what appeals to musicians and audience *in performance* may differ from what appears on the page (a point already emphasised in my introduction). '**The Winter it is Past**' is another favourite of mine which was probably adapted from an existing song.[17] Thorpe Davie thought this a disappointing specimen, although he liked the air. I find '**The Winter it is Past**' a satisfying song to sing, and I know other singers with whom it is a favourite. Any 'strained metaphors and . . . infelicitously expressed clichés'[18] in the text are more than compensated for when the song is sung with commitment. Similarly, I feel Thorpe Davie misjudges the earlier of the two versions of '**Ca' the Yowes**' when he says 'I take it that nowadays nobody would want to sing the earlier words . . . in preference to the version written some seven years later'.[19] I have heard several excellent performances of the first version,[20] although these are fairly recent, and Thorpe Davie may well never have heard it sung. If, as seems likely, this item is based more closely on a traditional song,[21] then we should not be surprised if it has some appeal amongst singers of that genre. It seems to me to have a more personal voice than the later version, and engages us more closely with the thoughts and dialogue of the courting couple in working out their relationship.

Another song seldom sung is the beautiful '**Jamie come try me**' (example 6), which is a simple but passionate plea to be loved. Burns says, 'This air is [James] Oswald's; the song mine'.[22] James Dick, the first twentieth-century editor of, and commentator on, Burns's songs, comments, 'The tune is interesting, but its compass is too great for ordinary voices'.[23] What is an 'ordinary voice', and is Dick's claim a reason not to sing such a wonderful song? '**Jamie come try me**' is discussed in some detail by Catarina Ericson-Roos,[24] who notes that the large melodic range parallels the large emotional range of a text whose potential may not be obvious on the page, but which comes to life as soon as one tries to sing it. The song certainly has a wide range (an octave plus a sixth) and is tricky to sing, but the physical effort to do so itself contributes to the feeling, requiring full concentration and commitment from the singer. Another option is to adapt this tune, keeping its character while reducing the high register hazards:[25]

Example 6

Jamie come try me,
Jamie come try me,
If thou would win my love
Jamie come try me.

If thou should ask my love,
Could I deny thee?
If thou would win my love,
Jamie come try me.

If thou should kiss me, love,
Wha could espy thee?
If thou wad be my love,
Jamie come try me.

Burns, as we have seen, was keen to preserve and pass on anything he saw as a good song. We have another example of traditional songs living on alongside substitute texts in the satirical Jacobite song **'Sow's Tail tae Geordie'**, referring to the love life of George I. The words were regarded as strong stuff for the *Scots Musical Museum*, so Burns wrote the following [example 7]:

Example 7

HE:
O Philly happy be that day
When roving through the gather'd hay
My youthfu' heart was stown away
And by thy charms, my Philly.

SHE:
O Willy, ay I bless the grove
Where first I own'd my maiden love
Whilst thou did pledge the Powers above
To be my ain dear Willy . . .

This tune also exists as novelty or 'special effects' fiddle piece (other popular examples include '**The Hen's March to the Midden**' and '**The Four Poster Bed**') with variations, the final one involving scraping the bow on the fiddle to suggest a pig squeaking.[26] A version of the original song was noted by North-East collectors Gavin Greig and James Duncan around the turn of the century [example 8].[27] It has great fire in its plain-speaking text and swaggering jig tune, complete with a grumphing soo later in the song:

Example 8

O Geordie's noo come here aboot,
O wae be on his sulky snoot,
A Pawky soo has foun' him oot
An turned her tail tae Geordie.

> The soo's tail tull him yet,
> The soo's birse will kill him yet,
> The soo's tail tull him yet,
> The soo's tail tae Geordie . . .

Although Burns is often portrayed as someone with an active interest in the local, national and international politics of his day, this is seldom fully reflected in the songs most people choose to sing. Some of the political songs like the election ballads are ephemeral, with their treatment of very specific contemporary events. Others, whose themes are still with us, may seem too close for comfort: my singing of '**Such a Parcel of Rogues in a Nation**', for instance, at a Burns Supper, once drew the comment 'that was very nice dear, but that's no' Burns!' Is this simply ignorance, or an unwillingness to be challenged by the breadth of subject matter treated in all Burns's songs?

The *Scots Musical Museum* is still an important song collection today: due to Burns's valuing of the tunes, their names and the need to record them, we have a book which is, as he and Johnson hoped, representative of a wider repertoire of Scots song. Between them they laid many clues regarding songs before and since their time which we can follow up today. Let me conclude with an example from recent tradition. The *Scots Musical Museum* ends with Burns's version of '**Goodnight and joy be wi' you a'**'[example 9], a parting song whose tune has carried its fair share of texts, including one by James Hogg.[28] The tune appears in the Skene manuscript (1620s) as 'Goodnight and God be with you'. Burns asked Johnson to print

Example 9

the old words, followed by his own masonic text ('Adieu! a heart-warm, fond adieu').[29] The traditional verse runs:

> This night is my departing night,
> The morn's the day I maun awa'.
> There's no a friend or foe o mine
> But wishes that I were awa'.
> What I hae done for lack o wit
> I never never can reca'.
> I trust ye're a'my friends as yet,
> Gude night and joy be wi you a' . . .

The tune was employed once more to accompany a poem by Dumfriesshire poet Thomas Cunningham, brother of poet Allan Cunningham. Published in various forms in the nineteenth century, '**Amang the Hills o Gallowa**' [example 10] was taken up as song, and sung to me some years ago in Galloway. The singer was retired shepherd and fiddler Robbie Murray (1907–87) of the Forrest Glen near Dalry, and he took great delight in explaining to me the meanings of 'they aul' words that naebody kens nooadays'. '**Amang the Hills o Gallowa**' reminds us that the creative engagement Burns enjoyed with the oral and the literary environments of his time is still fruitful territory today. Here is a tune from a seventeenth and eighteenth century song, reworked by Burns and others, used to carry a nineteenth century sentimental verse of rural courtship. In the light of what we know about our song tradition, we should not be surprised to find it behaving like a traditional song once more in the late twentieth century:

Example 10

'Amang yon birks sae blythe an gay
I met my Julia hameward gaun.
The linties chauntit on the spray,
The lammies loupit on the lawn.
On ilka howm the swaird wis mawn,
The braes wi' gowans buskit braw,
An' gloamin's plaid o'grey wis thrawn
Oot ower the hills o'Gallowa.

Wi' music wild the woodlands rang
An' fragrance wing'd alang the lea
As doon we sat the flooers amang
Upon the banks o stately Dee.
My Julia's arms encircled me
An' saftly slade the hours awa'
Till dawin coost a glimmerin' ee
Upon the hills o Gallowa.

It isna owsen, sheep an kye,
It isna gowd, it isna gear
This lifted ee wad hae, quoth I,
The warld's drumlie gloom to cheer,
But gie tae me my Julia dear,
Ye powers wha rowe this yirthen ba',
An O! sae blythe thro' life I'll steer
Amang the hills o Gallowa.

When gloamin dauners up the hill
An oor gudeman ca's hame the yowes,
Wi' her I'll trace the mossy rill
That o'er the muir meand'ring rowes
Or tint amang the scroggy knowes
My birken pipe I'll sweetly blaw
An' sing the streams, the straths an' howes,
The hills an' dales o Gallowa.

An' when auld Scotland's heathy hills,
Her rural nymphs an' jovial swains,
Her flowery wilds an' wimplin' rills
Awake nae mair my cantie strain,
Where frien'ship dwells an' freedom reigns,

Where heather blooms an' maircocks craw,
Gae dig my grave an' lay my banes
Amang the hills o Gallowa.

Notes

1. James Kinsley (ed.), *The Poems and Songs of Robert Burns*, (3 vols., Oxford, 1968); and for recent comments on singable versions of the tunes, see David Johnson, 'Note on the Music', in Donald Low (ed.), *The Song of Robert Burns* (London, 1993), xi.
2. Recent scholarship includes Cedric Thorpe Davie, 'Robert Burns, Writer of Songs', in Donald Low (ed.), *Critical Essays on Robert Burns* (London, 1975), 157–85; Catarina Ericson-Roos, *The Songs of Robert Burns — A study of the Unity of Poetry and Music* (Uppsala, 1977); Mary Ellen Brown, *Burns and Tradition* (London, 1984), ch. 4; John Purser, *Scotland's Music* (Edinburgh, 1992) XV; and Peter Davidson, 'Song Arrangements', appendix 1 in Low (1993), 931–48.
3. Brown (1984) gives some consideration to Burns's audiences, but these remain a fruitful and relatively untapped source of information.
4. J. DeLancey Ferguson & G. Ross Roy (eds.), *The Letters of Robert Burns*, vols. I & II (Oxford, 1985) (henceforth *Letters*), 147, 153A, I 168, 177.
5. Brown (1984), 30. The author discusses what can be ascertained of Burns's collecting technique, and quotes Letters 145, 193, 203, 598 as examples (Brown, 151, note 9).
6. For examples of other contemporary collections and their contents, see Thomas Crawford, *Society and the Lyric* (Edinburgh, 1979), especially ch 1, and the same author's 'Lowland Song and Popular Tradition in the Eighteenth Century', in Andrew Hook (ed.), *The History of Scottish Literature*, Vol. 2, 1660–1800 (Aberdeen, 1987), 123–38. Eighteenth-century tune collections are discussed by David Johnson in *Music and Society in Lowland Scotland in the Eighteenth Century* (Oxford, 1972) and *Scottish Fiddle Music in the Eighteenth Century* (Edinburgh, 1984).
7. A count of items in Low (1993) shows that 88 per cent have a range of an octave to an octave plus a fifth. The remainder are divided equally between ranges below and above this. Intervals of

sixths and octaves are common, and sevenths and ninths not difficult to find.

8. James C. Dick, *The Songs of Robert Burns, Now First Printed with the Melodies for which they were Written* (London, 1903, repr. 1962), ix. Dick also discusses Burns's general musicianship.

9. David Herd, *Ancient and Modern Scottish Songs* 1776, reprinted (2 vols.) 1869, 1973, II, 208.

10. Scottish Tradition 9, *The Fiddler and His Art* (School of Scottish Studies/Tangent Records TNGM 141, 1988), booklet 6–7 (ed. Peter Cooke).

11. In Francis George Scott, *Scottish Lyrics Set to Music* book 5 (low voice) (Bayley & Ferguson 1939). Thanks to Lillias Scott-Forbes for permission to use this example. For other information on Scott, see Maurice Lindsay, *Francis George Scott and the Scottish Renaissance* (Edinburgh, 1980) and Purser (1992), 248–50.

12. Low (1975), 9.

13. Low (1993).

14. David Johnson (1984), 20.

15. Letter 684, *Letters*, II, 368.

16. Thorpe Davie, in Low (1975), 164.

17. Low (1993), 283 (notes).

18. Thorpe Davie, in Low (1975), 171–2.

19. *Ibid.*, 170.

20. For a particularly imaginative interpretation, see Sileas: *Beating Harps* (Green Linnet Records SIF 1089).

21. Low (1993), 218 (notes).

22. Robert Burns, *Notes on Scottish Song* (ed. James C. Dick) (1908, repr. 1962).

23. Dick (1903), 390.

24. Ericson-Roos (1977), 44–6, 131, 133–5.

25. See Jean Redpath's version of the song, in *The Songs of Robert Burns*, vol. 6. (Greentrax TRAX 005S).

26. Johnson (1984), 239–43.

27. P. Shuldham-Shaw & E.B. Lyle (eds.), *The Greig-Duncan Folksong Collection* (Aberdeen, 1981), vol. I, 325 (song no. 121).

28. Hogg's version appears in R.A. Smith's *Scottish Minstrel* (Edinburgh, 1821–4), vol. VI. The tune, under the title 'Goodnight and God be with you', is in the Skene MS (1620s).

29. Letter 684, *Letters*, II, 370.

30. In chapbook printed in Stirling by W. MacNie in 1826 (Mitchell Library Collection, 668: 76168, 893245). Also in Malcolm Harper (ed.), *The Bards of Galloway* (Dalbeattie) 1889), where the editor says, 'Several of his [Thomas Cunningham's] songs have attained great popularity: "The Hills of Gallowa"' was the great song of the day, and is still well known in the South of Scotland' (251). A version is also in P. Shuldham Shaw & E.B. Lyle (eds.), *The Greig-Duncan Folksong Collection* (1987), vol. III, 307–8 (song no. 504). For discussion of Robbie Murray's repertoire and other information on local music, see Josephine L. Miller, 'Traditions of Music Making in the Glenkens, Galloway' (unpublished M. Litt. thesis, Edinburgh University, 1986).

11
Supperman: Televising Burns

Donny O'Rourke

This "paper" is a dickeyed up and pared down conflation of two talks delivered two years apart; the first a selective tour of the Burns archive, the second, a more personal rumination based upon my own work as a producer and director of Burns programmes. Both benefited from illustrative video clips. You probably had to be there . . .

Since most of you weren't, the (post) script will have to suffice. But first, the disclaimers: I'm not an expert; like all TV producers, I'm a mountebank to trade; nor am I an academic. My licence to pontificate is based only on a few TV programmes and the deep love of Scottish culture and Burns's place within it, that I hope my work reveals. But my enthusiasm for Burns is selective. So, to prevent anyone wasting valuable time, I should point out right away that my idea of an apt celebration of Burns Night is not a room full of men making whoopee over the equivalent of a cultural kissogram. If you like that, you won't like this. The approach here is partial in more ways than one.

In fact, Burns is joyously and variously celebrated far beyond such stereotyped and increasingly discredited confines: at suppers for women, at Gay gatherings, at get togethers where the poetry and the poet are enjoyed and remembered with sincere, unstilted affection. I'd like to think that over the last decade or so, television has not only reflected this change of emphasis, but helped bring it about.

In the beginning, was the Bard. From the outset, BBC Scotland and, later, Scottish Television wanted 'Rabbie' on their team. The inaugural broadcasts by both organisations featured well-known Burns songs rendered in the rather corseted style then prevailing. New Year shows also used Burns; and not just Auld Lang Syne. BBC and STV transmitted

Burns programmes on the first applicable January 25th after operations commenced in Scotland.

Scottish Television's debut, in 1958, was typical of the time. *O A' The Airts*, 'a portrait of Ayr and its people', ran sub-Griersonian shots of local places and faces over conventional (and usually abridged) versions of appropriate songs, poems and lushly orchestrated tunes. There is no commentary. And lest we are tempted to patronise the past, judging its shaky black and white footage in smug moral monochrome, it should be pointed out that given the mores and broadcast conventions of the day, it was an honest wee programme entertaining enough in its way. It really is too easy to sneer, deploying quips and clips, to indulge a talent to accuse. The station's 1962 effort did have a commentary and indeed an in-vision presenter teeing up the poems and songs in tones of sonorous sentimentality.

Much more than the mannered performance style preferred in such programmes, it was these seemingly authoritative and invariably florid interpolations that betrayed Burns in programme after programme until well into the seventies. That the emphasis was on the romantic Rabbie is unsurprising and would matter less in a country and culture with a larger selection of literary heroes to drink to. Although it's splendid that we do celebrate a national bard, given Burns's disproportionate and distorting place in the panoply, a great opportunity to delve deeper into our poet, and ourselves, kept on being missed.

Two examples of this. *Sweetly Played in Tune*, from 1984, was a big, showbizzy and rather tacky studio programme with the magnificent, but on that occasion somewhat somnolent, Andrew Cruickshank intoning the autocued pieties between pseudo-operatic 'numbers'. Looked back at, the whole venture teeters precariously, and hilariously, on the brink of camp. And all in colour too, for by then tartan spotters could indulge themselves to the full. This programme was the last of its kind. By the early eighties, other ways of presenting and re-presenting Burns's songs were edging this kind of thing off the screen. I think, though, of the seventies as the mixed-fibre ascendancy – all full-flowing, nip-waisted, tulip-collared, sorbet-shaded, nylon blouses; and that was only the baritones.

When that good-looking and mellifluous baritone, Peter Morrison, wasn't looking silly in a studio, he was often to be found, come January 25, looking silly (and chilly) in one tenuously relevant beauty spot or another.

Billy Connolly's skit on marching through the heather (a physical impossibility) is perhaps the funniest rebuttal of the Bens and Glens approach: not only in Burns programming, TV's bathetic fallacy.

The most significant development in Burns programming, however, wasn't a tendency, or an approach, it was a man. Previously, the Bardolators had no living image on which to focus their devotion. BC, that is. Before Cairney. Many Scots still believe John Cairney to be Robert Burns. Had Tom Wright had his way and secured the television role for his first choice in the theatre, Maurice Roeves, it would all have been very different. *There Was a Man* established John Cairney as Rabbie's representative on earth, eradicating the Nasmyth and other portraits with a single toss of his pony-tailed head. I don't doubt that in the original Traverse production Cairney's original conception of the character had its points, but on television feeling gave way to sentimentality, and Burns the man to Cairney the thespian. It will be a generation or two before Cairney's image stops being superimposed on that of Burns.

Television has always been more interested in the songs than in the poems and in this I don't think is very different from most of its viewers. Although the folk revival almost exactly coincided with the coming of television and of programmes about Scotland's greatest maker and mender of songs, Robert Burns, art-song settings predominated; the formal was normal. Only occasionally until the early eighties did the kind of folksong approach that Burns himself would have employed get anything like a regular look-in. Indeed not content with salon settings, when Scottish Television felt like a change for Burns Night in 1979 they aimed higher, not lower, commissioning from Peter Ebert and Scottish Opera a canty and kenspeckle production of Cedric Thorpe Davie's *Life and Liberty*, these Jolly Beggars, (Linda Ormiston and Bill McCue among them), typifying the classical style.

As the Corries and other folk acts became more popular throughout the sixties and seventies, achieving series of their own and high viewing figures to go with them, their influence began to be felt in some Burns programmes, particularly those of the BBC.

Whereas Scottish Television tended towards Light Entertainment in this period (the hey, or should that be hay-day of Thingummyjig), the Beeb flirted with folk, though folk mostly of the smoothed-out and broken-in sort popularised by Alistair McDonald and Jimmie MacGregor. Engagingly tuneful, agreeably accompanied, and always performed with conviction and verve, these folk settings began to turn up alongside classical settings in more and more programmes, influencing in their turn the next wave of folk performers whose singing drew more on primary sources than on commercial artistes such as the McCalmans.

The benchmark for the performance of Burns's songs contined to be 'classical', however, with polite condescension often characterising the reaction of the Burns establishment, and the general viewer conditioned by years of besporraned *bel canto* to regard folk music as being rather beneath both Burns and his admirers. Falsified records continued to sell well.

It is impossible to separate out wider changes in popular music and public tastes from those affecting Burns's songs in particular. The same hunger for a real, honest, sophisticatedly simple Scottish music that had roots in the past and relevance in the present increased the appetite for authentic-sounding Burns as well as the market for Silly Wizard, Dougie MacLean, Rod Paterson, Dick Gaughan, and older artists such as Archie Fisher whose time had finally come and with whose tastes the public was beginning to catch up.

Leaving aside the occasional presence of folk music on Burns Night, two more systematic assaults on the prevailing culture (or kilture) began to assert themselves. As more and more singers and groups specialising in folk-inflected Burns began to dominate a 'scene', previously presided over by the Corries and their cultural kin, TV producers saw advantages in basing programmes on that sort of music rather than the older norms. The orthodoxy could be seen to be shifting. And because television is a mass medium artistically and commercially, responsive to and influenced by popular taste, this change gathered momentum quite quickly. It is also true that as my generation of producers came into its own, the music we had grown up with – a music much influenced by Planxty and other innovative Irish bands of the seventies – came to represent our norm. Since 1984, there have been very few Burns programmes of the haggis, heather and hokum sort; and when Peter Morrison does turn up, it is usually in this new context with his performance style being judged against a non 'classical' standard.

Jean Redpath's artistry gracefully encompasses both folk club and salon. Her renditions of Haydn's Burns settings straddle the frontier between art song and folk music in just the way that Burns himself almost certainly did (a manoeuvre requiring less dexterity then than in the more recent past although we are all post-modern boundary busters now . . .) These, however, have received less notice than her extraordinary collaboration with the American composer, Serge Hovey.

Almost completely incapacitated physically, Hovey continued to work until his death on his heroic attempt to rediscover and arrange the original tunes for the poet's entire *oeuvre*. The generic tension between Redpath's traditional way of singing the songs, and the composer's Bartokian dissonances, divided listeners. No-one failed to appreciate the musicological ambition of the venture; to some, however, the chamber settings overwhelmed the songs. What everyone agreed upon, however, was the enormous importance of having, at last, first (and in many instances subsequent and therefore comparable and contrastable) versions of the songs. It is not, I think, to overstate the case to compare Hovey and Redpath's efforts with those of Johnson and Thomson. Two television programmes resulted from the project: Tim Neat's painterly and poignant film, *The Tree of Liberty*; and a Scottish Television programme, the execrably entitled *In Search of the Auld Sangs*. Despite the title, the STV programme managed to bring off a sparky and illuminating rapport between Jean Redpath and Scottish Opera's then newly appointed music director, John Mauceri. I should declare an interest here, since I was associated with the show, but director

Ross Wilson made the most of the culture shock tactic of harnessing the erudite and urbane New Yorker and the passionate and earthy Fifer. It complemented, and added to, Tim Neat's more substantial and considered film. Simple, compassionate (though not explicitly passionate), *The Tree of Liberty* is one of the most profound and important Burns programmes ever broadcast.

Once again, though, it was the music that was being celebrated. When plausible and appropriately rendered songs combine with narrative fluency and producerial grip, you get programmes like William McIlvanney's admirable retracing of Nicol and Burns's hoofprints in the television film Keith Alexander made for BBC Scotland in 1988 — another highlight in an area of broadcasting that should have more to be proud of.

The traditional Burns Supper itself, of course, offers just the variety and poetic range that many of the programmes lacked. True, it's the same few party-piece poems that tend to feature (cue nightshirt and 'Holy Willie's Prayer') but producers have sought to vary the format by filming Burns Suppers in the USSR or Canada or by finding an angle such as the fact that the Scots-American hostage Tom Sutherland had consoled himself in Beirut by reciting Burns. Burns in Beirut was an old-fashioned supper, lent new zest by an irresistible human interest story – a programme less about the Bard than the Hostage.

George Cathro's *That*, for BBC Scotland, had me feeling really envious. He got a selection of Scots pop stars to sing Burns in a series of polished pop videos. Accurate, informative captions conveyed useful information. Interviews with the stars were interspersed with the performances, and although one or two of them seemed to be straining a little to convince us of any deep or abiding interest in Burns, it was nonetheless comforting to hear so many successful young musicians affirming their Scottishness and the importance of national expression through traditional music.

My own work on Burns has mostly been more interesting (if it's been interesting at all) for its content than for its style; style costs money, and although local production has expanded enormously and improved in quality these have been lean times in the world of commercial television, at least as far as arts programmes are concerned. Frustratingly, most Burns programmes stay local because the ITV network, BBC London and Channel 4 believe Burns to be a parochial ploughman who couldn't be bothered to speak English. They would rather commission and subtitle a documentary about Lorca, a poet I love, than even think about getting to grips with Burns.

Everything I have tried to do in Burns programming flows from the same precepts and prejudices that have been implicit throughout this essay. The Redpath–Mauceri programme I have already mentioned, and Bob Clyde and Ross Wilson should take most of the credit for that. *Butterstone Burns* (1988) simply assembled a cast of leading Scottish folk musicians at Dougie MacLean's home in Dunkeld and encouraged them to perform various songs in various permutations.

I recall with especial fondness Cilla Fisher's account of the original, bawdy version of 'John Anderson' and Rod Paterson's tilt at 'Willie Wastle' with Dougie MacLean on didgeridoo, circular breathing and all. Michael Marra made a smoky, bluesy pass at 'Ae Fond Kiss'; Archie Fisher (*sans pareil*, the finest phraser in Scotland) let his burring bass voice and rippling guitar read us 'O a' the airts' (in a Canadian version minus the tune's second part), and Dougie MacLean got right to the modal heart of 'It Was A' For Our Rightful King'.

Next came a special edition of Scottish Television's arts magazine programme, *NB*. Alistair Scott and myself had started the show in 1989 and we worked together on a Burns 'special' which had some fine performances from Billy Ross among others and (even if I say so myself) some nice wee touches which would really have to be seen to be appreciated.

Its importance (again, if it had any) was that it tried to get serious, thoughtful, unhackneyed ideas across to a very large general audience. Emboldened by the fact that it seemed to work, my next Burns venture was a programme entitled *Supperman*, which set out, a touch self-consciously, to challenge some of the more manifest Burns Supper absurdities. In retrospect, it was akin to taking a sledgehammer to a pistachio nut, but o what fun it was to hear the crack! The 'crack', in fact, was excellent. Our gimmick was a sort of Mad Max, post-holocaust supper in a disused cheesemarket in Glasgow. It was so cold, plumes of frost accompanied the singers like cartoon voice bubbles. And what singers! Dick Gaughan, Andy M. Stewart, Dougie MacLean again, Gerda Stevenson. Dick's Dylanesque, introspective and slightly rearranged reading of 'Afton Water' had the crew mesmerised (a harder feat to pull off than you might think). Andy Byatt and Finlay Welsh did readings. It attracted hate mail on about the scale of a Blue Peter Appeal. Very gratifying; RB would surely have approved.

By this time, I was feeling in strong need of a break from Burns. To some extent this was personal: I reckoned I'd said what I most wanted to say. But I believed then, and believe now, that Burns can harmfully distort the balance in the broadcasting ecology. So few arts programmes get made at all, a tiny proportion of those are about poets, and very few of those poets aren't Robert Burns – good arguments, it seems to me, for letting the field lie fallow now and again.

And that's precisely what I persuaded Scottish Television to do the next year (1991). In *New Acquaintance*, the ghost of Burns appears at the start of the programme to urge, in a parody of Standard Habbie, which I don't intend to embarrass myself by quoting, that heed be taken of living bards. Which naturally enough the programme proceeded to do, offering the viewer verse videos from Robert Crawford, Ron Butlin, Tom Leonard, Kathleen Jamie and other contemporary Scottish poets. Dave Whyte, Rod Paterson and others sang settings of modern Scots poetry too. Bits of it were a bit too twee, I fear, but James MacMillan singing his own setting of Soutar's 'The Tryst' was beautiful to listen to, however corny my cackhanded visuals. I'd originally wanted to call the show *Bard Barred*, but found people (no wonder) unresponsive. I felt lucky enough to be making a poetry programme at all. It taught me many lessons, not least that not all poets are the best readers of their own verse.

I still feel that much of what I have any realistic hope of persuading Scottish Television to pay for has been done. It's difficult also to square some of my enthusiasms with the commercial imperatives of a company of necessity as committed to making money as to making programmes (though uniquely among Thatcher-traumatised ITV franchise holders, it retains a strong sense of cultural and national responsibility).

There are lots of 'Burns and . . .' programmes to be made: Burns and Fergusson; Burns and Boswell; Burns and Scott; Burns and Keats. Paul Muldoon's imaginative 'what if', in sending Southey and Coleridge to America, could be applied to Burns's near-thing in the Indies. George Rosie has recently spent a lot of time in Hollywood working on *Burns the Musical* for Gene Kelly; a film, one imagines, that ought to be called *Brig o' Doon*. Catherine Carswell's '30s biography spent too long out of fashion and print until it was reissued by Canongate in 1991. Dramatically written in its own right, it would form the basis for an outstanding screenplay.

The orthodoxy *has* changed. The Burns who believed his songs to be 'both beyond and above price', the Burns who could compose only once he had mastered a song in his own singing, that Burns can now be heard on television. The producers of Burns programmes can help ensure that Burns Night is more than just a sing-song, that Burns is more than the small onion produced annually from the nation's sporran to induce a seasonal greet. We have to take the con out of the icon, yes, but we also have to be true to the sheer complexity of an intricate heart and mind: Robert, Robin, Rob Mossgiel, Rab, Sylvander; not the simplistic, reductive, myth-misted 'Rabbie' but multiple Burns. That old Scottish saying, 'I canny place him', comes to mind. We need to place Burns in his historical and cultural context. We have to stop invoking his eloquent and safely posthumous shade to advocate or endorse policies he would never have supported. If I were compiling my ideal Burns programme from the archives, its range would be very wide, its editorial policy generous and inclusive. Communicado's revisionist and compelling multi-media ensemble piece *Jock Tamson's Bairns* would be there. So would an extract from David Hayman's Citizens' production of Joe Corrie's Burns play. It would have satire and social poetry in it as well as songs. But there would be songs sung in every conceivable style: art song, jazz, pop, classical, folk – the whole gamut. We'd hear Dietrich Fischer Diskau singing Burns as set by Beethoven (showing him to be the equal of Goethe in lieder). One could contrast the beauty of 'A Red, Red Rose' as performed by Kenneth McKellar, Joseph Hyslop, Jean Redpath (using the original tune), Pat Kane, Bobby Eaglesham and the late Ian Charleson – masterpieces every one.

Not all of my attempts at Burns programming have worked out satisfactorily. I have done my time on television's cutty stool. I hope the line I have taken in this paper doesn't seem self-righteous, or sanctimonious. The new orthodoxy must not become a tyranny in its turn. I enjoy Burns in many ways through the talents of many performers as well as privately on the page or singing his songs with friends.

I said this would be partial. I wish in respect of the material reviewed it were less so: nothing from Grampian or Border, less from the BBC than I'd have liked to look at. Astonishingly, a fair amount of Scottish Television's archive ended up in a skip, sometime in the seventies – unpardonable neglect. There is an enormous amount of material, however; and not just on TV. I do think that a researcher with a media studies background and methodology would find a howk through the complete trove of programmes worthwhile. I look forward to reading the ensuing paper in a future compilation of *Burns Now*.

12
Some Thoughts of Murdo

Iain Crichton Smith

Chairperson, ladies and gentlemen, and may I say how glad I am to see so many smiling poetic faces gathered here in honour of the Bard, I wish to say a few words anent Robert Burns. Last year in this very place we had a rather interesting disquisition on Burns and the Silicon Chip, and beforehand we had a talk on 'If Burns were alive today how old would he be?' Tonight I am going to talk about Burns and the Humble Mouse. We have all met the mouse at some time or another. Sometimes we see it in our houses and we do not welcome it, indeed we do not welcome the mouse. For we think of it as a pest, and we do not think that the mouse has his own life to lead. A mouse may not be a poet or a civil servant but it has its own mousely thoughts, its own griefs and its own sorrows, and it has to think of its own future. As indeed we all have. We are not as different from the mouse as we think, though of course we are not as small as the mouse, or not many of us. And what does the mouse want from us? Well, as we realise from this poem, all it wanted from the great poet was an icker in a thrave. Not much indeed. For we all know what an icker in a thrave means. Don't we? I do not need to explain an icker in a thrave to such friends of the poet and indeed I may say scholars as we have here in this distinguished assembly of poetic lovers. It would be an insult for me to translate an icker in a thrave for them.

Let us therefore picture the mouse, a mouse whom we cannot know individually for mice do not have names such as we have. No one has ever heard of a mouse called Alex or Jean, and indeed the very notion is laughable. You cannot call a mouse to you as you would a dog with some such name as Rover. Anyway, this mouse, dislodged from its hiding place, runs trembling from the great poet's ploughshare, for we know that Burns was a farmer as well as a poet, and we have it on good authority that he was a good farmer, as we would expect him to be though the land he was working on was very poor. What does the mouse do when he sees this ploughshare approaching? Well, he did what was natural for a mouse in such circumstances. He ran away.

Not only that, but he ran away with bickering brattle. A fine phrase in itself. Here is the mouse among the corn as we might say helpless, and here is the great poet who had by this time written many great poems. It is not a minor poet that we have here but a major poet withal at the height of his powers or pooers as I might say. What did this great poet, author of such famous poems as 'Death and Doctor Hornbook', do? He addressed the mouse. Most great poets would not see in this tiny animal matter for speculation. But Rabbie Burns did. That is why he is our National Poet. At this moment he would teach us a lesson.

How many of us would have assailed this mouse for stealing our icker in a thrave? We would say to ourselves, have I grown this icker in order that this impudent animal might steal it; this animal that neither tills nor reaps, nor uses a ploughshare? For whoever saw a mouse with a ploughshare? The very notion is laughable. We might have shouted at the mouse as it ran away with our icker, 'Stop, thief'. We might have done it but Burns didn't do it. And that is how he is a great National poet and we are not. He was a man who knew about destitution and corn. The mouse, as we may imagine, did not wait for Burns to deliver his address. For it is not the mouse's nature to wait. It is a very active animal. No indeed, it does not wait to see what the poet will do with his ploughshare. Perhaps it had a hint that this was a great poet but the poem doesn't tell us. Burns meantime stands there astounded. The divine afflatus has descended on him, for his Muse does not despise a mouse. Is there not a lesson here for us all? What indeed may a bickering brattle not signify? May it not call us to be human beings? And what indeed is an icker in a thrave? All of us can afford one if we think for a moment. There is not one of us that can't afford an icker.

Now the next thing to be said is that by the time Burns is composing his address the mouse had disappeared. It will not wait for the great poet. On the contrary it will escape because that is the nature of the mouse. Burns therefore is present and the mouse is not, and that is an example of a paradox, and all great poetry is full of paradoxes. And indeed we cannot imagine the mouse caught red-handed as it were among the ickers waiting for Burns to address it, however attractive that might be. Did Burns at that moment remember his dear Jean, Highland Mary who died of a fever, all his dear loves, even Clarinda who lived in Edinburgh and who had never seen a mouse in her life? Did he recall his first fumbling attempts at verse as he stared at the place where the mouse had been but now was no longer? We don't know; we cannot know; but I think he did. I think that as the hapless mouse ran away with his icker he thought of all these things, and of his attempts to succeed in farming with his brother Gilbert, and his future career in the Customs and Excise and perhaps of the French Revolution, and the works of Alexander Pope with which he was *au fait*.

I will not chase thee with my murdering pattle, said Burns to the mouse. I will chase other beings but not you. My pattle will be kept for dealing with others as the case may arise but not you, you helpless being. And the mouse hiding somewhere withal must have been aware of this. He must have been aware in his mouselike mind that a great decision had been made, that the great poet in a murderous rage would not rush at him with his pattle. We do not know if the mouse knew what a pattle was: perhaps not. Suffice it to say that it was at least safe from the pattle of Burns.

The poet now sees that he has laid the mouse's tenement low. Did he blame himself? The point of this great poem is that he did. And he was sorry for it. He regretted it. He would have put the tenement back again but he didn't know how. And he stood there shivering, for in those days they did not have thermal clothing that we have now — nor indeed would he have deigned to wear it for he was a proud passionate man whom wet weather could not frighten, a man's man, and that is of course why he died at such an early age of rheumatic fever as we are told; and he stood there shivering like the mouse, perhaps more than the mouse for the mouse does not feel the cold as we do. What a picture fit for the heart we have here! And beside them is the cruel coulter. And the mouse and the man have to thole the cranreuch. What poetry is in these words, for the cranreuch as we know is the Scots word for frost. If this had been written in English, how much less cold it would have been.

Ladies and Gentlemen, I find myself moved at this moment. Here we have a great poet who has written poems such as 'The Banks of Ayr', and other such masterpieces and gems, face to face with the vanished mouse, and one of the greatest moments of his life is here. Did he shrink away from it? No, no, he did not. His murdering pattle in his hand, he stood there, not ashamed to weep, this great poet who knew, as scholars have reminded us, French and who was *au fait*, as scholars have also reminded us, with Alexander Pope and poets of that ilk. Here they stood, as on the field of Bannockburn about which Burns wrote, as we know, 'Scots Wha Hae'. But this was another Bannockburn, for Burns did not wave his pattle but stood with it at his side in a peaceful manner, as if to say to the mouse whose name we shall never know, 'I'll not harm you'.

Ladies and Gentlemen, I would like you now to be upstanding and to raise your dram, for this is a literary occasion, and to say with me, 'Burns and the Mouse. Burns and the Mouse'.